War and Peace in the Worlds of
Rudolf H. Sauter

War and Peace in the Worlds of Rudolf H. Sauter

A Cultural History of a Creative Life

Jeffrey S. Reznick

ANTHEM PRESS

Anthem Press
An imprint of Wimbledon Publishing Company
www.anthempress.com

This edition first published in UK and USA 2026
by ANTHEM PRESS
75–76 Blackfriars Road, London SE1 8HA, UK
or PO Box 9779, London SW19 7ZG, UK
and
244 Madison Ave #116, New York, NY 10016, USA

First published in the UK and USA by Anthem Press in 2022

The author completed this work as part of his official duties as a historian employed by
the United States Federal Government in its National Library of Medicine.
He asserts the moral right to be identified as the author of this work.

All rights reserved. Without limiting these rights,
no part of this publication may be reproduced, stored or introduced into
a retrieval system, or transmitted, in any form or by any means
(electronic, mechanical, photocopying, recording or otherwise),
without the prior written permission of both the author
and the above publisher of this book.

British Library Cataloguing-in-Publication Data
A catalogue record for this book is available from the British Library.

Library of Congress Control Number: 2025942650

ISBN-13: 978-1-83999-668-9 (Pbk)
ISBN-10: 1-83999-668-4 (Pbk)

Cover image: photograph of Rudolf H. Sauter, 1928
© E.O. Hoppé Estate Collection/Curatorial Assistance Inc.

This title is also available as an eBook.

CONTENTS

List of Figures   vii

Acknowledgments   xi

    Introduction: Reconstructing a Creative Life   1

1. Beginnings, 1890–1914   11
2. Internment, 1914–19   41
3. Recovery, 1919–24   73
4. Artistry I, 1924–39   93
5. Artistry II, 1939–50   125
6. Reflections, 1950–77   141

    Conclusion: Legacy   181

Epilogue: In His Own Words   185

Selected Bibliography   197

Index   207

FIGURES

1.1	Rudolf H. Sauter family tree	12
1.2	George Sauter, *Maternity*, ca. 1899, oil on canvas, 69.9 × 49.5 cm	21
1.3	George Sauter, *Comrades*, ca. 1900, oil on canvas, 68.6 × 55.9 cm	22
1.4	Sauter family photograph of Joseph Conrad and his son Borys, ca. 1900	24
1.5	Rudolf H. Sauter, sketch, 1910, pencil on paper, 12.7 × 8.8 cm	26
1.6	Rudolf H. Sauter, drawing of sailboats, 1913, pencil on paper, 10.79 × 13.97 cm	27
1.7a and 1.7b	Rudolf H. Sauter, letter to George Sauter, May 21, 1911	38
1.8	"Harrow School Champion Torpids 1911," Rudolf H. Sauter and William K. McClintock	39
2.1	Rudolf H. Sauter, letter to Viola Wood, August 4, 1918	50
2.2	Rudolf H. Sauter, untitled (studies of fellow internees), above ink on paper and below pencil on paper, ca. 1918–1919, 23.4 × 30.4 cm	57
2.3	Rudolf H. Sauter, "B" *Battalion from the Workshops*, 1919, pen and ink wash on paper, 47.3 × 49.2 cm	58
2.4	Rudolf H. Sauter, *The Canteen, Alexandra Palace*, 1919, sepia ink wash on paper, 26.6 × 36.8 cm	59
2.5	Rudolf H. Sauter, *The Watchmaker, Alexandra Palace*, 1919, sepia ink wash on paper, 12.7 × 17.7 cm	59
2.6	Rudolf H. Sauter, letter to Viola Wood, June 13, 1919	63
2.7	Rudolf H. Sauter, untitled (Firth Hill Camp, Surrey), sepia ink wash on paper, 24.1 × 29.2 cm	66
2.8	Rudolf H. Sauter, *Plan of Aliens Internment Camp, Frith Hill*, 1919, mulicolored ink on paper/board, 31 × 43.8 cm	67
3.1	Rudolf H. Sauter, *Suburban Back Gardens in Snow*, ca. 1920, watercolor on paper, 40.5 × 58.5 cm	76

LIST OF FIGURES

3.2	Rudolf H. Sauter, self-portrait, ca. 1920, oil on board, 51 × 41 cm	76
3.3	Rudolf H. Sauter, frontispiece, in John Galsworthy, *Awakening*, illustrated by Rudolf H. Sauter	78
3.4	Rudolf H. Sauter, "And a lovely smell of whitewash," in John Galsworthy, *Awakening*	79
3.5	Rudolf H. Sauter, *The Poet, John Masefield*, 1923, charcoal, 62.5 × 45 cm	90
3.6	Rudolf H. Sauter, *Map of the Story*, 1934, pen and black ink with turquoise and pink wash on paper, 25 × 34 cm	91
4.1	Rudolf H. Sauter, untitled (The Puente Nuevo), ca. 1925, drypoint etching	96
4.2	Rudolf H. Sauter, *Carnations in a Glass Vase*, 1926, oil on canvas	105
4.3	Rudolf H. Sauter, *New York from South End of Central Park*, 1931, pastel on buff paper, 36.8 × 57.2 cm	110
4.4	Rudolf H. Sauter, *Plan of Bury Studio 1931–32*	112
4.5	Rudolf H. Sauter, holiday greeting card for 1932	114
4.6	Photograph, "The Etching Room," in Rudolf and Viola Sauter, *Book of the Studio*	115
4.7	Clockwise from top: Rudolf H. Sauter, bookplates designed for Viola Sauter and himself, for his aunt Ada Galsworthy, and for his uncle John Galsworthy	117
4.8	Rudolf H. Sauter, change-of-address card, 1934	118
4.9	Rudolf H. Sauter, holiday greeting card for 1935	119
4.10	Rudolf H. Sauter, *Windmill*, oil on board, ca. 1940, 71 × 58.5 cm	121
4.11	Rudolf H. Sauter, *NEVER MORE…! (a modern Triptych)*, 1936, oil on panels, unknown dimensions,	122
4.12	Rudolf H. Sauter, holiday greeting card for 1936	123
5.1	Rudolf H. Sauter, *Homo Sapiens: MCMXL*, 1940, unknown medium, unknown dimensions	126
5.2	Rudolf H. Sauter, *After the Raid*, ca. 1940, watercolor on paper, 49.5 × 60 cm	127
5.3	Rudolf H. Sauter, *Not to be Removed*, ca. 1940, watercolor, 39 × 58 cm	128
5.4	Rudolf H. Sauter, *Searchlights along the Thames Estuary*, October 1940, gouache and pastel, 59.5 × 38 cm	132
5.5	Rudolf H. Sauter, *Paths in the Moonlight—Bombers Going Out Over the Channel*, October 16, 1944, watercolor on paper, 29 × 40 cm	133
5.6	Rudolf H. Sauter, *Doodlebug Alley—Death on the Way*, 1944, watercolor over pencil on paper, 25 × 35 cm	133

5.7	Rudolf H. Sauter, *Plants Springing from a Barren Landscape*, ca. 1947, oil on board, 51 × 61 cm	137
6.1	Rudolf H. Sauter, *Our Time and Age*, ca. 1957, oil on canvas, 71 × 58.5 cm	143
6.2	Rudolf H. Sauter, untitled illustration on the cover of the theatrical program for *Four Hungers*, May 1960, unknown medium and dimensions	147
6.3	Rudolf H. Sauter, *Annunciation*, 1940s, tempera on board, 50 × 62.5 cm	147
6.4	Rudolf H. Sauter, *Crie du Coeur* (Stroud, Gloucestershire: Stroud Typewriting, Rotaprinting and Duplicating Services, 1968)	156
6.5a and 6.5b	Rudolf H. Sauter, "Four Hungers," in *A Soothing Wind*, 16–17	164
6.6	Rudolf H. Sauter, *Creational Theme*, 1967, oil on board	167
6.7	Rudolf H. Sauter, *The Last Glow*, 1976, oil on board, 23.4 × 41.9 cm	176

ACKNOWLEDGMENTS

This book would not have been possible without the generous support of Robert Oldmeadow and his family and Alan Arthur Meyer, co-trustees of the estate of Rudolf Helmut Sauter (1895–1977) and joint holders of the copyright in his work. I thank them for appreciating my interest in reconstructing Sauter's creative life in its own right—out of the shadow of his famous uncle, John Galsworthy. Whereas Sauter has been a supporting player in works about Galsworthy—including my own 2009 study—here he is the lead.

My research for this book took me physically and virtually to the many archives, art galleries, auction houses, libraries and museums that hold Sauter's work and related materials about his creative life. I am grateful to the outstanding professionals in all of these institutions for their time and talent. I would especially like to thank Nicole Allen, Nikita Brady, Jenny Childs, Vicky Clubb, Beth Cutts, Mark Eccleston, Hamda Gharib, Catherine Martin, Mark Williams, Cadbury Library, University of Birmingham; Jenny Childs and Anna Young, Research and Cultural Collections, University of Birmingham; Anna Chen, Elizabeth Garver, Rick Watson and Richard Workman, Harry Ransom Humanities Research Center, The University of Texas at Austin; Michael Lange, Dean Smith and Lee Anne Titangos, The Bancroft Library, University of California, Berkeley; Carlos D. Acosta-Ponce, Jennifer Donner and Jacalyn Pearce, Department of Special Collections and University Archives, University of Tulsa; April Armstrong, AnnaLee Pauls and Adrienne Rusinko, Department of Special Collections, Princeton University Library; Nanette Hardison and Kelly Spring, Joyner Library, East Carolina University; Adele Adrian and Aimee Campbell, UK Army Personnel Centre; Liliya Gusakova and Mary Wassum, National Library of Medicine, National Institutes of Health; Samuel Ali, Pauline Allwright, Sara Bevan, David Bell, Emily Dean, Barry Smith and Sally Webb, Imperial War Museum; Morex Arai, The Huntington Library; Alexandra Aslett, St. Paul's School; Charles Ashton, Cheffins Fine Art; Andi Bartelstein, Peter Carini, Myranda Fuentes and Scout Noffke and Jay Satterfield, Rauner Special Collections Library, Dartmouth College; Julia Beaumont-Jones, Royal

Air Force Museum; Jeremy Bigalke, Graham Howe and Marika Lundeberg, Curatorial Assistance; Katie Blackford and Marta Cappella, Tate Library and Archive; Peter Boswell and Rebecca Moore, Archive Digital; Elizabeth Botten and Marisa Bourgoin, Archives of American Art, Smithsonian Institution; Betsy Boyle, Massachusetts Historical Society; June Can, Beinecke Rare Book and Manuscript Library, Yale University; Shaun Carroll and Helen Timlin, Gloucestershire Archives; Kevin Chambers, Kayleigh Pearson and Rodney French, UK National Archives; Salma Chen and Madelon Monté, Letterkundig Museum/ Kinderboekenmuseum; Terry Clifford and Steve Goodwin, Cotswold Playhouse; Ron Cookson and Elizabeth Trout, Mills Archive Trust; Sarah Colegrave, Sarah Colgrave Fine Art; Pip Dodd, National Army Museum; Katherine Degn, Kraushaar Galleries; John Doyle and Dina Frank-Rice, National Institutes of Health Library; Helen Durndell, University of Glasgow, Special Collections; Jack Eckert and Scott Podolsky, Countway Library, Harvard University; Simon Edsor, Flure Grossart and Cordelia Lingard, The Fine Arts Society; Will Ellin, Burstow & Hewett Auctioneers & Valuers; Richard Everett and Simon Chaplin, Wellcome Collection.

I also wish to thank Frank Egerton, Clare Hills-Nova and Jessica Semeniuk, Taylor Institution Library, Oxford University; Tace Fox, Luke Meadows, Angharad Meredith and Christine Ryan, Harrow School; Catherine Flynn, Naomi Greenway and Jean Rose, Penguin Random House Archive; Shannon Harmer and Ben Vargas, PARS International Corporation; Fran Hazlewood-Mosby, Nigel Smith and Joanna Watson, Morphets of Harrogate Ltd.; Antony Hopkins, Witt and Conway Libraries, Courtauld Institute of Art; Felicity House, The Pastel Society Archives; Vinny Bamrah, Freya Levett and Glena Isaac, Victoria and Albert Museum; Thomas Jenner-Fust, Chorley's Auctioneers; Ellie Jones, Andelli Art; Louise Kosman, Louise Kosman Modern British Art; Deirdre Lawrence and Linda Paleias, Brooklyn Museum; Nicole Licavoli and Liz Valentine, Gale|Cengage Learning; Paul Liss, Sacha Llewellyn and Petra van der Wal, Liss Llewellyn; Magee Lawhorn, Archives & Special Collections at Phillips Exeter Academy; Alice Millard and Matthew Jones, West Sussex Record Office; Dana Miller, Rare Book and Manuscript Library, University of Illinois Urbana–Champaign; Henry Moore-Gwyn, Moore-Gwyn Fine Art; Isabel Planton, Lilly Library, University of Indiana; Michael Prince, Pearson; Michael Pritchard, The Royal Photographic Society; Judith Ratcliffe and Rachel Tompkins, Britten Pears Arts; Simon Rayner, Simon Rayner Fine Art; Lori Reese, Redux Pictures; Alexandra Reigle, Smithsonian American Art Museum/National Portrait Gallery Library; Charlotte Robinson, Westminster School; Jessica Scantlebury, Mass Observation Archive, University of Sussex; Lynne Shipley, Dominic Winter, Ltd.; Amy Silverman, The Wolfsonian, Florida International University; Bernhard Stalla, Comenius-Expertenforum;

Susan Stanbury, Haberdashers' Aske's Boys' School Library and Archive; Elizabeth Trout, Mills Archive Trust; Nigel Walsh, Leeds Art Gallery; and Andy Wood, Royal Institute of Painters in Water Colours.

My research also took me to Stroud, Gloucestershire, where Sauter lived during the last two decades of his life. I thank Robert and Jane Oldmeadow for their warm hospitality in Fort William, Sauter's former residence, located high atop the town at the end of its Rodborough Common. They showed me the nearby places where Sauter painted, walked and found creative inspiration—including the Cotswold Gliding Club where Sauter marked his 80th birthday, in 1975, by taking his first glider flight—and they fundamentally helped me to appreciate and understand Sauter's many landscapes of Stroud. They also introduced me to John Oldmeadow with whom Sauter worked to create his collections of poetry during the late 1960s. I deeply appreciate all of these unique experiences and how they informed and inspired my thinking about this book.

Many more individuals helped me complete aspects of this book, and I am grateful to all of them for their kindness, enthusiasm and inspiration and interest in my research. Thanks especially to several anonymous holders of Sauter's artwork and to Johnny Ak, Phylomena Badsey, Michael Biard, Hannah Billcliffe, Rachael Blundell, Amanda Boyd, Ba Ba Chang, Belinda Clark, Daniel Deegan, Eric and Maya Boime, Alex Godwin-Brown, Hannah Briscoe, Sabine Lee, Colin Close, Netta Cohen, Daniel Dullaway, Sophie Dupre, Tom Dupre, Philip Errington, Tom Ewing, Josephine Fairey, Juliet Franks, Jason Gaiger, Steve Goodman, Ron Gordner, Christoph Gradmann, Stephen Greenberg, Alan Griffiths, Chris Griffiths, Mark Harrison, Brenda Hayton, Thomas Hahn, Ann Hambley, Timothy Hoey, Patrick Howell, Janet Hudson, Jae Hwang, Patricia Jenkins, Richard Kay, Georgianne Ensign Kent, John Knowles, Ken Koyle, Jeffrey Lesser, Janette and Jim McCaffrey, Wendy McLean, Nicole Milano, Jill Newmark, David Northrup, Trevor Owens, Penny Page, Patricia Phillips, James Perry, Aliya Rahman, Geoffrey Roberts, Gabrielle Robilliard, Ginny Roth, Scott Ross, Stacy Ross, Mair Salts, Michael Sappol, Marilyn Shatz, Sue Stafford, David Stewart, Julie Taddeo, Carsten Timmerman, Patricia Tuohy, Arnold Victor, Rebecca Warlow, Linda Watson, Oliver Wilkinson and John Wilson. I also thank Daniel Deegan for his skillful digitization of the unique recordings of Sauter's voice held by Cadbury Library, University of Birmingham, which enabled my assessment of Sauter's later life, and Jan Pohl for his expert knowledge of German which helped me make meaningful Sauter's poetry of the Great War period.

I appreciate the institutional support I received during my research and writing of this book, and updates to it, as part of my official duties as a historian employed by the United States Federal Government in its National Library of Medicine. None of the opinions presented here represent the views of the library. According to Section 105 of the United States Copyright Act, the intellectual work I produce through my official duties belongs to the United States Federal Government and is not subject to copyright within the United States. Therefore, I cannot claim the copyright in portions of this book which I have authored, transfer any copyright, or accept any royalties. So as my work as a federal historian advances the greater good, so too does this book through its copyright status and focus on the creative outlook and existential concerns of its subject in times of war and peace.

During the course of completing this book, I had the privilege of connecting with many likeminded scholars who supported my inquiries, stimulated my thinking and offered me critical feedback. This occurred particularly at conferences and institutions where I presented aspects of my work, including the Imperial War Museum, Mid-Atlantic Conference on British Studies, Harvard University and University of Wolverhampton. Thanks to everyone I met on these wonderful occasions and for our keeping in touch about mutual interests.

I am grateful to the entire team at Anthem Press for their expertise, patience and assistance as the project transformed from proposal to peer-reviewed manuscript in production. Every scholar should be so fortunate to work with such an outstanding group of professionals.

Completing this book was a remarkable professional and personal journey and I am deeply grateful to my family to whom I dedicate it. They indulged me every step of the way as I shared excitement about the complexity of my research and what it revealed about Sauter's life and creative mind. I especially appreciate the unwavering support of my wife, Allison, in making my love of writing part of—not apart from—our daily life, as well as the enthusiasm of our daughters, Danielle and Rachel, who always asked me supportively "how's the book going" and even sometimes willingly lent a hand by helping me decipher handwriting and sort my notes. I also thank my father and mother, Bernard and Ellen Reznick, for listening patiently to my ideas and thoughts, and for their love and support. While my cultural-historical scholarship has developed through my professional trajectory, it has always remained rooted in my upbringing in Rochester, New York, where, thanks to my father, I first began to appreciate how art, history and literature combine to illuminate the human condition.

Any errors in this book are mine alone and I will appreciate being in touch with anyone who would contact me with corrections. Beyond securing written permissions to use Sauter's body of work, I have made every effort to trace the copyright holders of other material reproduced here, which does not otherwise fall into the public domain. Should holders step forward after publication, due acknowledgement will gladly be made.

August 2025

Introduction

RECONSTRUCTING A CREATIVE LIFE

On June 16, 1977, the *Birmingham Post* informed its readers that "a Gloucestershire artist and author, Mr. Rudolf Sauter, has died at Stroud hospital, aged 82." The announcement continued: "Mr. Sauter, of Butterow, Stroud, was the nephew of John Galsworthy. He wrote poems, plays and a biography of Galsworthy."[1] Sauter's passing was noteworthy to the Birmingham community because he had donated papers of his uncle—the famed Nobel Prize-winning novelist—to the University of Birmingham. As the newspaper reported a few months later, Sauter left additional Galsworthy papers to the institution, including "many family papers," therefore making the collection "the most comprehensive in the world."[2] Significantly, the *Birmingham Post* was silent on the fact that Sauter's further bequest to the university included his own papers which documented his life as an artist and trustee of the Galsworthy legacy.

These newspaper articles are an ideal touchstone for introducing this first book to examine Sauter's creative life and legacy. They rightly reflect his close and public association with his uncle who loved him like the son he never had. Yet, these articles obscure the richness and complexity of Sauter's life as an artist and the variety of events that shaped it, particularly his internment during the Great War as an "enemy alien," due to his German identity. At the same time, these articles provoke many questions about his life: As an artist, poet, playwright and writer, what were the subjects of his work? What were his inspirations and motivations in choosing these subjects? Where, when and under what circumstances did he display and publish his work? How were his various productions received?

---

1. "Mr. R. Sauter," *Birmingham Post*, June 16, 1977, 6, https://www.britishnewspaperarchive.co.uk/viewer/bl/0002135/19770616/130/0006.
2. "Forsyte Bequest Completes Archive," *Birmingham Post* (Birmingham, England), September 1, 1977, 2, https://www.britishnewspaperarchive.co.uk/viewer/bl/0002135/19770901/033/0002.

This book answers these questions and many more, revealing Sauter as a singular creative figure and cultural observer whose body of artistic, literary and theatrical work spanned three-quarters of the twentieth century and reflected the subjects of war, love, memory and concerns of modern times, including the environment and nuclear war. It is organized chronologically and thematically, with emphases throughout on places and spaces as frameworks to reconstitute and contextualize Sauter's creative worlds in war and peace. Broad physical environments, like neighborhoods and landscapes, figure prominently in the narrative, as do smaller spaces, namely studios, around which Sauter's creative life took shape and grew meaningfully.

Chapter 1, "Beginnings, 1890–1914," examines Sauter's birth and formative years before the Great War. It opens a window onto his upbringing in London's posh Holland Park, his schooling in Elstree and Harrow and his relationships with his father, the noted artist Georg Sauter and his mother, the suffragist and sister of John Galsworthy, Lilian Sauter. This chapter also examines Sauter's early life in the context of Georg and Lilian's circle of notable friends whom they regularly welcomed into their home, making it a center of sociability and rich literary and artistic creativity. Here, Georg and Lilian and their friends nurtured Rudolf's early talent in the arts, forming the basis of his future career before the Great War changed their lives.

Chapter 2, "Internment, 1914–19," focuses on Sauter's experiences as an "enemy alien" interned in two camps within the network of such facilities established by the British government to restrict the activities of nationals of enemy nations residing in the country. Sauter fell into this category due to his German birth and because he had not become a naturalized citizen of the country in which his parents had raised him in their very English manner. Drawing on his illustrated correspondence, contemporary poetry and related drawings of the scenes and routines of his daily life, this chapter reveals how Sauter conceived and transformed the stark and utilitarian spaces of his captivity into ad hoc studios. Herein, he documented his captivity through words and images, seeking to endure the experience through these creative efforts.

Chapter 3, "Recovery, 1919–24," investigates Sauter's creative life during the years immediately following his release from internment. It focuses on how, through patronage of his uncle which yielded home studios and various creative projects, he sought both to forget and remember his experiences during the Great War and develop his reputation as a sensitive artist. The success Sauter achieved during this period of his life would yield a career involving exhibitions in Britain, the United States and the Paris Salon, as well as memberships in numerous professional organizations, including the Pastel

Society, Royal Institute, Royal Society of British Artists and Royal West of England Academy, among others.

Chapter 4, "Artistry I, 1924–39," reveals the further establishment of Sauter's artistic career as he became a naturalized British citizen and international travel expanded his creative horizons, inspiration and productions as a sensitive artist. Near the midpoint of this period—arguably at the pinnacle of his career—Sauter achieved his bespoke Bury Studio along with documentation of its conception, design, construction and decoration that was as remarkable as that which inhabited his wartime letters and drawings of his ad hoc studios in captivity. Whereas those sites were his prisons which simultaneously constrained and fostered his creativity, Bury Studio was his castle wherein his creativity could flourish and have no bounds.

Chapter 5, "Artistry II, 1939–50," opens a window onto Sauter's creative life during his residence in Kent, along Doodlebug Alley, and his enlistment with the British Eastern Command of the British Army, covering East Anglia and the Central Midland Counties, where he served the nation which had previously interned him as an enemy alien. Within his renovated millhouse studio and through duties across this region which enabled him to paint en plain air, Sauter focused on a variety of subjects symbolizing the realities and physical force of the nation at war, productions which stood in stark contrast to the images of captivity he created during the previous war. Although he was never an official war artist, he documented Britain at war as accurately and meaningfully as his counterparts who painted in formal service to the nation at war.

Chapter 6, "Reflections, 1950–77," tracks Sauter's later years in his studios of Coddington Court and Stroud, and as a member of the creative community of the latter locale. During this period, he moved beyond painting to experiment with different creative formats through which he rediscovered, reshaped and re-represented some of his earlier work for new audiences. The outcome was a diverse portfolio of art, theatre plays in the tradition of masque entertainment and bespoke books of poetry which focused on the arc of his life, including his experiences in two world wars and perspectives on life during the Cold War.

Historiography

As this book recovers Sauter's creative life and makes it meaningful, it sits at the intersection of several fields of scholarship, connecting and contributing to each one. Broadly speaking, these fields include cultural biography, art history and the history of modern war.

Cultural Biography

A biography is traditionally understood to be a written account of a person's life. This book has such elements but offers much more as it deliberately excavates and reconstructs Sauter's life through a historical lens focused on a variety of primary textual and visual sources. The result is part life study and part cultural history—indeed a cultural biography—located in a growing constellation of such works which exist dynamically and valuably between traditional historical studies and strict biographical narratives.[3] Moreover, this book unpacks the depth and breadth of history embedded in the fleeting and unsatisfying treatments of Sauter, which appear in studies of his uncle.[4] Like the abbreviated announcement of Sauter's passing in the *Birmingham Post*, these passages provoke questions, prompt inquiry and inspire research into an underappreciated life and unexplored corners of history. Both sources motivate the curious reader to ask: Who was this man Sauter on his own terms

---

3. Barbara Cain, *Biography and History* (Basingstoke, Hampshire: Macmillan Education, 2010); Peter J. Conn, *Pearl S. Buck: A Cultural Biography* (London: Cambridge University Press, 1998); Kate Culkin, *Harriet Hosmer: A Cultural Biography* (Amherst: University of Massachusetts Press, 2010); Robert W. Gutman, *Mozart: A Cultural Biography* (New York: Houghton Mifflin Harcourt, 1999); and Linda Merrill, *The Peacock Room: A Cultural Biography* (New Haven, CT: Yale University Press, 1998). For an excellent overview of the field of cultural biography, see Harold K. Bush. "Cradling Lives in Our Hands: Towards a Theory of Cultural Biography," *Christianity and Literature* 57, no. 1 (2007): 111–29.

4. Such brevity on the subject of Sauter's life itself, if not outright silence, is found in Dudley Barker, *The Man of Principle: A Biography of John Galsworthy* (New York: Stein and Day, 1969); Catherine Dupré, *John Galsworthy: A Biography* (New York: Coward, McCann & Geoghegan, 1976); Alec Fréchet, *John Galsworthy: A Reassessment* (Totowa, NJ: Barnes & Noble Books, 1982) and R. H. Mottram, *For Some We Loved: An Intimate Portrait of Ada and John Galsworthy* (London: Hutchinson, 1956). The notable exceptions to this brevity, albeit with their foci on Galsworthy, are James Gindin, *The English Climate: An Excursion into a Biography of John Galsworthy* (Ann Arbor: University of Michigan Press, 1979) and Gindin, *John Galsworthy's Life and Art: An Alien's Fortress* (Ann Arbor: University of Michigan Press, 1987). In writing *The English Climate*, Gindin met and interviewed Rudolf, described his later creative work and, albeit briefly in the narrative, revealed his warm character and engaging artistic personality. In *John Galsworthy's Life and Art*, Gindin rightly pointed out that "in one sense, Rudo's imprisonment helped him participate in the experience of his generation" (375), but then did not explore this observation. This book, therefore, picks up substantially where Gindin left off, pulling Sauter completely out of the shadow of his uncle and recognizing him as a creative figure on his own terms. In this regard, too, this book builds on my own work on Galsworthy, wherein Sauter plays a supporting role; here, he is the featured subject. Jeffrey S. Reznick, *John Galsworthy and Disabled Soldiers of the Great War* (Manchester: Manchester University Press, 2009).

as an artist, poet, playwright and writer? This book answers this question while uncovering the motivations and roots of his creative life, his artistic energy and inspiration during two world wars and the Cold War and the diversity and historical value of his creative portfolio. In doing so, it gives Sauter agency heretofore largely if not completely denied to him, essentially unearthing and granting him his own voice in the experiences and narrative of his own creative life. Additionally, this book gives Sauter the respect he deserves from a legal perspective, rescuing his work from being treated as orphaned as it remains in copyright until the year 2047. It is unclear when the copyright in Sauter's work began to be treated as orphaned.[5] Regardless, it should never have been so since the names of Sauter's executors and copyright holders—Patricia Scrivens and Alan Meyer—appear in his last will and testament held by the University of Birmingham, deposited there among his other papers. While identifying these copyright holders was one challenge achieved in realizing this book, locating them was another matter entirely, involving persistent inquiries to auctioneers hand in hand with consistent respect of privacy rights. In the end, after many years of effort, contact was made, permissions were granted, and this first study of Sauter was realized, fundamentally with all due thanks to the copyright holders in his body of work.

Finally, this book helps to correct the public record of Sauter's first name which he formally spelled Rudolf. During the course of his increased public profile following the Great War, due at worst to anti-German sentiment or perhaps to the more common spelling of Rudolf as Rudolph, observers of his art and trusteeship of his uncle's legacy began to refer to him by the latter. This book, then, correctly names him by the former and, in so doing, will hopefully lead twenty-first century appreciators of his creative life to do the same as part of reflecting critically upon his multifaceted body of work and its associated events, ideas and individuals.

---

5. For what was perhaps the earliest instance of this treatment, see Edward Hudson, ed., *Poetry of the First World War* (London: Wayland, 1989), wherein Sauter's poem "Barbed Wire" appears among several works for which the copyright had "proved impossible to trace" and therefore the publishers apologized for "this apparent negligence" (118, 126). A later example of such treatment appeared in Mandy Kirkby's *Love Letters of the Great War*, wherein there is acknowledgement of the institutional holder of his letter reproduced, namely the Imperial War Museum, but no mention of copyright or permission sought or granted. See Kirkby, *Love Letters of the Great War* (New York: Macmillan, 2014), 193–96, 212.

Art History

Since his passing in 1977, many auctions have scattered Sauter's large body of work around the world and into a large number of private and public hands.[6] The decade of research underpinning this book entailed extensive stocktaking of his oeuvre, only a small fraction of which is reproduced here to frame and contextualize a narrative of his life, and to contribute to dialogue on art as a meaningful source of biography and history. Readers will see many more works by Sauter cited in the footnotes. I hope this direct and indirect surfacing of Sauter's oeuvre will inspire a future project which will reveal the full scale of his creative output. In the meantime, as this book rescues Sauter's body of work generally from neglect and foregrounds the various studios in which he created it, it is in dialogue with the field of art history, particularly the disparate body of work which recognizes the multifaceted character of the artist's studio, encouraging more explorations of this creative, meaningful and provocative space.[7] Sauter conceived some of his studios out of necessity,

---

6. The largest of these auctions occurred in 1993 and involved over forty works. Writing in the *Independent*, Dalya Alberge described the event as being "a visual record of a little-known chapter in British history—Alexandra Palace as a wartime internment camp for enemy aliens," adding the (inaccurate) statement that Sauter "did not follow an artistic career after being freed" from his internment. See The Fine Art Society, *Rudolf H. Sauter, 1985–1979 [sic] Internment Drawings—Alexandra Palace 1918–19, 7–25 June 1993* (London: The Fine Art Society, 1993) and Dalya Alberge, "Sketches record life in London prison camp: Drawings by German interned in Alexandra Palace during First World War go on sale," *Independent* (London, England), June 2, 1993, http://www.independent.co.uk/news/uk/sketches-record-life-in-london-prison-camp-drawings-by-german-interned-in-alexandra-palace-during-first-world-war-go-on-sale-1489178.html.
7. Alice Bellony-Rewald and Michael Peppiatt, *Imagination's Chamber: Artists and Their Studios* (London: Gordon Fraser, 1983); Daniel Buren and Thomas Repensek, "The Function of the Studio," *October* 10 (Autumn 1979): 51–58; Daniel Buren, "The Function of the Studio (Revisited): A Conversation between Daniel Buren and the Curators/Editors Jens Hoffman, Christina Kennedy and Georgia Jackson," in *The Studio* (Dublin, Ireland: Dublin City Gallery, 2007); John Goodrich, "The Private Language of Painting, Revealed in Artists' Images of Their Studios," *Hyperallergic*, April 13, 2015, https://hyperallergic.com/198769/the-private-language-of-painting-revealed-in-artists-images-of-their-studios/; Jens Hoffmann, *The Studio: Documents in Contemporary Art* (London: Whitechapel Gallery and the MIT Press, 2012), especially his introduction, "The Artist's Studio in an Expanded Field," 12–17; Liza Kirwin with Joan Lord, *Artists in Their Studios: Images from the Smithsonian's Archives of American Art* (New York: Collins Design, 2007); Lilly Lampe, "What Goes on in the Artist's Studio." *New Yorker*, April 16, 2015, https://www.newyorker.com/culture/photo-booth/what-goes-on-in-the-artists-studio; George Philip LeBourdais, "A Brief History of the Artist's Studio," accessed June 30, 2021, https://www.artsy.net/article/artsy-editorial-why-do-we-care-about-an-artist-s-studio; Trevor Leonard, "'Guilded Squalor': An Evaluation of Francis Bacon's 7

some he designed, and some were the results of his uncle's patronage. One he built with remarkable attention to detail, documenting each and every step in his realization of the space. Some were ephemeral and en plein air as a result of his travels. Regardless of their origin and shape, Sauter embraced every one of his studios with gusto. These spaces are hallmarks of his creative life. Uncovering and focusing on them gives him agency as an artist, indeed as an historical figure who experienced periods of war and peace in his own unique ways.

By extension, this book draws on and contributes to the branch of art history which examines the artist's book, a distinctive medium conceived and created in the artist's studio through the process of offset lithography, involving lightweight metal plates rather than heavy metal type in a letterpress.[8] Such work was a central part of Sauter's later life when he continued to draw and paint, as well as take up multimedia theatrical productions, all as means to assess the arc of his creative life and re-present and reshape his earlier poetic and visual work. Through such achievement in the local creative ecosystem

---

Reece Mews Studio," https://www.igs.ie/education/list/category/trinity-college-dublin/p6; John Minford and Claire Roberts, eds., *China Heritage Quarterly* 13 (March 2008), http://www.chinaheritagequarterly.org/editorial.php?issue=013; Allison Malafronte, "The History of the Plein Air Movement," *American Artist* (October 2009): 20–24; Alex Taylor, *Perils of the Studio: Inside the Artistic Affairs of Bohemian Melbourne* (North Melbourne, Victoria: Australian Scholarly Publishing, 2007); Ian Wallace, "The Evolution of the Artist's Studio, From Renaissance Bottege to Assembly Line," *Artspace*, June 14, 2011, https://www.artspace.com/magazine/art101/art_market/the-evolution-of-the-artists-studio-52374; Tom Wilkinson, "Typology: Artist Studio," *Architectural Review*, February 17, 2017, https://www.architectural-review.com/essays/typology-artist-studio/10017316.article.

8. On the subject of artists' books, see especially Johanna Drucker, *The Century of Artists' Books* (New York: Granary Books, 2004). On the process of offset lithography, see Dennis Bryans, "The Double Invention of Printing," *Journal of Design History* 13, no. 4 (2000): 287–300; Rob Dunn, Ray Hester and Andrew Readman, "From Letterpress to Offset Lithography," in *Print and Electronic Text Convergence*, ed. Bill Cope and Diana Kalantzis (Champaign, IL: Common Ground, 2001), 81–108; Jesse Adams Stein, "Masculinity and Material Culture in Technological Transitions: From Letterpress to Offset Lithography, 1960s–1980s," *Technology and Culture* 57, no. 1 (January 2016): 24–53. See also Elizabeth Baker, *Printers and Technology. A History of the International Printing Pressmen and Assistants' Union* (New York: Columbia University Press, 1957); Alan Marshall, Changing the Word: The Printing Industry in Transition (London: Comedia, 1983); Michael Twyman, *The British Library Guide to Printing: History and Techniques* (Toronto: University of Toronto Press, 1998), 76–82, and A Century of Artists Books, exhibition at the Metropolitan Museum of Modern Art, October 23, 1994–January 24, 1995, https://www.moma.org/calendar/exhibitions/439.

of Gloucestershire, Sauter participated in broader dialog about the existential concerns of modern times.

History of Modern War

With its cultural-biographical and art-historical foci, this book connects with and contributes to multiple histories of modern war, particularly those which define and elucidate gradations of the experience of the Great War, from core studies of the "generation of 1914"—that cohort born between the years 1880 and 1900 whose lives were forever altered by direct experiences loss and trauma—to newer examinations of the experiences of prisoners of war.[9] Born in 1895, Sauter came of age with the "generation of 1914," his upper-class English privilege placing him in the same educational and social circles with those young men who would eventually serve king and country at the front, losing their lives in battle or surviving forever changed through their war experience. However, Sauter's German birth and lack of British citizenship would seal his fate as an "enemy alien," placing his comfortable life on a different path—to internment—with which he sought to cope through his creative skills of drawing, painting and writing. Following the war, like many former "enemy aliens," Sauter both recalled his captivity and sought to forget it as a means of moving forward with his life. Two and a half decades later, during the Second World War, and many years after he had become a

---

9. Robert Wohl, *The Generation of 1914* (Boston: Harvard University Press, 1979) and the many works inspired by it, including Stephen Lovell, ed., *Generations in Twentieth-Century Europe* (Basingstoke: Palgrave Macmillan, 2007). On prisoners of war during the Great War, see especially David Cesarani and Tony Kushner, eds., *Internment of Aliens in Twentieth Century Britain* (London: Routledge, 1993); Richard Dove, *"Totally Un-English"?: Britain's Internment of "Enemy Aliens" in Two World Wars* (Amsterdam: Rodopi, 2005); Edgar Jones and Simon Wessely, "British Prisoners-of-War: From Resilience to Psychological Vulnerability: Reality or Perception," *Twentieth Century British History* 21, no. 2 (2010): 163–83; Panikos Panayi, *Prisoners of Britain: German Civilian and Combatant Internees during the First World War* (Manchester: Manchester University Press, 2012) and Alon Rachamimov, *POWs and the Great War: Captivity on the Eastern Front* (Oxford: Berg, 2002). See also Harold Mytum and Gilly Carr, eds., *Prisoners of War: Archaeology, Memory and Heritage of 19th- and 20th-century Mass Internment* (New York: Springer-Verlag, 2013); Anne-Marie Pathé and Fabien Théofilakism, eds., *Wartime Captivity in the Twentieth Century: Archives, Stories, Memories* (New York: Berghahn Books, 2016); Robert Jackson, *The Prisoners, 1914–18* (London: Routledge, 1989); Matthew Stibbe, *Civilian Internment during the First World War: A European and Global History, 1914–1920* (London: Palgrave MacMillan, 2019); Oliver Wilkinson, British *Prisoners of War in First World War Germany* (Cambridge: Cambridge University Press, 2017) and John Yarnall, *Barbed Wire Disease: British and German Prisoners of War, 1914–18* (Gloucestershire: History Press, 2011).

naturalized British citizen, his life could not have been more different than it had been during the Great War. He enlisted in the British army, serving the nation that had previously interned him as an enemy alien and marshalled his artistic skills yet again, but this time to capture national mobilization, readiness and the resulting experience of war on the home front. Sauter held onto these and previous wartime experiences for the remainder of his life, later recalling them, creatively recasting them and investing them with new personal and professional meaning. Therefore, in the constellation of histories of war experience, captivity and modern memory, we can now include this cultural history of the wartime and peacetime worlds of Rudolf H. Sauter and his creative life.

Chapter 1
BEGINNINGS, 1890–1914

In 1890, 26-year-old Blanche Lilian Galsworthy lived in 8 Cambridge Gate, London, with her parents John and Blanche and her siblings: 23-year-old John, 21-year-old Hubert and 19-year-old Mabel Edith (Figure 1.1). One day, Lilian's friend Frances Knight-Bruce visited the home accompanied by a handsome 24-year-old Bavarian painter named Georg Sauter.[1] He had recently arrived in the city through the generosity of a patron of his promising artistic career begun at the Royal Academy and developed through work in various parts of Europe, including Holland, Belgium, France and Italy.

Frances had seen Georg in the National Gallery sketching Titian's *Bacchus and Ariadne* and was "struck by the excellence of the copy he was making."[2] She "opened conversation with him" and "soon became strongly impressed by his talent" and his determination "to stand on his own two feet and half-starved perhaps, but wholly indomitable [in his] fight for recognition in London." Frances became interested to find him paid work, so she brought him to the

---

1. The recollections of Mabel Edith Reynolds-Galsworthy, "Memories of Georg Sauter," appear in Bernhard Josef Stalla, *Lebenswege eines Malers und Zeichners: George Sauter* (Brannenburg: Peter Drexler, 2011), 73–87. They are an invaluable source for reconstructing the relationship between Georg and Lilian and their roles as parents to Rudolf. Evidently, these recollections were unknown to Galsworthy biographers Dudley Barker and James Gindin who offered a different account of how Lilian met Georg. Citing no sources, Barker suggested that it was Lilian who saw Georg painting in the National Gallery, "brought him home to Cambridge Gate" where Georg first "began on Mabel" who "fell in love with him," but then "things turned out even worse" when the family learned that he was not "in love with Mabel but with Lilian and she with him." Dudley Barker, *The Man of Principle: A Biography of John Galsworthy* (New York: Stein and Day, 1969), 34–35. Citing a May 22, 1974, interview with Muriel Galsworthy, Galsworthy's niece, Gindin offered that Lilian and Mabel together saw Georg painting in the National Gallery and invited him home where he "started with Mabel," who rejected his marriage proposal. Georg then proposed to Lilian. James Gindin, *John Galsworthy's Life and Art: An Alien's Fortress* (Ann Arbor: University of Michigan Press, 1987), 48–49. See also James Gindin, *The English Climate: An Excursion into a Biography of John Galsworthy* (Ann Arbor: University of Michigan Press, 1979), 10.
2. Reynolds-Galsworthy, "Memories of Georg Sauter," 74.

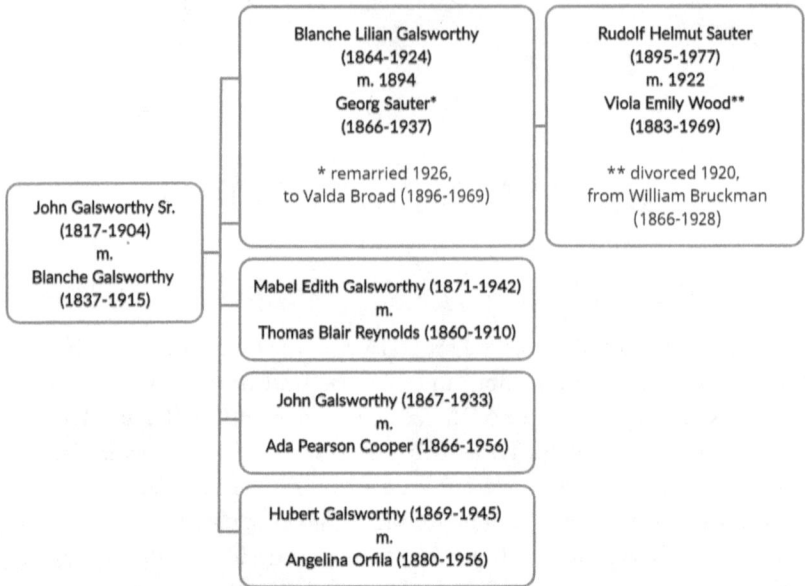

Figure 1.1 Rudolf H. Sauter family tree, abridged to include key individuals mentioned in this book.

Galsworthy's home, hoping that the elder Galsworthy might let him paint his portrait.

The household into which Georg entered was "very 'Victorian'" and likely had a "devastating effect [...] on his art-loving eyes and soul," beginning with "the vast conventional drawing-room [which] must have been a shock." Therein, he saw "carpet and curtains [...] of crimson velvet [...] Buhl cabinets, white marble, consol-tables, gilt-edged mirrors, Dresden china ornaments, a Collard grand piano and water-colours by popular Royal Academicians." At the same time, Georg likely made his hosts as "uncomfortable" as he felt in their orderly Victorian home, as he was

> a somewhat uncouth figure [...] clad in unconventional garments, but the head was striking...with rather long dark-brown hair, strong Wagnerian profile and keen blue eyes. He knew very little English as yet; but Lilian's German was fairly equal to the occasion, though the translation of a philosophical work by Teichmüller on which, I remember, she was working at the time, was not, perhaps, the most useful preparation

for colloquial conversation in homely German tinged with strong Bavarian dialect.[3]

Despite his appearance and background, or likely due to it, the Galsworthys became enthralled with his experience and expertise:

> He talked vigorously and picturesquely and some of his opinions gave us rough, if healthy shakings, He had, for instance, a lively contempt for what he called the [informal chocolate-box] portraits in the R[oyal] Academy; and doubtless found equally contemptible our comparative ignorance concerning such gods as Rembrandt, Whistler and Matthieu Maris. He waxed enthusiastic over Lenbach of Munich, in whose studio/workspace he had received kindness and helpful advice and he talked about many another painter, both "ancient and modern," of whom we had never heard. His eyes constantly strayed in my Father's direction and once or twice, in complete oblivion of surroundings and company, he would shoot out a broad hand—considerably constrained by paint and cigarettes—and caress the air, with a curious, semi-circular, sweeping movement. He was composing the possible future picture in his mind's eye![4]

Embraced by the family for his obvious skill and "infectious enthusiasm," Georg eventually embarked on his portrait of the elder Galsworthy, visiting the home on multiple occasions and transforming its drawing room into his studio. With each visit, Lilian not only observed his painting take shape but also Georg himself as he worked. "In the bay window sat my sister always," Mabel recalled, "her translation or other work on a table in front of her—artist and canvas well within her view." She observed Georg with her "eager shining eyes" which "seemed to drink in his excitedly-expressed ideas humbly, thirstily, without reservation" because

> to watch him paint was a revelation. He worked with feverish intensity. Darting at the canvas as though he wanted to annihilate it, he would lay the paint on with a kind of fierce tenderness, impossible to describe. Then, springing back, he would survey the picture from a distance, his eyes ablaze and his broad hand—in which the slender brush looked as much out of place as a pin in the jaws of a steam-hammer—waving wildly, or stroking the air with the 'composing gesture', before violently

---

3. Ibid., 74.
4. Ibid., 75.

attacking tubes and palette again with a view to some fresh and subtle combination of colour.⁵

Beyond falling in love as she observed Georg and he inspired her intellectual pursuits, Lilian was navigating her lifelong interests and desired future goals influenced by the lingering Victorian separate spheres. Expected by her parents—and wider society—to remain and grow in her domestic role, self-sacrificing and managing the household, she desired otherwise to live and grow in the public domain and participate in its prevailing ethic of work and achievement. According to Mabel, Lilian was

> quiet and studious [...] [a] rare spirit in a frail body [...] who brought to us three younger ones the greater part of such mental stimulus as our very normal, ordinary lives ever knew. Always quietly busy herself with her painting, reading, needlework or writing, it was she who would start interesting subjects for discussion; she who told us stories when we were little; she who opened our eyes and minds to beautiful things to be seen or heard or read.⁶

Closest in character to her brother John, Lilian's literary interests stretched back over a dozen years when, around 1892, she "had discussed with him a book which she thought of writing."⁷ During the same period, she recorded in her personal notebooks the substantial depth and variety of her intellectual interests, ranging from philosophy to nature to women's rights.⁸ Over time, her desire to learn and create would drive her to be "ferociously literary," as Henry James would later describe her, and to suggest "alterations" to her brother's 1900 novel *Villa Rubein,* a story about "the love of a young Austrian

---

5. Ibid., 76.
6. Mabel Edith Reynolds, *Memories of John Galsworthy* (London: Robert Hale, 1936), 17. Lilian's lifelong frailty was due to a number of ailments, including curvature of her spine and occasional rheumatism. Rudolf H. Sauter, *Galsworthy the Man: An Intimate Portrait* (London: Peter Owen, 1967), 34–35, and Lilian Sauter to Georg Sauter, May 5, 1910, JG(II)/9/1/59, Cadbury Library, University of Birmingham.
7. H. V. Marrot, *The Life & Letters of John Galsworthy* (London: William Heinemann, 1935), 109.
8. Lilian Sauter, diaries and related papers, JG(II)/10/1–7, Cadbury Library, University of Birmingham.

painter for an English girl," which was inspired by and dedicated to her and Georg.⁹

So as Georg conveyed his inspiration, passion and enthusiasm for the arts, he tapped into creative interests which Lilian held dear. As Mabel later explained the situation, for her sister,

> a new door to spiritual freedom was rapidly opening—new aspects were swiftly presenting themselves of existence and of art. The very crudity and violence of his feelings and expressions were an attraction; their independence [sic] fascinated her diffident nature and drew her wonder and covert applause. To both of us, indeed, it was an exciting upheaval— the sudden encounter with his volcanic nature, with its combination of the elemental (Ursprünglichkeit) and the artistic (Künstlerschaft), its almost fanatical urge for work and its detestation of "Pfuscherei" [bad-job] of any kind.¹⁰

Bavaria

Following their courtship of several years and engagement in 1892, Georg and Lilian married in 1894, her parents ultimately understanding her love for Georg and supporting her wish to be with him.¹¹ Shortly thereafter, they left London for Bavaria. Their destination was the Kneipp health resort in Wörishofen, the center of the Natural Cure Movement of Germany, a form of hydrotherapy practiced by Father Sebastian Kneipp.¹² Here, Georg hoped to find artistic inspiration and Lilian hoped to find comfort and relief from her frail health. As they found what they were seeking, they became parents. On May 9, 1895, Lilian gave birth to a boy with assistance from a midwife, a close friend of Georg's mother who had assisted her in Georg's birth 29 years earlier.

The days that followed brought out the best in Georg and Lilian as new parents, but they also provoked understandable frustration given the new rhythm of their lives, which impinged upon their hopes for rejuvenating in the baths of Wörishofen. Visiting the pair and their child as they all resided

---

9. Marrot, *The Life & Letters of John Galsworthy*, 108–9, 120; Ford Madox Ford, *Memories and Impressions* (Harmondsworth, Middlesex: Penguin Books, 1979), 366. See also Barker, *The Man of Principle*, 80–81.
10. Reynolds-Galsworthy, "Memories of Georg Sauter," 76.
11. Friedrich Max Müller to Georg Sauter, December 24, 1892, MS G/MüLLER.4, Taylor Institution Library, Oxford University. See also Barker, *The Man of Principle*, 38.
12. Serena Gianfaldoni, et al. "History of the Baths and Thermal Medicine," *Open Access Macedonian Journal of Medical Sciences* 5, no. 4 (2017): 566–68, https://www.ncbi.nlm.nih.gov/pmc/articles/PMC5535692/.

in an apartment of the historic Castle Mattsies, Mabel recalled one day when Georg

> laying his little 'Madonna' tenderly on the bed [...] sat down with me to await events. They did not tarry. Soon there was a wriggle, a little waving fist and sound which I would fain have called musical but which afterwards confessed to finding hideous and exasperating beyond words. Ge[org] proved surprisingly equal to the occasion. His broad hands handled the tiny rebellious morsel of humanity with a certain dexterity. He laid his little Bubi in his Wife's arms; and peace reigned again in Schloss Mattsies.[13]

However, even as Lilian "was up and could take charge of the child" with her "newly-recovered strength," such "peace" did not last long. Georg dismissed the midwife, "declaring" her "superfluous," and neither she nor Lilian "had dreamt of questioning" his judgment. The result was love still expressed by Georg, yet mitigated by his artistic temperament, and a miserable situation for Lilian, because as

> tenderly as he loved his little "madonna" he seemed incapable of realizing the additional strain put upon her so much frailer person by the nervous imagination of a delicately-bred organism, which sent a thrill of panic to her heart at every cry or whimper from the by-no-means easy-going babe. He took his own part gallantly at night, it is true; often walking up and down for half-an-hour at a time when the child in his arms, when convinced of legitimate cause for the trouble. But he has great ideas on the education of the baby and if these ideas came uppermost, as they generally did in daytime, when he wanted to work in the adjoining room, he would insist on its being left to scream in its cot, regardless of all pleading in favour of more soft-hearted measures.

This dynamic became the norm for some time before the couple struck a balance. Lilian regained her health while Georg returned from his occasional outings in the countryside with flowers for her and "more proud of his 'Bub', more careful and tender to his little 'Madonna.'"[14]

Several weeks later, Father Kneipp christened Georg and Lilian's son, an honor that was likely the result of Georg having "great admiration" for Kneipp as well as an eagerness to paint his portrait. However, the christening

---

13. Reynolds-Galsworthy, "Memories of Georg Sauter," 80.
14. Ibid., 81.

itself did not go smoothly. When Georg and Lilian indicated that they wished their child to be named "Ian Helmuth," Kneipp "flatly refused to permit it" because there was no saint named Ian and they could not convince him that "Ian and John, or Johann, were really the same." Then and there, after some "hasty whispered consultations," Georg and Lilian chose another name: Rudolf. Kneipp was satisfied, the boy was christened Rudolf Helmuth, and all was well, including Georg's relationship with Kneipp, whose portrait he eventually painted.[15]

Georg and Lilian remained in Wörishofen through most of 1896 and then spent time in Rome before moving to London with Rudolf the following spring. They settled in 8 Cambridge Gate where they had met and fell in love.[16] Soon after, the couple moved to 1 Holland Park Avenue, Kensington, through the generosity of Lilian's father who had bought the lease to the property.[17] Settled among notables in this fashionable neighborhood helped Lilian and George to become notables themselves and their son to grow up and be influenced by the artistry, activism and sociability of their home. This culture would infuse their lives for 18 years before the Great War would change everything.

Holland Park

Taking its name from the nearby grounds of the Jacobean mansion called Holland House, Holland Park was an idyllic hub of upper-middle-class Edwardian sociability. The neighborhood encompassed the impressive Phillimore Estate and the ornate, well-to-do areas of Campden Hill Square and The Royal Crescent designed by the planner Robert Cantwell. During the late nineteenth century, a number of notable artists and art collectors lived in the area, most notably "The Holland Park Circle" of artists including Lord Frederic Leighton, Valentine Prinsep and George Fredric Watts, among others.

In this historic and well-respected milieu, the Sauters lived among prominent authors, educational leaders, businessmen, religious leaders, and physicians and

---

15. Count de Soissons, "George Sauter," *Artist* 30 (June 1901): 173; and Peter Schäfer, "Georg Sauter und seine Jenaer Professorenporträts," *Das kulturhistorische Archiv von Weimar* 1, no. 2 (2008): 97–109.
16. Reynolds-Galsworthy, "Memories of Georg Sauter," 83.
17. Lilian and Georg also settled in 1 Holland Park thanks to sister Mabel who, with her new husband Thomas Reynolds, had noticed the property during the course of their own house hunting. Mabel and Thomas settled into 10 Tor Gardens, Campden Hill, near to brother John who lived in 16a Aubrey Walk. See also Barker, *The Man of Principle*, 53.

surgeons.[18] Down the street and above the poulterer's and fishmonger's shops of 84 Holland Park Avenue was the home of Ford Madox Hueffer (later Ford), editor of the *English Review*, the major literary journal of the day in which Lilian would later publish her poetry. Like the Sauters, Ford frequently hosted "congenial parties that brought literary people together."[19] Other prominent neighbors included the physician and author Thomas Dutton; Joseph Lichtenfeld, London's leading wig-maker; Miss Evans Bell, a member of the executive committee of the Royal Institute of Painters in Watercolors; the cabinetmaker John Sollie Henry; and Mrs. Ada S. Ballin, the well-known author, editor and magazine proprietor of children's and women's magazines.[20]

Comfortably situated and following in the footsteps of The Holland Park Circle, the Sauters established their own circle in their new home which had its own prominent history. Originally built in the early 1820s by the London developer James Brace, 1 Holland Park was augmented with a studio in the 1860s around the time when Alexander Constantine Ionides, the prominent shipping owner and art collector, purchased it for himself and his family.[21] Before the Sauters moved to the residence, it was occupied by William Holman Hunt, the pre-Raphaelite painter and one of the founders of the Pre-Raphaelite Brotherhood who held that artists should interpret the world as a system of visual signs.[22]

Boosting the prestige of 1 Holland Park was the loving investment of Lilian's father in converting its top floor into a large studio naturally lit by twenty-foot-high windows on the north and south sides, overlooking "the expanse of northern

---

18. *Royal Blue Book: Fashionable Directory and Parliamentary Guide, January 1899* (London: Kelly's Directories, 1899), 320.
19. Ralph Herman Ruedy, *Ford Madox Ford and The English Review*, PhD diss., Duke University, 1976, 44, 87.
20. University of California, Davis, "Household Books Published in Britain," accessed June 30, 2021, http://householdbooks.ucdavis.edu/authors/2326. See also W. J. Gomersall, Correspondence to the editor, *Westminster Review* 166, no. 1 (July 1906): 114.
21. University of Glasgow, "James McNeill Whistler: The Etchings, A Catalogue Raisoneé: Alexander Constantine Ionides, 1810–1890," accessed December 28, 2020, https://etchings.arts.gla.ac.uk/catalogue/biog/?nid=IoniAC. See also Charles Harvey and John Press, "The Ionides Family and 1 Holland Park," *Journal of the Decorative Arts Society* 18 (1994): 2–14.
22. Historic England, "Holland Park," accessed June 30, 2021, http://www.imagesofengland.org.uk/details/default.aspx?id=480017. See also British History Online, "Campden Hill Square area," in *Survey of London 37, Northern Kensington*, ed. F. H. W. Sheppard (London: London County Council, 1973), 87–100, http://www.british-history.ac.uk/survey-london/vol37/pp87-100.

London."²³ According to Ralph Hale Mottram, a close friend of the family, this impressive space had

> all the impedimenta—easels, curtains, frames and paints, pushed against the walls or stacked in a gallery to make room, in a more domestic and 'homey' atmosphere than is perhaps common in such places, for a large and well-stocked tea-table, the cups, plates and hit-water dish upon which were dominated by a Russian samovar, covered by a special straw-woven cosy.²⁴

The setting, Mottram described further, was

> presided over by Mrs. Lilian Sauter, who won my rather overawed provincial heart with the first glance of her beautiful grey-blue eyes. Smaller-boned and more obviously hypersensitive than her brother, either from the strain of being a painter's wife, or uneasily accepted maternity, or merely the new awareness of social injustice around, she was already slightly grey and worn. Or it may have been from the extra effort she put into the delicate verses she somehow contrived to write amid her other pre-occupations. Beautifully dressed, with just a touch to show her devotion to the arts and to the current internationalism that differentiated her from the average Kensington hostess, she made me welcome. She was supported, on one side by Jack [John Galsworthy] and Ada and on the other by her husband. I had visited the Continent sufficiently to recognize in him a dark-haired, tan-cheeked, square-shouldered central European mountaineer, who had assimilated his environment so equitably and so well controlled his inevitable accent, that one thought of him first as a painter and only remotely as of foreign birth.²⁵

And completing the group, Mottram observed:

> at their feet, half-concealed in his mother's robe, or a rug, was the jolliest and least ordinary of little boys. He was Rudo (Rudolf Helmut Sauter), then seven years old, showing in his bright glance and the gleam in his ducky hair just that fine edge with which some outside strain endows the otherwise plain British race.²⁶

---

23. Rudolf H. Sauter, "'The Other Side of the Coin': John Galsworthy as We Knew Him," typescript, ca. 1967, n.p., JG(II)/12/6, Cadbury Library, University of Birmingham.
24. Ralph Hale Mottram, *For Some We Loved: An Intimate Portrait of Ada and John Galsworthy* (London: Hutchinson, 1956), 28.
25. Ibid., 28–29.
26. Ibid., 29.

The "framework" of this home, Mottram concluded, "the house itself, the money that kept it going, the lightly-held social rules that governed it, were utterly English," even while "much of the furniture, many of the sentiments, were derived thankfully from anywhere beyond these islands."[27] Herbert Furst of the *Art Record* echoed Mottram's perspective on the residence, observing it to be exquisitely representative of Georg's artistic identity and rising international reputation:

> No sooner have you entered Sauter's house than a mysterious atmosphere surrounds you—a peaceful harmonious feeling and though you may not have seen the man yet—you feel his presence. His staircase is white and the carpets dark green. The walls are hung with reproductions from the artist's paintings and his invisible presence greets you: Welcome in *my* house. His studio is large and not crowded—in fact, you are able to see everything that is in it and everything has its reason to be where it is; the easels, the chairs, the crowded writing-table; the huge red brick fireplace and the large old-fashioned bellows, everything seems conscious of its duty which consists in making a *milieu* for the man to whom they belong. All this, though you may not think so, is very important and concerns Sauter the man more than you probably admit. [...] You enter his studio and if you are possessed of the gift of looking into and not at things you know at once that you have entered the domains of a real artist [...] Sauter's house is very quiet—full of harmony—the noise has been transformed into a silent music and the theme is *adagio consolante*.[28]

This creative milieu placed Georg at the very center of the artistic community in which he would further establish his international reputation. For Lilian, it constituted the base for her own intersecting artistic and political engagements, as well as her participation in the monthly salons which she and Georg hosted in his studio and called their "Fourth-Sunday At-Homes."[29] For Rudolf it was a milieu of love and learning as exemplified by two distinctive portraits completed by his father shortly after the family moved into the residence. *Maternity* depicted Rudolf and his mother in a warm and tender embrace (Figure 1.2), while *Comrades* depicted him with his arm around his

---

27. Ibid.
28. Herbert Furst, "George Sauter...An Impression," *Art Record* 2, no. 41 (January 1902): 665.
29. Lilian Sauter to Georg Sauter, May 5, and October 2, 1910, JG(II)/9/1/59 and 63, University of Birmingham. Rudolf H. Sauter, *Galsworthy the Man: An Intimate Portrait* (London: Peter Owen, 1967), 35.

Figure 1.2 George Sauter, *Maternity*, ca. 1899, oil on canvas, 69.9 × 49.5 cm, © Research and Cultural Collections, University of Birmingham.

grandfather, John Galsworthy Senior (1817–1904) as the two gazed at a large sea-shell (Figure 1.3).[30] Both images portrayed Rudolf with his large eyes, high cheekbones and thick hair, offering a glimpse of the handsome young man he would become.

The Sauters in Holland Park

Georg and His Circle

Comrades and Maternity stood among dozens of portraits and landscapes Georg produced in his Holland Park studio, all contributing to his burgeoning career and reputation for having, as one critic observed, "a special psychological

---

30. Complementing these portraits of Rudolf's home life are contemporary photographs held by the Cadbury Library, University of Birmingham, depicting him enjoying the outdoors with his family including his grandfather from whom Rudolf inherited thousands of pounds. This was the first of several inheritances that would come Rudolf's way over his lifetime—those of his uncle and aunt would follow, respectively in 1933 and 1956—all helping to support his artistic endeavors and household expenses. Barker, *The Man of Principle*, 16, 99.

Figure 1.3 George Sauter, *Comrades*, ca. 1900, oil on canvas, 68.6 × 55.9 cm, © Research and Cultural Collections, University of Birmingham.

perception, an interest in and instinctive understanding of human character" in addition to

> power of seeing finely, i.e. a natural faculty for seeing and selecting phase, pose, lighting, that which is beautiful, interesting, out of the common, distinguished and individual. He also has the sense of arrangement in the sense of so placing in the canvas and grouping and balancing the masses as to form a whole, harmonious in line and colour; feeling for equality in the work, i.e. sense of and a love of, the beautiful; rich and atmospheric qualities of texture to be obtained in painting; a mastery of technique, i.e. drawing and brush work; feeling for tone, accurate and fine perception of values and appreciation of effects and atmosphere; and finally, above all, deep devotion to Nature and a wide, open-minded view of her. These qualities and the fulfillment of these conditions have opened for his pictures the doors of museum in Brussels, Venice and the capital of his own country Munich.[31]

---

31. Count de Soissons, "George Sauter," *Artist* 30 (June 1901): 169–80, 171.

Georg's career reached its pinnacle in 1909 when his painting *The Bridal Morning* won second prize in the thirteenth annual exhibition of the Carnegie Art Institute. The work caused "much astonishment"[32] due to its eroticism, received by the public in much the same way that Manet's *Dejeuner sur L'herbe* had been in 1863.[33] Georg reluctantly responded to the protests, explaining that "it is a symbolical [sic] picture [...] universal & intended to embody an idea expressed through form and colour."[34] Public outcry eventually subsided and Georg continued his painting but never with the impact as he had experienced with *The Bridal Morning*.

A key driver of Georg's professional success was his association with the International Society of Sculptors, Painters and Gravers, established in 1898 under the presidency of James McNeil Whistler.[35] Georg served as honorary secretary of the group and became a member of the intimate circle of Whistler followers who, with Whistler himself until his death in 1903, regularly participated in the Fourth-Sunday At-Homes of 1 Holland Park.[36] Also in attendance was young Rudolf, who later recalled these occasions involving not only Whistler

> who was very fond of my mother [but also] the American etcher, Joseph Pennell, tall and thin, joyously disputing with everyone, Mark Twain, discussing philosophy, religion and Survival with my mother [...] Prince Pierre Troubetskoy, humanitarian and best-man at my parents wedding in 1894 [...] Ezra Pound and Richard Aldington, fresh from contributions to the magazine *Blast!* Blasting everything and everybody, including John Galsworthy for having bourgeois opinions.[37]

---

32. Frank Moore Colby, ed., *The New International Year Book 1909* (New York: Dodd, Mead, 1910), 549.
33. Albert Boime, "Georg Sauter and the *Bridal Morning*," *American Art Journal* 2, no. 2 (1970): 72–80.
34. Georg Sauter to Harrison Morris, May 14, 1909, box 118, folder 4, papers of Harrison S. Morris, Princeton University Library.
35. George Sauter, "The International Society of Painters, Sculptors and Gravers," *Studio* 14 (1898): 109. See also David Bernard Dearinger, "George Sauter," in *Paintings and Sculpture in the Collection of the National Academy of Design, 1826–1925* (Manchester, VT: Hudson Hills, 2004), 491.
36. The International Society of Sculptors, Painters and Gravers, of London, *Catalogue of the First American Exhibition. March 3 to March 27, 1904* (Chicago: Art Institute, 1904), 3.
37. Rudolf H. Sauter, *Galsworthy the Man: An Intimate Portrait* (London: Peter Owen, 1967), 35. Other participants in the salons organized by Georg and Lilian included G. F. Watts, Hubert Herkomer, James Gutherie, Laurence Binyon, Campell Dodgson and curators of the British Museum. See James Gindin, *John Galsworthy's Life and Art: An Alien's Fortress* (Ann Arbor: University of Michigan Press, 1987), 49.

Figure 1.4 Sauter family photograph of Joseph Conrad and his son Borys, ca. 1900, JG(II)/15–16 (box 3), Cadbury Research Library, University of Birmingham.

Other salon participants included John Macallan Swan, the award-winning English painter and sculptor, who Georg selected to be Rudolf's mentor,[38] as well as Joseph Conrad, who, as a father himself to a young son, appreciated Rudolf and his interests[39] (Figure 1.4). A few years later, the two "talked boats," Conrad observing that for

> "Rudo"—then age thirteen—"model sailing seems to be his hobby just now." Conrad recalled further that they "got on very well," adding "he is an engaging boy and no mistake."[40] The following year, after seeing Rudolf and his mother at a performance of Galsworthy's play *Strife*,

---

38. Mottram, *For Some We Loved*, 31.
39. This image is one among several held by the Cadbury Library, University of Birmingham, which attests to the closeness of the Conrad family with the Galsworthys and Sauters.
40. Joseph Conrad, *The Collected Letters of Joseph Conrad*, volume 4 (Cambridge: Cambridge University Press, 1983), 75. Young Rudolf was also interested in aviation, as suggested by Galsworthy sending him, at the urging of Ada, "the standard work on aviation," which "looks heavy enough to kill all your aspirations." John Galsworthy to Rudolf H. Sauter, December 22, 1910, JG(II)/20, Cadbury Library, University of Birmingham.

Conrad observed that Rudolf "struck me as very big and nice with a most sympathetic glance of any boy I ever knew."[41]

Complementing the nurturing environment of 1 Holland Park was Rudolf's summertime travel with his parents. In 1906, the family visited towns and galleries in Holland.[42] Subsequently, from as early as 1909 through 1912, they visited the mountains of Switzerland. It was likely during one of these later trips that Rudolf sketched figures in town squares, reflecting his emerging interest in the human form (Figure 1.5). Around the same period, he completed a sketch of boats reflecting his love of the subject and perhaps also his growing interest in landscapes[43] (Figure 1.6).

Lilian and Her Circle

With her "sensitive intellect," "consuming desire to be a poet" and devotion to contemporary literature, Lilian achieved her own professional success in Holland Park as she actively participated in the Fourth-Sunday At-Homes which she and Georg hosted and wrote and published poetry with enthusiastic support of her brother John.[44] While her sketchbooks of a decade earlier reveal her nascent interest in poetic forms and themes, she began to compose poetry formally as early as 1904.[45] A few years later, she began to establish her reputation as a socially conscious author. In September 1910, she achieved her first publishing success when her fellow Holland Park neighbor Ford Madox Hueffer featured two of her poems in his prestigious *English*

Rudolf's interest in this subject remained with him throughout his life, likely inspiring his aviation-themed works during the Second World War and his interest to take his first glider flight on his 80th birthday.

41. Joseph Conrad, *The Collected Letters of Joseph Conrad*, 225.
42. Lilian Sauter to Harrison Morris, September 17, 1906, box 118, folder 4, papers of Harrison S. Morris, Princeton University Library.
43. Rudolf sent this sketch to his lifelong friend Curtis O'Sullivan (1894–1967). O'Sullivan received his early education in St. Aubyns, Rottingdean, Sussex and at Westminster School before moving to California to enroll in the University of California at Berkeley. He subsequently enlisted in the US Army, serving as Captain of Infantry during the Great War and, during the Second World War, as colonel of infantry. "California Militia and National Guard Unit Histories, Outline History of the California National Guard (1950), The Adjutant General," accessed June 30, 2021, www.militarymuseum.org/cng50.html.
44. Barker, *The Man of Principle*, 69. also John Galsworthy to Lilian Sauter, March 21, 1910, JG(II)/10/7, Cadbury Library, University of Birmingham.
45. Mottram, *For Some We Loved*, 29.

Figure 1.5 Rudolf H. Sauter, sketch of a woman, 1910, pencil on paper, 12.7 × 8.8 cm, private collection, © Trustees of The Estate of Rudolf H. Sauter.

Review.[46] "The Aviator" and "The Pause" appeared in the company of works by two respected contemporaries, Charles Newton Robinson and James Stephens, and by notables including Hilaire Belloc, R. A. Scott-James, James Stephens, H. G. Wells and Hugh Walpole, among others. With its powerful existential inquiry, "The Pause" was well placed in this impressive collection:

> Surely our life, in essence, is concrete
> Eternal verity and death
> Only the pause in the incessant beat

---

46. *The English Review* 6 (September 1910): 193.

Figure 1.6 Rudolf H. Sauter, drawing of sailboats, 1913, pencil on paper, 10.7 × 13.9 cm, private collection, © Trustees of The Estate of Rudolf H. Sauter.

Of many-pulsing life, the breath
Indrawn, the wave receding, that returns? ...

Declaring "The Aviator" to be "a quite notable effort," the *Globe* quoted one of its impressive verses:

For once to measure with an infinite span
The little things of earth, from heaven's great height,
And thence to view the works and ways of man,
And judge their values with a clearer sight!
O Joy! To race the winds and hear them singing,
To cleave the clouds and spring and swoop and rise,
And on and on, in the infinite, up-winging,
With throbbing pulse and sun-confronting eyes![47]

Noting the previous appearance of "The Aviator" in the *English Review*, the editors of the *Living Age* reprinted it alongside work by William Watson and

---

47. "The English Review," in *Globe* (London, England), August 31, 1910, 5.

Guy Kendall. The *Argonaut* did the same, placing it with other current verse by Arthur Chapman, William Watson, Berton Braley and Richard Wightman.[48]

With these publications, Lilian joined the literary company of her increasingly well-known brother John and other notables who had also published in the pages of the *English Review*, including Joseph Conrad, Thomas Hardy, D. H. Lawrence, Wyndham Lewis and Ezra Pound. Lilian's reputation grew and more poems followed. In just over a year, the *Englishwoman* featured six of her works,[49] namely "Astrantia," "Trevone," "To Love," "Storm-Cry," "Still Life," and—standing among her most powerful works—"Woman," which concluded:

> Hail! Hail to her full revelation!
> No queen and no slave shall she be!
> But strong for the weal of the nation
> A voice shall be hers with the free!
> Acclaim her the comrade of men!

Additionally, the *Vineyard* featured her poem "Poet's Work," which seemed to encapsulate her lifelong literary dreams:

> To pluck a thought out from the heart of life,
> Plunge it in molten words and fling it high!
> A flaming banner in the gloom of strife,
> A beacon blazing in a storm-swept sky ...[50]

Soon after the appearance of "Poet's Work," the Women's Printing Society published Lilian's poem "Women's Highest Plea for Suffrage." This achievement likely brought her to the attention of the Women Writers' Suffrage League (WWSL), which had been supporting many notable authors including Beatrice Harraden, Laurence Houseman, Violet Hunt, Marie Belloc Lowndes, Alice Meynell, Elizabeth Robins, Olive Schreiner, May Sinclair, Evelyn Sharp, Margaret Woods and Edith Ayrton Zangwill.[51] In

---

48. *The Living Age* (November 12, 1910): 386; *The Argonaut* (January 6, 1912): 10. "The Aviator" also appeared in the *Jackson Daily News* with the notation that it was published originally in the *English Review*. *Jackson Daily News*, January 14, 1911, 3, https://www.newspapers.com/image/194327250/.
49. Respectively, these six poems appeared in the *Englishwoman* 5, no. 14 (1910): 199; 5, no. 15 (1910): 262; 6, no. 18 (1910): 264; 7, no. 21 (1910): 267; and 9, no. 26 (1911): 188–89.
50. Lilian Sauter, "The Poet's Work," *Vinyard: A Monthly Magazine* 2 (September 1911): 511.
51. Founded in 1908 by Cicely Hamilton and Bessie Hatton, the WWSL sought to "obtain the vote for women on the same terms as it is or may be granted to men and its method

1911, the WWSL published Lilian's poem "Women's Plea," and shortly thereafter supported the publication of her book *Through High Windows*, a collection of her poems.[52] Dedicated to Georg, the volume included "The Aviator" and "The Pause," as well as "Woman's Song of Freedom," which Annette Hullah, a noted writer on the subject of music, had set to music and the London Society for Women's Suffrage had published to advance the cause. "Raise the song of liberation!" Lilian's song began and continued:

> Rouse the fire in every heart!
> For the weal of all the nation!
> Women claim their equal part!
> Raise the song of freedom!
> Call the low land and the valleys,
> Wake the wide and wind-swept hills,
> Voice the slums and crowded alleys,
> In the work-room and the mills,
> Breathe the song of freedom!
> Life the heart to high endeavour,
> Fire the thought and nerve the will,
> Though the bonds be hard to sever
> Clasp your faith in justice still!
> Break the way for freedom
> Like a wide and flowing river.
> Rolling onward to the sea,
> Woman's life shall deepen ever!
> O thou River wide and free!
> Bear us on to freedom!
> On to larger duty, flinging
> Wide the mother-heart to all!
> Till the nations hear our singing,

---

was to employ the pen to achieve this." Elizabeth Crawford, *The Women's Suffrage Movement: A Reference Guide 1866–1928*, 712–13.

52. Lilian and her work were in good company at the WWSL which also published *How the Vote Was Won: A Play in One Act* (1909) by Cicely Hamilton and C. Hedley Charlton; *The Suffrage Question* (1909) by Madeleine Lucette Ryley; *A Pageant of Great Omen* (1909) by Cicely Hamilton; "Women's Cause" (1909), a poem by Laurence Housman; *Why* (1910) and *Under His Roof* (1912) by Elizabeth Robins; *Lady Geraldine's Speech* (1910) by Beatrice Harraden; and *Feminism* (1912) by May Sinclair, and a cartoon postcard of "Justice," by W. H. Margetson. Elizabeth Robins, *Way Stations* (London: Hodder and Stoughton, 1913), 225–28, and Elizabeth Crawford, *The Women's Suffrage Movement: A Reference Guide 1866–1828* (London: Taylor and Francis, 2003), 713.

Till they answer freedom's call
Raise the song of freedom!

Lilian's political affiliations extended beyond the WWSL. She served as temporary secretary of the Spiritual Militancy League for the Women's Charter of Rights and Liberties, established in 1913 "with the object of showing in a militant manner without violence that Woman Suffrage has a spiritual connection and is not a purely secular movement."[53] Despite its pledge of nonviolence, newspapers on at least one occasion associated the organization with the broader militant suffragist movement,[54] certainly to the dismay of its members and very likely also to Lilian's brother John who was, by his own public testimony, "a supporter of woman's suffrage, but not of militant suffragism."[55]

While the suffrage movement enthusiastically embraced Lilian and her writings, at least one reviewer, publishing in the *Guardian*, offered a tempered view of her book *Through High Windows*:

> Mrs. Lilian Sauter has concentrated a great deal of vigorous and vivid feeling into a small collection of verses. [...] The half-dozen sonnets are a rather weak spot in the volume and Mrs. Sauter's energetic plea for the suffrage, an excellent plea, is, as a poem, too explanatory. She suffers from a tendency to allow poetic seriousness to overheat itself as it take form; yet several of her shorter lyrics—and we should like to mention in particular that called "To Love"—burn with a clear heat of which no part is wasted.[56]

Despite such criticism, Lilian continued her writing, publishing "The Cause" in the June 1914 issues of the *Englishwoman* and *Jus Suffragii*.[57] The war

---

53. "Militancy for Non-Militants: A Spiritual Militancy League," in *Votes for Women* (London, England), February 21, 1913, 301. See also "A New League: The Woman's Charter," *Devon and Exeter Gazette*, March 18, 1913, 2, https://www.britishnewspaperarchive.co.uk/viewer/BL/0000511/19130318/001/0002.
54. "Suffragists Burn a Pavilion at Kew, Two Arrested and Held without Bail—One Throws a Book at a Magistrate. Shots Placed in Keyholes. Men Getting Home Late at Night Made to Suffer—'Wasps' Attend Church in Startling Gowns," *New York Times*, February 21, 1913, 5, https://timesmachine.nytimes.com/timesmachine/1913/02/21/issue.html.
55. John Galsworthy, Appeal to the Press (A Letter to *The Daily News*, 1911), as reprinted in Galsworthy, *A Sheaf* (London: William Heinemann, 1916), 184–85.
56. "Recent Verse," *Guardian* (London, England), March 13, 1912, 5, https://theguardian.newspapers.com/image/259003876/.
57. "June Magazines," *Common Cause* (June 5, 1914), 189, https://www.britishnewspaperarchive.co.uk/viewer/BL/0002226/19140605/034/0009.

eventually interrupted her career. The traumatic experiences of Georg and Rudolf being interned ended it. A decade later, shortly after her death due to persistent ill-health made worse by her wartime anxiety, the *Sackbut* reprinted her poems "Heart-Lighted" and "Trevone."[58]

Georg and Lilian's respective accomplishments—indeed their mutual support within and beyond their loving, intellectual and creative home—profoundly shaped Rudolf's attitudes, outlook and later creative work that addressed the human condition in times of war and peace. Equally influential was his experience of the "Victorian phenomena" of the preparatory and public schools of Elstree and Harrow and their focus on the classics, cult of athleticism and dedication to the Empire.[59] These institutions defined Rudolf's life as they did the lives of so many of his generation, but in his case, his artistic identity blossomed not as a result of his education in these institutions but very much despite it.

Elstree

Rudolf entered Elstree in 1905, during the headmastership of the Reverend Franklyn Lushington, the prize-winning classical scholar and sportsman who set the prevailing classical, masculine and imperial tone of the school.[60] Here, under the guidance of the "great games player" J. F. Morris,[61] Rudolf learned Latin, taking "great interest in his work" and "making favorable progress."[62] He learned mathematics under William McGregor Hemingway, a "scholar of King's College and a cricket and athletics Blue," who reported that Rudolf "show[ed] considerable ability and [was] keen in his work."[63] Under the

---

58. *The Sackbut* 4 (1924): 309 and 314, respectively. Ninety years later Lilian's "Women's Song of Freedom" would be included in the seminal collection *Literature of the Women's Suffrage Campaign in England*, but she would remain a largely unknown literary figure whose life, like so many, was upended by the Great War. Carolyn Christensen Nelson, ed., *Literature of the Women's Suffrage Campaign in England* (Peterborough, Ontario: Broadview Press, 2004), 173.
59. J. A. Mangan, *Benefits Bestowed? Education and British Imperialism* (Manchester: Manchester University Press, 1988), 57; Melanie Tebbutt, *Making Youth: A History of Youth in Modern Britain* (London: Palgrave, 2016), 34, 51, 117. See also Jeffrey Hill, *Sport, Leisure and Culture in Twentieth Century Britain* (Houndmills, Basingstoke: Palgrave, 2002); H. Branston Gray, *The Public Schools and the Empire* (London: Williams & Norgate, 1913).
60. I. C. M. Sanderson, *A History of Elstree School and Three Generations of the Sanderson Family* (privately printed, 1979), 35–41. See also Mangan, *Benefits Bestowed?*, 62.
61. Sanderson, 37.
62. Rudolf H. Sauter, Elstree School report, 4 November 1905, JG(II)/9/7, Cadbury Library, University of Birmingham.
63. Ibid.

instruction of the Reverend N. V. Ridgeway, scholar of Worcester College, Oxford, Rudolf learned French and English, "getting along quite satisfactorily" in the former and ranging from "fair" to "very fair" to "good" in the latter and equally so in the subjects of divinity, history and geography.[64] As for Rudolf's "General Conduct" by the end of 1905, Lushington reported that it was "excellent" and that he was "glad to read such good reports of him."[65] In 1907, Rudolf brought home two prizes, one for mathematics and another for Latin.[66]

Three years later, the Reverend G. A. Scott reported that Rudolf was "a very painstaking worker" in Latin and "making good progress." R. F. Bailey reported that Rudolf was making "progress in geometry [...] equal to the top boys [while] still rather fussy over his work." And William Hemingway reported that, in French, Rudolf "works very hard" but he was "not making as much progress [...] as [...] hoped." In English, his reading and writing were "fair" and his history and geography "very fair." And as for Rudolf's "General Conduct" in this later report, Lushington simply stated that it was "very good."[67]

Harrow

Harrow solidified Rudolf's experience in Elstree, as well as his upper-class upbringing. He entered in the Easter-Midsummer term of 1909, following in the footsteps of his uncles John and Hubert, who entered in 1881 and 1884, respectively.[68] Upon his own arrival, Rudolf stood among the "the boys with London addresses" and many others from across the United Kingdom and the empire.[69] Under the primary instruction of John Cottam Moss, an award-winning classics expert, Rudolf began his time by "working very well," making "an excellent start," and deserving "the highest praise."[70] Testifying

---

64. Ibid.
65. Ibid.
66. Lilian Sauter to Harrison Morris, December 31, 1907, box 118, folder 4, papers of Harrison S. Morris, Princeton University Library.
67. Rudolf H. Sauter, Elstree School report, December 18, 1908, JG(II)/9/7, Cadbury Library, University of Birmingham.
68. *Harrow School Register*, 1900–1911, comp. and ed. R. Courtenay Welch (London: Longmans, Green, 1911), 583 and 618.
69. Christopher Tyerman, *A History of Harrow School, 1324–1991* (Oxford: Oxford University Press, 2000), 376.
70. Rudolf H. Sauter, Harrow School reports, June 20 and July 31, 1909, JG(II)/9/7, Cadbury Library, University of Birmingham.

to his early accomplishments was his receipt of prizes for his achievements in mathematics and science.[71]

Such accomplishment levelled off as Rudolf proceeded through his studies. Overall, Moss reported that Rudolf's performance in French and mathematics was consistently "good" and "satisfactory," and his Latin to be "weak" even while he regularly "work[ed] well" at it. And perhaps as a foreshadowing of his nurtured and growing focus and discipline in art and literature, Rudolf's work in science was occasionally "weak" but more regularly "excellent," "neat and tidy," "promising," "methodological," and "steady and industrious." Toward the end of his time at Harrow, Rudolf received a prize for his achievements in science,[72] and around the same period Moss observed that Rudolf's "essays show real promise: the best work I have had for a long time from a beginner."[73]

As for Rudolf's own view of his studies and experiences at the school, he told his mother in late 1909 that, with regard to a recent lecture, it was "very badly delivered and was a little too scientific. The general opinion was that it was the worst lecture we have had for a very long time." Here, Rudolf informed his mother further that he had "chosen science for specials as Mr. Moss thinks it would be the best and even suguested [sic] it himself." He wrote further, "I hope you do not mind," suggesting that he was worried about his mother's literary interests informing a negative view of his decision. He quickly changed the subject of his letter first to music, informing her about his friend "Gearies [who] plays the piano quite well" and an "informal concert the other day in which only boys performed," and then to cricket, informing her that his team was "beated B-1 in semi-finals".[74]

---

71. *Harrow School Register*, 1900–1911, 906. Moss was a former Porson and Craven Scholar, recipient of the Powis Medal, two-time recipient of the Greek Epigram and three-time recipient of the Browne Medal for Latin Ode and the Greek Odo. *Harrovian* 22, no. 6 (October 23, 1909): 83. See Harrow School, "Harrow Terminology," accessed 30 June 2021, https://www.harrowschool.org.uk/news-events/explore-harrow/harrow-terminology.
72. *The Harrovian* 24, no. 3 (May 27, 1911): 36.
73. Rudolf H. Sauter, Harrow School report, April 8, 1911, JG(II)/9/7, Cadbury Library, University of Birmingham.
74. Rudolf H. Sauter to Lilian Sauter, December 14, 1909, JG(II)/9/1/54, Cadbury Library, University of Birmingham.

These accounts of Rudolf's academic achievements in Harrow belie his poor state of mental health which understandably concerned his parents. As Lilian wrote to Georg in the spring of 1910, "Rudo has just gone through one of his bad crises of depression which are dreadful to me." She continued:

> it accumulated for days, & finally all came out in a great talk with me. Dreadful unhappiness at feeling that he is *unable* to do all he wants, & to *feel* all the joy in beautiful things that he ought to feel, & that Harrow is killing this power more & more. After a good fit of crying he got better a little, but he is all the time feeling slack & sleepy, & tired after walks & rides etc.—& he looks unhealthy. I don't really know what to do. This fine air ought to have done some good & doesn't seem to. We have been unfortunate in the weather—only two really fine days—gales & rain all the time!—most disappointing & depressing …[75]

A few weeks later, Lilian wrote to Georg that she

> went to Harrow. […] It was a *heavenly* day—The most beautiful we have had. The young green sang against the pure delicate sky. I found the dear boy cheering up—pleased I think at beginning to feel his undoubted position in many ways—& not finding himself overwhelmed by the work as I had feared. Fancy, in Geometry he is now in the first division in the whole school!—On his hardest day last week he got up before 5.30 to do his preparation! but he says this term he will have more time for it, than last, because they only play cricket on half holidays, not every day as they did foot-ball. He says that the 1st & 2nd fifth forms do practically the same work, all together, under Mr. Crutwell. He is hoping so much for a letter from you.[76]

Lilian visited Harrow again that fall, finding "Rudo very subdued" but, with his friend, a boy named "Fitch,"

---

75. Lilian Sauter to Georg Sauter, April 20, 1910, JG(II)/9/1/57, Cadbury Library, University of Birmingham.
76. Lilian Sauter to Georg Sauter, May 5, 1910, JG(II)/9/1/59, Cadbury Library, University of Birmingham.

very pleased that they have at last a room alone together again—& a large room—intended for 3 but with no third boy this term. It looks out on the opposite side, but over the Vicarage garden, with a large branching yet tree just before the window, where birds come, & no bars to that window. There is another, barred, window in the room as well. Rudo *is* of course in the 1st fifth. When I was at "bill" it seemed to me this time there were very few boys who marched past before the boy appeared & even those were not all above him as the classical 1st fifth march in first but is not really above the [Middle 5th]. He sent his *very* best love to you dearest—Do write him a few lines very soon, he cares so much for it.[77]

Georg did write to his son on multiple occasions. In reply to one letter, composed shortly before the coronation of King George V, Rudolf responded lovingly:

Dearest Father, Thank you ever so much for your lovely letter; it was such a pleasure for me to receive it. I was just longing to hear from you again. I am so glad the work is going well but I do hope you will be here with us again soon. At the time of the coronation I shall be able to come home [...] so that I shall get at least two good days with you then; and then also at the Harrow and Eton Exeat. The spring here is lovely too but I do not get much time to enjoy it, so there is always too much to be done. Today however is a most melancholy and miserable day, drizzling rain all the time. On my birthday mother came down and I had a most lovely afternoon with her, the weather could not have been more beautiful.

He continued:

As the term goes on I like my room more and more; it is much quieter than the one the other side of the house that I had last term. I am so sorry you are kept awake by the too-joyful birds in the morning and so can get very little sleep. Dear father do write to me often even if it is only a postcard from some place where you have gone on a motor

---

77. Lilian Sauter to Georg Sauter, October 2, 1910, JG(II)/9/1/63, Cadbury Library, University of Birmingham.

tour or something. I do so love to hear all about what you are doing and what is happening over there and what you are enjoying. The last evening of the holydays mother took me to see 'A Midsummer Night's Dream.' I do not think I have ever enjoyed a comedie more than I did this one. It was very well acted and staged. Mother also took me to see Ibsen's play 'The Master Builder' which I also enjoyed very much. Now I think I have exhausted everything I have got to tell you, once already through mother. I do so wish you were here so that I could give you a real good hug and thousands of kisses. With ever so much love, from your loving son.[78]

As Rudolf's words revealed his sensitive and thoughtful character and relationship with his parents, his sketches in the margins of this letter revealed his nascent artistic mindset. He embraced his new dormitory room as a studio, offering his father his window view of "St. Mary's Harrow" (Figure 1.7a) and his playful vision of a sleeping kangaroo (Figure 1.7b).

Suggesting that he dedicated significant time to these sketches, Rudolf concluded his letter with an explanation and loving apology: "I wrote the letter a long time ago but has been waiting for the drawings please forgive my not having sent it before dear father [sic]."[79]

As with peers of his generation, a fundamental part of Rudolf's education at Harrow was his regular participation in that most Victorian of activities which had "character-building value"—cricket.[80] Rudolf was a member of Torpids, the under-16 House cricket team made up of boys who had been enrolled in Harrow less than two years.[81] By spring 1911, the school considered Sauter's team, led by Mr. Moss, alongside the team led by Mr. Warner, to be "the two strongest." As the *Harrovian* reported,

> In the torpid fives, the match between Mr. Moss' [sic] and Mr. Warner's [...] ended in a victory for Mr. Moss's—no unexpected result, for McClintock had already on his first year proved himself the best torpid fives player in the School. They had, however, a good deal of difficulty in

---

78. Rudolf H. Sauter to Georg Sauter, May 21, 1911, JG(II)/9/2/7, Cadbury Library, University of Birmingham.
79. Ibid.
80. Article appearing in the *Harrovian* throughout Sauter's tenure attest to his participation in cricket. See especially *Harrovian* 23, no. 4 (June 20, 1910): 51; 23, no. 6 (October 22, 1910): 95; 23, no. 8 (December 17, 1910): 135; 24, no. 2 (April 8, 1911): 28; 24, no. 8 (December 16, 1911): 143, 145.
81. *Harrovian* 23, no. 2 (April 2, 1910): 26.

beating Mr. Warner's and the game between the two pairs produced the best torpid fives we have seen, all four players hitting hard and playing with sense. McClintock was really the mainstay of his side, being very safe, getting up first cuts well and hitting excellent ones. Sauter wisely left him all he could, but played steadily in the back court.

Acknowledging that Warner's team played well and "made a lot of good shots," the *Harrovian* went on to reveal that

the first game went easily to Mr. Moss's: the second went point by point, Mr. Warner's leading at first and they led afterwards at 13–11. Here they got in and won. In the last game, the scopes were level at 6: then Mr. Moss's made 5 in one hand. Mr. Warner's replied with five 13 all was reached and both sides went in and out pointless, McClintock

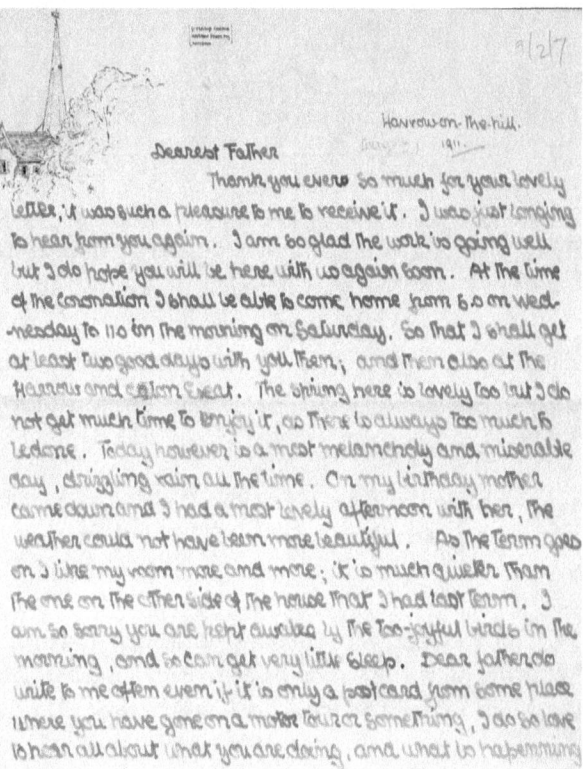

Figure 1.7a and 1.7b (*Continued*)

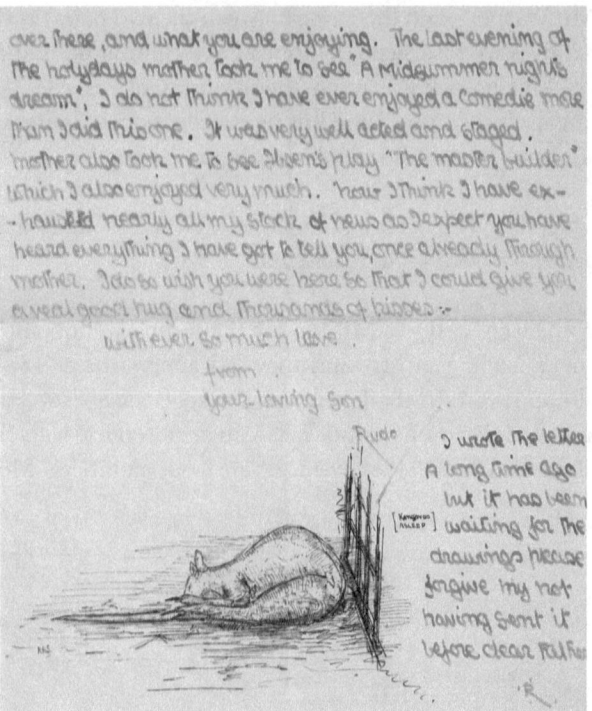

Figures 1.7a and 1.7b Rudolf H. Sauter, letter to George Sauter, May 21, 1911 (recto, left, and verso, right), JG(II)/9/2/7, Cadbury Library, University of Birmingham, © Trustees of The Estate of Rudolf H. Sauter.

making one magnificent save that very likely turned the game. Then Mr. Moss's made the needful 2 points and won. Their other games were easy victories.[82]

This victory led to Rudolf and his teammate William K. McClintock being photographed together, an image of youthful athleticism which belied the different paths they would take in the coming years, and their different fates (Figure 1.8).

Born to William and Edith McClintock on March 7, 1896, McClintock had entered Harrow only a few months after Rudolf, in the January Easter term of 1910. While Rudolf left the school in February 1912,[83] McClintock

---

82. *Harrovian* 24, no. 3 (May 27, 1911): 44.
83. *Harrovian* 25, no. 1 (February 24, 1912): 5.

Figure 1.8 "Harrow School Champion Torpids 1911," Rudolf H. Sauter (left) and William K. McClintock (right), Harrow School Archives.

remained, eventually playing in the 1914 Schools Match and then leaving to follow in his father's military footsteps by enlisting and serving at the front in the Connaught Rangers.[84] After the war, he became a right-hand batsman for Gloucestershire.[85] Rudolf's future would stand well apart from McClintock's just as it would from most of the 27 boys with whom he entered Harrow in

---

84. "Eaton v. Harrow," *Manchester Courier and Lancashire General Advertiser*, July 11, 1914, 2, https://www.britishnewspaperarchive.co.uk/viewer/BL/0000206/19140711/001/0002. The UK National Archives, "Lieutenant William Kerr McClintock: The Connaught Rangers," accessed June 30, 2021, http://discovery.nationalarchives.gov.uk/details/r/C1057007?descriptiontype=Full&ref=WO+339/3060.
85. ESPN Cricinfo, "William McClintock," accessed June 2021, https://www.espncricinfo.com/england/content/player/17468.html.

1909. Approximately half of them would go on to serve at the front during the Great War, and at least eight would be killed in combat.[86]

* * *

For Rudolf, the mottos of his alma maters Elstree and Harrow—respectively, "Clarior Ex Obscuro" (Brighter, Out of the Darkness) and "Stet Fortuna Dormis" (Let the Future of the House Stand)—held remarkable irony. The days ahead for him, and for his mother and father, would in fact be far darker compared to the brightness that had long illuminated their lives. As Joseph Pennell, a family friend, reflected on their Holland Park home in 1921, it "now stands for tragedy—the life in it wrecked by the war as was the life in so many other houses not only in London, but the world over."[87]

---

86. Rudolf's class at Harrow included the following boys who would go on to serve at the front* and who would be killed in combat†: Ronald Anson†, Kenneth Edward Brown*, Marshall Lord Curtis Brown, Jack Oliver Cooper†, Guy Leslie Crosland, Frederick Hugh Palliser Clermont de Costobadie, Christen Albert de Linde, Eric Robert Donner†, Philip Julius Donner*, William Whitworth Fox*, Ronald Edward Oliver Goetz*, Horace George Seale Hallam†, George Herbert Harrison†, Cyril Leigh Heseltine*, Lance Alfred Holland, Edward William Rigbye Jacques†, Charles D'Arcy Jessopp, Robert Keith Makant*, Cecil George Ochs*, Alfredo Pacheco; Samuel Herbert Arthur Rathbone Proctor, Alistair Brand Hautonville Richardson, Roland Ruffer *, Maurice James Peel Scully*, Owen Brice Smyth*, John Maurice Stewart†, and Ralph Bertram Van Praaagh†. This assessment is based on studies of *Harrow School Register*, 1800–1911, comp. and ed. R. Courtenay Welch (London: Longmans, Green, 1911) and *Harrow Memorials of the Great War*, volumes 1–6 (London: Philip Lee Warner, publisher to the Medici Society, 1918).
87. E. R. and J. Pennell, *The Whistler Journal* (Philadelphia: J.B. Lippincott, 1921), 149.

Chapter 2

INTERNMENT, 1914–19

On August 5, 1914, one day after England declared war on Germany, Parliament passed the Aliens Restriction Act, requiring foreign nationals, particularly Germans, to register with the police and, when necessary, be interned or deported.[1] As Georg described the situation to his friend Ethel Fiedler, "the calamity which has come over us is so terrible and paralysing, we [are] dumb."[2] Despite this climate of widespread anti-German sentiment and fear of spies, Georg and Lilian sought to live as usual. He continued to paint. She continued to write, publish her poetry and expand her involvement in suffragist circles. Rudolf continued the studies he had begun in Munich a few years earlier. He also spent time in Manaton at Wingstone, his uncle's farmhouse, riding horses and walking in the countryside.[3] The normalcy all three Sauters attempted to achieve belied the fact that "the shadow of war was creeping closer to them."[4]

Indeed, the rule of wartime law eventually caught up with them when authorities interned Georg on December 7, 1915.[5] The action appalled his family and friends, and especially his brother-in-law. Galsworthy soon petitioned strongly for Georg's release, sending a letter to the Home Secretary Herbert Samuel and visiting the Home Office where he argued personally for Georg's

---

1. Matthew Stibbe, *Civilian Internment during the First World War: A European and Global History, 1914–1920* (London: Palgrave MacMillan, 2019), 91–93.
2. Georg Sauter to Ethel Fiedler, September 3, 1914, MS.G/SAUTER G.10, Taylor Institution Library, Oxford. More generally, with regard to "the present unhappy state of affairs in Europe & our own feelings for all the millions of sufferers through it," as he conveyed to Ethel Fiedler, Georg soon thereafter suggested a similar state of mind to his friend Harrison Morris, writing that "it absolutely paralises [sic] my thoughts" Georg Sauter to Harrison Morris, September 17, 1914, box 118, folder 4, papers of Harrison S. Morris, Princeton University Library.
3. H. V. Marrot, *The Life and Letters of John Galsworthy* (London: William Heinemann, 1935), 413.
4. Ralph Hale Mottram, *For Some We Loved: An Intimate Portrait of Ada and John Galsworthy* (London: Hutchinson, 1956), 184.
5. Georg Sauter to Harrison Morris, December 9, 1919, box 118, folder 4, papers of Harrison S. Morris, Princeton University Library.

case. Ultimately, Samuel did nothing except refer the case back to the tribunal dealing with internees. In May 1916, with a petition in hand signed by himself and many other well-known writers and artists, Galsworthy appealed in person to an Advisory Committee in Westminster Hall, but without success.[6] The news about Georg's likely fate, as well as the near-certain fate of Rudolf, made Lilian all the more frail and full of worry. The artist Leon de Smet captured her poor physical and mental state in his contemporary portrait of her.[7]

Lilian continued to worry even as the police permission she and Rudolf had received, thanks to her brother, allowed them to travel to Manaton to avoid the anti-German feeling in London where they had been restricted to a five-mile radius of their home in Holland Park.[8] Anxiety and fear continued to mark their lives through the winter of 1916–17, when, in January, Georg was repatriated to Germany, "able to take nothing with him but his trunk which was robbed on the way & leaving practically all his work locked up in hostile countries."[9] This terrible news, combined with the persistent and pervasive anti-German climate, prompted Rudolf to decline to volunteer for national service, thinking that this action would put him in even greater jeopardy if he would be repatriated to Germany like his father. As he explained in a letter to government authorities:

> While gratefully recognizing the kindness with which I have been, hitherto, treated here, I feel that, seeing that my Father [...] has, after internment, been repatriated to Germany and that the feeling in England against Germans is such, that in all probability he and I will be forced to live there and not here after the war, I cannot put myself in the wrong

---

6. Lilian Sauter to Harrison Morris, May 25, 1916, box 118, folder 4, papers of Harrison S. Morris, Princeton University Library.
7. Leon de Smet, portrait of Lilian Sauter, 1916, red and brown crayon with charcoal, 52 × 37 cm, National Library of Medicine, National Institutes of Health. Created by de Smet for Lilian, he inscribed it, "Très respectuesement au cher maître G Sauter, Leon de Smet 6.7.16."
8. Dudley Barker, *The Man of Principle: A Biography of John Galsworthy* (New York: Stein and Day, 1969), 174–75.
9. Lilian Sauter to Harrison Morris, January 21, 1921, box 118, folder 4, Princeton University Library. En route to Germany, Georg spent five weeks "with dear friends in Holland" where he was "nursed back to strength & health & reintroduced in the most charming way to civilized habitation." Georg Sauter to Harrison Morris, December 9, 1919, box 118, folder 4, papers of Harrison S. Morris, Princeton University Library. Soon after arriving in Germany, he began to travel around Europe, living and working in various locations and eventually traveling with Rudolf throughout Italy, as discussed below.

with the Government in Germany and incur the penalties there, that would follow my signature of the National Service Form.[10]

Internment therefore became Rudolf's fate even as the tranquility of Manaton and the company of his mother and uncle provided a temporary sense of security. His visual works of this period reflected his state of mind as he pondered the impact of events on himself and his family.[11] Some of these images, like *Meadows with Yellow Flowers, Sun through a Thin Mist* and *Windswept Clouds*, channeled his hope as they belied his anxiety, fear and sadness. Others, like *Dark Hills, Dusk* and *Storm over a Tor*, reflected his emotions more directly, as did his contemporary poems, some of which he composed in German perhaps as a way to connect culturally with the fate of his father. Such works included "Im Stillen" (In Silence)—dated November 13, 1917—"Traum!" (Dream!)—composed two days later—and "Choral—Zu Weihnachten, 1917" (Choral—for Christmas, 1917).[12]

During the months that followed, Rudolf composed more poems which further revealed his worry—if not his depression—about his likely fate. "Mein Herz ist grau!" he proclaimed in "Klage" (Legal Action), dated February 21, 1918. "Die Trauer tönt: Gefängnis!" he announced in "Gedanke" (Thought), also dated February 1918. And in "Morgengesang" (Song at Dawn), he longed for the boundless possibilities of life despite his anticipated captivity. Many more poems took shape after authorities arrested Rudolf in March 1918, transported him from Wingstone to London and imprisoned him in the Alexandra Palace.[13] From "Verborgenheit" (Seclusion) to "Der Gefangene" (The Prisoner) to "Eintonig ... In der Gefangenschaft" (Monotonous ... In Captivity), these works represented the very rupture of his life from all he had known in idyllic Manaton and comfortable Holland Park. To cope with this rupture, he would continue to draw, paint and write, embracing the certainty of his prewar life—indeed his artistic identity and skills—in the face of uncertainty.

---

10. Rudolf H. Sauter to unknown recipient, as reprinted in HO 144/5759, "Nationality and Naturalisation: Sauter, Rudolf Hellmut. No Nationality. Resident in Bury, Sussex. Certificate 14038 issued 3 November 1926." UK National Archives.
11. Harry Moore-Gwyn British Pictures, "Rudolf Sauter Observations from Nature Spring 1916 works in pastel by Rudolf Sauter, PS, RI, RBA (1895–1977), exhibition as part of stand C6, Art Antiques London (June 12–19, 2013), accessed June 30, 2021, http://www.mooregwynfineart.co.uk/pdf/Sauter_catalogue_mk_1_Layout_1.pdf.
12. Rudolf H. Sauter, poems, JG(II)11/5, Cadbury Library, University of Birmingham.
13. Marrot, *The Life and Letters of John Galsworthy*, 441.

Alexandra Palace

Located atop Muswell Hill in North London, the Alexandra Palace was, by 1916 and according to the *Lancet*, one of Britain's "best known" civilian internment camps.[14] It held more than two thousand aliens in its "vast halls" that were "split up for disciplinary purposes to hold battalions of 100 to 600 men….[and] divided up by partitions," an arrangement which yielded a distinctly utilitarian environment:

> On each side of the screens are the low beds, consisting of three longitudinal planks raised an inch or two from the ground, with straw mattresses, pillows and blankets upon them. Ventilation strikes the incomer as distinctly good. The heating is carried on by means, for the most part, of hot-water pipes beneath the floor, which produce an upward current of air passing out at the louvres in the high roof and drawing in fresh air through the cracks in doors and windows without the necessity of any artificial system.[15]

Outside the building:

> Each battalion of prisoners has its own particular portion of the Palace ground to exercise in, the area being marked off by wire entanglements, besides the use of the Italian garden in the Palace. […] Occupation for these men, who are all interned civilians, is, of course, purely voluntary. […] Some of the aliens assist with the cleaning and housework. Large numbers are content with lying on beds idling about, or playing games.[16]

And inside:

> A considerable minority occupies a narrow enclosure running around the whole extent of the hall with benches on each side, on which skilled handiwork is carried out. Some are engaged in carving and fretwork inlay of no mean quality; others make wooden toys, models of boats and ships and the like; while others are occupied more seriously in tailoring and cobbling for their comrades.[17]

---

14. "The Alexandra Palace Internment Camp," *Lancet* 187, no. 4835 (April 29, 1916): 919–20, https://www.sciencedirect.com/science/article/pii/S0140673601120167.
15. Ibid.
16. Ibid.
17. Ibid.

And as the Young Men's Christian Association (YMCA) later recalled "this huge exhibition building," here

> was gathered a crowd representing all groups of society, from the humble German waiter in a Soho restaurant to the merchant prince; all professions from the Navy to the cubist artist; all degrees of education, from the absolutely illiterate to the holder of a university doctor's degree; every degree of national sympathy from the man who had a son in the British Army to the most earnest German patriot. It was a society in miniature held together by no spiritual bonds, not even those of nativity, but by the implacable barbed wire. It was a society shot through with discontent and a sense of injustice. Even those who had been interned to protect them from mob violence succumbed to the all-pervading sentiment and came to regard themselves as victims of a cruel and unnecessary deprivation of liberty.[18]

The YMCA offered a blunt verdict on the Alexandra Palace, stating that "from the physical point of view [it] was satisfactory enough; but the high glass-roofed building was a cheerless abode, mentally depressing to a high degree."[19]

Upon his arrival in these stark environs, shortly before his twenty-third birthday and labeled "P/W [prisoner of war] 15691," Rudolf stood among the thousands of internees held in comparable sites across Britain and Europe. They were a cohort whose psychological state the Swiss surgeon Dr. Adolf Vischer had been studying intensely and writing about at length for his book *Barbed Wire Disease: A Psychological Study of the Prisoner of War*.[20] In that publication, as the *Lancet* reported, Vischer accepted the dictum of the noted British biochemist Dr. F. W. Mott "that hysteria and severe neurasthenia are seldom seen in prisoners' camps," but what contributes to the depressed state of mind of the prisoner of war was

> the monotonous and scanty food-supply, the absence of fresh air, the circumstances of their incarceration, the loss of personal freedom and the loneliness; summing up in one sentence the three basic factors as

---

18. Frederick Harris, ed., *Service with Fighting Men: An Account of the Work of the American Young Men's Christian Associations in the World War*, volume 2 (New York: Association Press, 1922), 247.
19. Ibid., 247.
20. Adolf Lukas Vischer, *Barbed Wire Disease: A Psychological Study of the Prisoner of War* (London: John Bale Sons & Danielsson, 1919).

follows—loss of liberty for an unknown period in close company with many others. The result is a continual longing with entire inability to perform.[21]

Drawing on writings from various camps, Vischer illustrated the condition of loneliness among those suffering from "barbed wire disease." As the *Lancet* reported further about Vischer's work,

> in the midst of this loneliness the barbed wire draws itself like a red thread through his whole world of thoughts […] [T]he camp community consists of people who hope and wait together and in so doing become wearied in mind and soul. Some find outlet in gambling, many in the familiar occupation of "grousing." Rumour plays a large part in camp life. Reports which are not at first actually believed circulate freely, so that the whole camp population may pack their things at night in preparation for a departure on the morrow, of which there was no reasonable prospect. […] Even the best-educated has to struggle to perform mental work of any kind. Concentration becomes ever more difficult. Restlessness sets in, with mental fatigue, on the slightest exertion, whether of mind or body. Lack of memory is a frequent complaint.[22]

Viewing Rudolf's internment through the lens of this contemporary study helps to reveal how he embraced what he knew best—his artistic mindset—as a way to mitigate suffering from potential "barbed wire disease." He actively conceived his utilitarian environs as de facto studios—in the spirit and practice of those spaces he had come to appreciate previously in Holland Park, Wingstone and Harrow—wherein his fellow prisoners and their daily activities became sources of creative inspiration for writing, painting and sketching.

Rudolf's motivation to face his captivity in this way emanated in part from his father with whom he had been corresponding extensively. "I'm convinced that you will bear the misery with courage and you will do me credit," Georg wrote to his son a few weeks after he arrived at the Alexandra Palace. He advised Rudolf further:

---

21. "The Mentality of the War Prisoner," *Lancet* 192, no. 4968 (November 16, 1918): 675–76, https://www.sciencedirect.com/science/article/pii/S0140673601029749. For a contemporary review of Vischer's book. See "Barbed Wire Disease," *British Medical Journal* 2, no. 3056 (July 26, 1919): 107.
22. "The Mentality of the War Prisoner," *Lancet* 192, no. 4968 (November 16, 1918): 675–76, https://www.sciencedirect.com/science/article/pii/S0140673601029749.

Even if we are physically constrained, our spirit can never be captured! I hope and wish that these experiences will contribute to your personal liberation, just as mine paved the way for my liberation. You will soon find friends and plenty of subjects for painting. You will also be able to play your flute over time, to the delight of your fellow sufferers. I'm happy when I think of that! I often wish you were here with mein Wakefield. You in particular, with your talent in pastels, will find an infinite amount of motifs in the camp to create fine colourings. A camp can be incredibly picturesque! And you'll be able to draw, even to sketch portraits. There are plenty of models. Choose the finest people among them and time will pass quickly. Life isn't dull if you look at it from the right perspective! [...] Have a look if you can participate in sports—tennis, gymnastics or whatever is on offer, maybe you're already in the thick of it. Take the whole thing as a lesson of life! Use your time! I know it's possible and I have no doubt that you will do it.—Write only in German to me, to keep up to speed on the language. You'll experience a lot now: stay pure in body and mind! Don't ever lose faith in the good in people and you'll make friends for life! [...] It's your birthday in a few days. My dear Rudo! I will think of you, wishing you all the best. [...] Your loving father, G. Sauter.[23]

More than this, Georg told his son that he could—and should—remain an artist not despite his internment, but rather as an outcome of the very experience of it. "If you're able to spend your time doing nice work, it'll all work out! It's so much easier for us than for thousands of others who have been torn away from their professions." He continued:

I hope your captivity doesn't last longer than mine did. [...] Take care of your health in all aspects, it is man's most sacred and valuable commodity. [...] In days to come, you'll think back on the time of your internment with a smile if you are as lucky as I have been to meet and acknowledge some wonderful people. Shared suffering has a habit of bringing together the best people. May God grant that you enter their circle! [...] With fondest love, my dear son, from your loving father G. Sauter. Send my love to your mother.[24]

---

23. Georg Sauter to Rudolf H. Sauter, May 7, 1918, JG(II)/9/4, Cadbury Library, University of Birmingham.
24. Georg Sauter to Rudolf H. Sauter, June 2, 1918, JG(II)/9/4, Cadbury Library, University of Birmingham. Georg's message to his son in this letter and related others evokes a certain perspective he held about the artist's studio, according to his second wife, Valda. "A studio where one dreams, thinks, acts, fights & suffers is in a way a

Along with his own motivation, therefore, Rudolf took his father's advice to embrace his life in the Alexandra Palace and his creative skills to cope with it.

Testifying to Rudolf's initiative and offering a unique and multifaceted record of his captivity are the letters he wrote to Viola Ada Emily Wood, a companion to his aunt Ada. Viola had met the Galsworthys and Sauters in 1906 when she and her husband at that time, the artist William Leendert Bruckman, attended one of Lilian and Georg's salons in 1 Holland Park.[25] Viola grew close to the families as her marriage to Bruckman ended and the couple had fully separated by the war.[26] She and Rudolf also grew close, the pair eventually becoming soulmates.

* * *

"Was it not a wonderful day," Rudolf wrote to Viola on August 4, 1918, shortly after she had visited him in the Alexandra Palace:

> We held together in the cup of our hands, when last you pilgrimaged to see me! And, though we could not have any time alone—did that keep us apart or make any real difference? All the earth was richly robed in summer, veiled with light and crowned with one great turquoise set in a silver wreath—for us, all of us and for those others, to whom this day is the greatest of all days.[27]

He continued, lamenting the "oceans of sorrow [which] have poured over the land [whose] angry waves beat on against the sheltered peaceful homes of all these millions […] [and] what ages of pain have passed in each short moment of that time." Rudolf then offered Viola remarkably detailed written and illustrated descriptions of his confines (Figure 2.1):

> Out of the flashing sunlight, through a narrow passage way and door— narrow, that only one person may pass at a time and built about with

---

holy place. In my heart are prayers & my mind is turned towards the Highest & my desire is to create something beautiful which shall bring help and pleasure to many." Valda Sauter, "Some Strokes of a Pen-Portrait," undated, Valda Sauter papers, MS.G/SAUTER V.4, Taylor Institution Library, Oxford University.

25. Rudolf H. Sauter, *Galsworthy the Man: An Intimate Portrait* (London: Peter Owen, 1967), 32–33.
26. Viola Ada Emily Sauter. "Close Links with the Galsworthy Family," *Stroud News and Journal*, May 22, 1969, n.p. See also James Gindin, *John Galsworthy's Life and Art: An Alien's Fortress* (Ann Arbor: University of Michigan Press, 1987), 32–33 and Rudolf H. Sauter, *Galsworthy the Man: An Intimate Portrait* (London: Peter Owen, 1967), 36–37.
27. Rudolf H. Sauter to Viola Wood, August 4, 1918, Documents.8056, Imperial War Museum.

iron fencing so that people cannot rush out quickly in case of uproar—along a little gangway, gay with the light of sun on yellow-painted boards and into—blackness, absolute darkness it seems after the brilliant light outside (though sometimes there is a faint gas-jet burning, it seems to give light) then to stumble, fumbling up 14 bare steps, then 9 more (and now it begins to get lighter, for there is a little skylight far above us) then another 9 & still 9 more; and we are at the entrance of our sanctuary.[28]

Drawing Viola further into his world—and pulling both of them further apart from the idyllic one in which they had lived together before the war—Rudolf continued:

Now through two 1/4" solid iron doors, heavy and stiff to open and we are inside that mysterious place, shut off completely from the rest of the camp, whose secrets only a few know:—

Noting that his sketch "shows direction along which photo I showed you," Rudolf explained further that this "mysterious place" was the "General & Mess Room: A-Tower with Kitchen & Small Bed-room," which encompassed

a great hall about 25 foot square and the same height with windows almost the whole height [...] out of this the kitchen is boarded off and a small bedroom for three. The general arrangement of the room you will see from the diagram. From the main window we have a most wonderful view into the distance. From here a sort of "gloryfied" ladder leads up into a gallery in which are two baths, a sink, table with wash bowls and one cubicle for two beds and a large mirror. At each end of a window and at any time we can manufacture a draught capable of blowing away all cobwebs. In fact, there is not a single place in the tower, through which we cannot turn a river of wind at any moment, if we wish.[29]

He wrote further:

From this gallery two flights of still steeper ladder-steps (circa) of 9 steps each lead to our dormitory, which is the same size as the Mess Room and the passage outside it together and contains at present 12 beds each of which is built into a cubicle or "hut" of blankets hung on scaffolding. Higher still is a gallery to which a ladder leads and which contains two

---

28. Ibid.
29. Ibid.

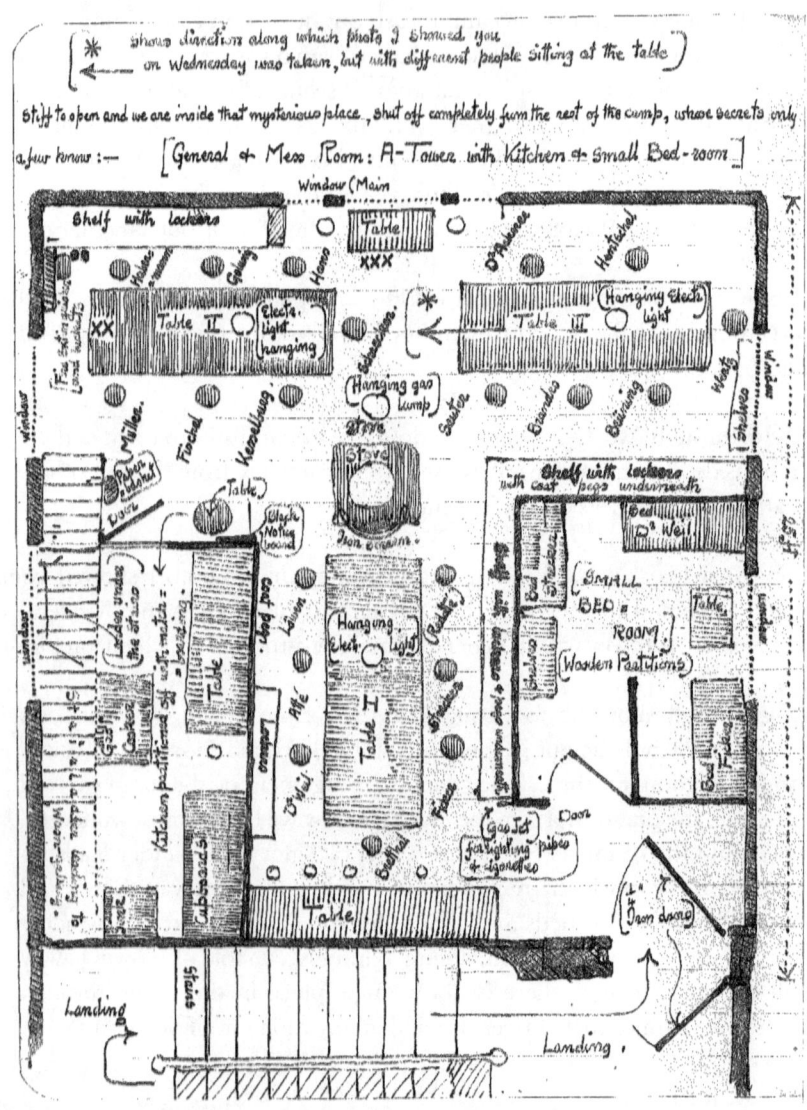

Figure 2.1 Rudolf H. Sauter, letter to Viola Wood, August 4, 1918 (detail), Documents.8056, Imperial War Museum, © Trustees of The Estate of Rudolf H. Sauter.

beds, built most wonderfully with roof, oil cloth floor, paper walls etc—most luxurious and unnecessary—where Hentschel & Dr. Achner sleep, although they did not build them.

Rudolf proceeded to offer Viola an apology for his "sketch plans" being "so rough and scratchy," hoping they "are sufficiently clear [...] to have some idea how the tower of our castle is arranged." Clear they very likely were to her, as she learned through their remarkable detail the character of the space Rudolf occupied, as well as the names of his fellow internees and who spent time doing what, and where within their quarters. Viola also learned details of the furniture and fixtures as well as Rudolf's own "special places," labeled as "XX," where he also sat "writing in the evenings; when the window is open," and labeled as "XXX," where he sat when "it is warm [...] otherwise my corner XX."

Pulling back from these details as if offering Viola a moment of calm in the center of the storm that was his new life, Rudolf suggested that what was taking place atop Muswell Hill, only miles from the life they had known in Holland Park, could have been scenes of a land located thousands of miles away, like the famous mountain of Ararat in Western Armenia. "I wonder if this will help you to follow things that happen here," he explained to Viola, "and help you more easily to take part in this queer and unnatural life that goes on within this ugly and ungainly ark, which from its Ararat looks over the whole of London."[30]

More detail followed, as Rudolf gave Viola insight into the very characters, layout, sights, sounds and pace of his world:

> In the evening we all sit about the tables and by degrees each has, so to speak, become associated with some particular place & employment. Thus Table I is reserved for readers and is mostly used by the people who also at meal times sit there. The far end of Table III you can be sure of finding a game of cards in progress—always the same people playing most noisily surrounded always by a number of people who never do anything else in the evening but watch the others play. At the near end people look at newspapers or talk. At Table II I usually sit writing; here too sit usually a pair of chess players and a few others writing—next

---

30. Ibid. Rudolf echoed this imagery of Ararat in his contemporary poem "Chor der Gefangenen" [Chorus of the Prisoners], and in one of his few oil paintings of this period, *An Aeroplane: View from the Compound Alexandra Palace Civil Internment Camp*, 1918, oil on panel, 27.5 × 35.4 cm, Art.IWM ART 16491, Imperial War Museum, accessed June 30, 2021, https://www.iwm.org.uk/collections/item/object/23787.

me on the left sits always a man who most assiduously and ineffectively tries to learn Russian […] he is a queer (lack of) character; &, deprived of his one great joy in life, his glass of beer, he makes a very pathetic figure—bright red hair, face almost as red, vacant eyes and a loud voice; usually quiet, when once he starts talking there is no end short of absolutely refusing to take on any notice, when the stream automatically & cheerfully ceases.

Shifting to the subject of time in his new world, Rudolf believed that his love for Viola helped him find and pass time, and be hopeful for the future:

And now, my wonderful Darling, […] do not fear; I am not worrying—not letting myself worry—about things; but just letting that come, which will come and, meanwhile, living in the golden hours you bring me; in the sunshine of our love; and in your happiness, that makes the worlds so beautifully bright.[31]

Rudolf also conveyed his acute sense of the pace of his days through several contemporary poems, including "Time" wherein he observed:

This unrelenting stratagem of life,
how should we measure it—unknowing!
By ripples, that drip minutes round the hem
and shore of future where the winds are blowing?
By sickled hours or by a planet's swinging?
Dare we account it growth? or must we lock
and bar the greatest moment of man's singing
within the sullen pulses of a clock? …

Challenged and lost time also featured in Rudolf's poem "Sleepless," where he recounted tossing in his bed as:

sleep scurries from the room;
I turn again; the darkness closes down.
Who's that hauling luggage overhead?
And someone's dragging chains across the sky,
harrowing the wind for stars—A thousand thieves
are picking all the locks (there are no locks

---

31. Rudolf H. Sauter to Viola Sauter, November 6–13, 1918, Documents.8056, Imperial War Museum.

to pick). Who's there? Who's there? *Who's
   there?*
A cupboard creaks reply and, everywhere
in the wainscote, shadow-footed things
run up and down, like rumours in a town.
There! something taps the blind and taps again.
My heartbeat shakes the bed's foundations, till
the entombed springs groan, reverberating down
deep between the interstices of dark.
The lithe-fingered dusk is tickling for a hair
along my scalp (as country children snatch
at trout that will not rise). And then,
my conscience swoops and perches on the bed
owl-eyed, unwinking-and glares great holes in me!
till all the worries leak in sweaty drops
out of my mind, to writhe and cling congealed
like rows of naked, pallid little "I"s.
My gleaming wrist-watch grins.
It's two o'clock
at least; and all the hidden pains, I've ever
had, creep from their holes and march along
my bones in armies—Sleep! It will not come.

* * *

Then, as I flick a match, the white walls stand
sentinel, within reach of my hand,
and mock at my imaginings and smile-
"it's only owls and rats which scratch awhile"—
and phantasy, that usurer of night,
extorting humour from imagined plight.

In "Doing Time," Rudolf explained how he lived in "a six-foot cube carved out of space" which included

a cupboard, camp-bed, trunk and chair,
one shelf (officially right bare
of things to eat—this year of grace)
my world, this lidless thing of rude
brown blanket, reinforced with stick,
hall-marked with arrows. [...] To be sick
in its slow-moving solitude,

what fitting sentence for the crime
of being alive!—That's doing time.

Among the many other spaces of the Alexandra Palace where Rudolf passed time was the "big hall" of A-Tower, where, one night, as he recounted in his poem "Night in the Big Hall," he heard a "DRIP, drip!" and observed:

> A monster morgue—a dismal vault,
> this, framed in dusk! [...] And ranks on ranks
> of living corpses on their planks,
> still dripping cold and miserable with thoughts
> that never halt... .
>
> Thick, thick
> with smoke! A little smudge of light
> is all that smears the sodden half-breathed air
> of yesterday with life. And, there,
> among the shadows thieving through the cold
> a face shows white.
>
> Drip, drip!
> Rain taps the floor. The minutes lag,
> a funeral, past the graves of sleep;
> the shadows toss and rats, they creep
> and gnaw the woodwork [...] . Figures huddle round
> a glowing "fag."
>
> Sick, sick!
> A cough—a cough! another spark
> of coughing grips its tinder, where
> the pillars echo. With a stare
> like glass, one dream-torn creature mutters:
> "Light!"
> The rest is dark.

Outside "A-Tower" the assault on Rudolf's senses—indeed his very existence—continued, as he wrote in "Barbed Wire All Round":

> Below, a hidden town!
> Lights swimming in the mist—Snow underfoot,
> it crunches as we stumble up and down—
> we creatures coralled in this narrow track
> (forty paces [...] Turn [...] And forty back,
> for miles on miles of purple dark we boot)

what spectacle of man's humanity!
Far quwheeting of an owl. [...] Then, suddenly,
his quivering call – so near it makes us start.
A shout! [...] A creak! Ghostlike a horse and
   cart
crawl in the yard; two men at head, with feet
lost wading in their shadows on the snow,
pass through the gate beyond the edge of sight.
A bayonet winks. [...] The sentries tick their beat
out on the boards and clock the hours [...] and
   sneeze!
(Poor fellows, shut up there and like to freeze!)

A challenge: "Who goes there?"—"Monotony."
Our prison tower gropes for the fringe of God—
to spit a star upon its lightning-rod.
And thousands of us, packed inside like blight... .

Well, *some* have walked across the world to-night!

Writing further about barbed wire in his eponymous poem, Rudolf began by asking:

I

WHAT bramble thicket this—grown overnight
on the clean earth-unflowering? In the dusk,
some mad end, loosened, taps upon its pole:
thorns tapping like the ghosts of dead delight.

II

WIRE, barbed wire!—A dour
and monstrous serpent round our lives.
And we're like creatures mesmerised;
it glares at us, all day, malignant, sour.

III

WIRE—fifteen feet of crouching coils to lock
man out from Heaven's wonder!
And yet, each evening, grey moths come to mock
and conjure it asunder.

IV

A NO-MAN'S-LAND, where little things can creep
and love and dance together;

flowers live ensanctuaried and crickets "cheep";
birds sing in silent weather.

V

WIRE—In Winter-time the snow
comes writhing down to perch on it
in great festoons. White-tented, now,
the distance marches in a bit.

Over the course of a tumultuous week in the middle of November 1918, as the armistice was being signed, Rudolf wrote another lengthy letter to Viola. It opened a further window onto how he was embracing his artistic identity by conceiving his environs as a studio. "This is how I spent the day," he began:

> Directly after count I walked up and down for an hour and a half, watching the grayness of the day, wondering and thinking about many things and, in between doing breathing exercises […] then in, to work at a little picture that was just in the right state of drying to be worked on. […] In the afternoon I worked again (had to, for my picture would otherwise have been dry by next day) and you may imagine with what thoughts the day was filled. […] All, all my love! … that is near and about you wherever you are. Love knows no distance, time is ours & beauty finds no breaking shore.

While Rudolf offered no details about the specific "little picture" to which he referred, it was one among dozens of works he completed during this period. Standing in stark contrast to the style and technique of his prewar work, these images in pen and ink and wash on paper immediately reflected his illustrated letters to Viola, and they underscored his diligence and commitment to capturing every possible perspective of his experience as a means of coping with it. Studies of his fellow internees (Figure 2.2)—perhaps individuals who he identified by name and located in his letters—guided him to complete detailed images of their various activities and routines in and around the private, semi-private and communal spaces of "A-Tower" wherein he and his fellow prisoners sought rest, refuge and hope for their freedom and an end to the war (Figures 2.3, 2.4 and 2.5).[32]

* * *

Despite the Armistice, Rudolf remained interned like many other enemy aliens and prisoners of war. Writing from Germany, Georg continued to offer

---

32. See The Fine Art Society, *Rudolf H. Sauter, 1985–1979 [sic] Internment Drawings—Alexandra Palace 1918–19, 7–25 June 1993* (London: Fine Art Society, 1993) for additional evidence of Rudolf's visual productions of this period.

Figure 2.2 Rudolf H. Sauter, untitled (Studies of Fellow Internees), ink on paper (recto, above) and pencil on paper (verso, below), ca. 1918–19, 23.4 × 30.4 cm, private collection, photographs by Stacy Ross, © Trustees of The Estate of Rudolf H. Sauter.

him words of encouragement as they both looked to the postwar world, as father and son, and as fellow artists. "I wonder how the atmosphere is for you and your fellow sufferers?" he wrote to Rudolf on December 4, 1918:

> It's important not to get thrown off the track. The sun will shine again! I'm always glad to hear that you enjoy your work—it helps us overcome

Figure 2.3 Rudolf H. Sauter, *"B" Battalion from the Workshops*, 1919, pen and ink wash on paper, 47.3 × 49.2 cm, © Trustees of The Estate of Rudolf H. Sauter, photograph by Lynton Gardiner, The Wolfsonian–Florida International University, Miami Beach, Florida, The Mitchell Wolfson, Jr. Collection, TD1993.98.1.

all those tragic experiences. Don't worry on my behalf and put your mother's mind at rest: I really feel well in every perceivable way, sitting here perfectly undisturbed, just as if it were the quietest of times. We have to be patient for a while about getting together; I think it's wiser if your mother stays put where she is now, until such a time when we are able to enjoy peace again and circumstances are back in order. I'd love to give you advice, help and encouragement, but for the time being I can only say hold out and trust that the bad times are coming to an end soon and that you'll be free again and can devote yourself to your art without any qualms of conscience. Militarism is hopefully a thing of the past by now, unless the world turns even crazier than before. From the newspapers, you'll be bound to be amply informed about all that's going on here. You know that you're free to make your own choices and that I understand and appreciate self-determination. I don't shed any tears for militarism and many other things of the past. My heart is full of hope that the new times will bring plenty of beautiful and noble things even if they are born of misery. We've seen plenty of examples how wealth only

Figure 2.4 Rudolf H. Sauter, *The Canteen, Alexandra Palace*, 1919, sepia ink wash on paper, 26.6 × 36.8 cm, courtesy of Dr. Colin Close,© Trustees of The Estate of Rudolf H. Sauter.

Figure 2.5 Rudolf H. Sauter, *The Watchmaker, Alexandra Palace, 1919*, sepia ink wash on paper, 12.7 × 17.7 cm, courtesy of Louise Kosman Modern British Art, © Trustees of The Estate of Rudolf H. Sauter.

leads to pride and parvenuism if misused and not made to be a blessing for peoples—just breeding hatred, envy and conceit instead of tolerance and all-embracing love. Look to the future with a calm and clear view. There's something great about walking or sailing through a storm.

And again, the following week, after receiving a reply from Rudolf, Georg responded with more fatherly guidance about life and art:

All your signs of life are a great joy and make me very happy. Even if our experiences in the past 3 years have been mixed with much grief and our separation was hard, the hope remains that we will see each other again, each of us equipped with rich experiences that will give us a new perspective about love and the foolishness people are capable of. Even if foolishness is a bitter spice—it's love that towers above it all like a shining pillar, dominating everything with its enthralling brilliance. Your ability to trust in people will come back. I can see that you feel lonely when it comes to art but my dear Rudo, the higher you climb on your path through this almost celestial field, the more you're going to feel lonely, like a mountaineer, trying to reach the summit. All great artists have been lonely—they alone are daring enough to walk the unknown ways of life. Was this not the case for our beloved Beethoven in particular? His heart beat for millions, for countless generations, but few hearts beat for him. [...]—I worry about your near future: whether you'll soon be free and in what form. Unfortunately, there's nothing I can do as our prisoners—heaven knows—can be held back, according to the armistice treaty.— [...] My lucky star is faithful to me as ever! May yours shine on you too, leading you along beautiful paths on your journey, into freedom and into my arms in the New Year. You always have the freedom of thought.[33]

Georg continued to encourage Rudolf to have faith in himself as an artist, prompting him to

find that, in the circles in which you find yourself, you are missing the company of those who appreciate the arts, then you will come to be all the more grateful once you come across it again. True understanding of the arts is most rare in these times that are eaten away by materialism. Don't let it discourage you. Shine and triumph are short lived. Keep

---

33. Georg Sauter to Rudolf H. Sauter, December 14, 1918, JG(II)/9/4, Cadbury Library, University of Birmingham.

the flame of what is true alive and burning: it's a most sacred flame and motivates us to keep going. Your mother writes that you managed to do a lot and even write poetry despite all the difficulties you've had to face. There will come a time when both will come into their own. Always think of humanity for which artists and poets are noble servants; don't think of nationalities. Among all of them, fools are equally and abundantly distributed. My heart goes out to you and to your mother—I'll be with you in spirit at Christmas! Somehow, some time, we'll see each other again in the New Year. Love to your mother and all the best from your loving father.[34]

Two weeks later, Georg wrote with a similarly positive and hopeful message, as well as much advice about how Rudolf should plan to travel to meet him, as he had evidently planned to do:

A few days ago, I received a message from your dear mother, telling me that you will regain your freedom in the not too distant future and today, I received your letter from the 18th December with the same happy news. God grant it will be soon and that we'll meet again, all healthy and in good spirits. So, it won't be too long until we three can see each other again.

However, news about Rudolf's release turned out to be either untrue or inaccurate. He spent several more months in the Alexandra Palace before authorities transferred him to Frith Hill Camp, Frimley, Surrey, in late spring of 1919. There, he faced the next chapter of his life in confinement.

Frith Hill Camp

Frith Hill Camp was a massive site encompassing two separate compounds, one for Germans and another for Austrians, Hungarians, Galizians, Moravians and Bohemians.[35] In the former—specifically camp #16 and tent #191—Rudolf continued to write letters, compose poems and paint and sketch images of his environs. Finding comfort and hope in the surrounding remnants of nature, he wrote to Viola:

---

34. Georg Sauter to Rudolf H. Sauter, December 24, 1918, JG(II)/9/4, Cadbury Library, University of Birmingham.
35. Graham Webster, "Frith Hill Internment and Prisoner of War Camp," accessed June 30, 2021, https://www.surreyinthegreatwar.org.uk/wp-content/uploads/2016/07/SHC-Frith-Hill-revised.pdf.

> My darling. [...] There is a tiny five-petalled purple flower (I don't know what it is called) which hides here in the trenches between our tents. The only flower, almost the only plant, with the exception of some few scraggy little clumps of dried-up grass, which dares to grow in the waste of this encampment. And very bold it is, though so shy as it smiles up at the sun—for no sparrows or mice, no beasts or birds come near us here. Only a few crows perch on the barbed wire and crow disconsolately, an occasional lark or two praises the dawn with its song, the jay-bird with its friendly not gargles at the moon, one or two cats (brought by the men from Alexandra Palace) prowl about & look miserable, which a few canaries, also pets, try their meagre best to outsing the wind—otherwise the creatures of the earth leave us severely alone. Even the insects (and perhaps this is an advantage) do not approach us too closely [...] a couple of small beetles, one butterfly—that is all. But this little flower looks at us so cheerfully out of the ditches, in spite of the sand which does its level best to silt up over its head; loving the sun and almost closing its beauty to the rain (shrinking before the rough weather.) it is like a beautiful thought in an arid place. Love in the wilderness!

He continued:

> One lives through each day, one much as the other, but it is seldom, so seldom that the arms of one's soul can reach the dim knees of the heavens that sit with their crowns of stars about the silence, waiting for mankind while the centuries swing by like comets, leaving trails of that fine flame that has inspired their being, white wakes that flare & fade again into their Mother-dark. [...] This is a queer sort of half-gypsy life—very interesting and amusing.

Rudolf explained further that "the camp itself is a mixture between army 'lines' and a gypsy encampment," and proceeded to offer Viola "a rough sketch of it"[36] (Figure 2.6).

Complementing this sketch was another in the same letter which illustrated an "account of the day," beginning around 6:00 a.m. when he awoke and proceeded to the washhouse, "a corrugated iron affair open at one side with more enclosed shower baths at the end, & running along the length of each a sort of table with taps and tubs."[37] There, Rudolf proceeded with

---

36. Rudolf H. Sauter to Viola Wood, June 13, 1919, Documents.8056, Imperial War Museum.
37. Ibid.

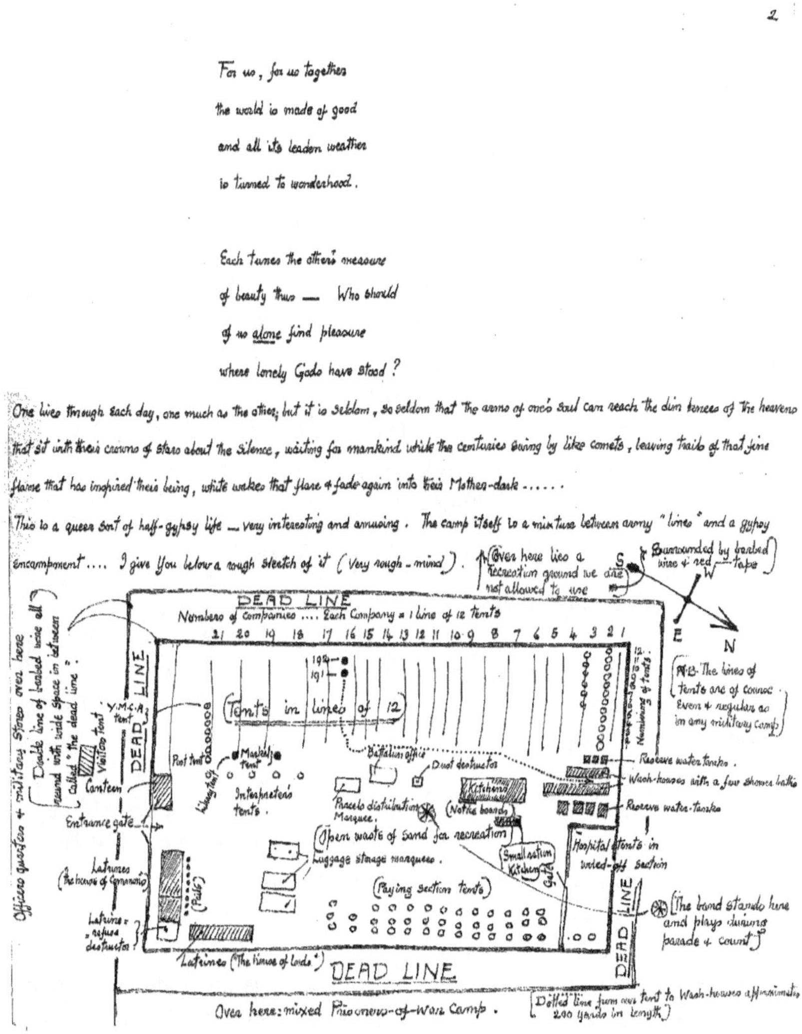

> For us, for us together
> the world is made of good
> and all its leaden weather
> is turned to wonderhood.
>
> Each turns the other's measure
> of beauty thus — Who should
> of us alone find pleasure
> where lonely Gods have stood?

One lives through each day, one much as the other; but it is seldom, so seldom that the arms of one's soul can reach the dim terraces of the heavens that sit with their crowns of stars about the silence, waiting for mankind while the centuries swing by like comets, leaving trails of that fine flame that has inspired their being, white wakes that flare & fade again into their Mother-dark......

This is a queer sort of half-gypsy life — very interesting and amusing. The camp itself is a mixture between army "lines" and a gypsy encampment.... I give you below a rough sketch of it (very rough - mind).

Figure 2.6 Rudolf H. Sauter, letter to Viola Wood, June 1919 (detail), Documents.8056, Imperial War Museum © Trustees of The Estate of Rudolf H. Sauter.

"shower-bath if there is still any water left (there is never any in the showers after 7:30 and sometimes not even in the taps)," and then he returned to his tent to "shave, dress, knock out my blankets, make the bed & put things a little straight, by which time the whistle will have gone and the stewards fetched one official breakfast (coffee—porridge *once* a week, nothing else."[38] He ate "in or just outside" his tent "for there are no big tents at our disposal either for meals or recreation." After breakfast, he explained further he

> put up the tent flaps and we clear up—then it is time for count at 9.0. For this we parade in companies side by side in the "recreation space" and march past four abreast to the sound of our band. After that we have the morning pretty well to ourselves except when it is ten—washing day or inspecting or something of that kind. On inspection mornings we must clean our tents more thoroughly that usual and at 10:30 are driven out of the lines ("Clear the lines!" "Clear the lines!!") and scuffle up and down in the sand for an hour or so until his Lordship has satisfied himself that there is sufficient red-tape tied to each tent, when we are allowed back again. At 12:30 we have lunch consisting of stew—a rather tasteless but wholesome corn conglomeration of unknown & international quantities.[39]

As for the remainder of the day:

> Usually we sleep or read in the afternoon it if is hot in the cold of our tent; if it is cold in the natural warmth of our tent, if it is windy its shelter, if it is not very windy in the beautiful drought which comes in under the lifted flaps—A wonderful contrivance ... a tent! About 4:30 we have tea (coffee & with it we get our daily ration of bread & biscuits, also sugar)—Supper is at 7:30 & consists of rice & beans, a good sloppy mess which we know we shall get tomorrow because we have had it yesterday & the day before & even the day before that, together with (sometimes) some under-cooked pig and our daily issue of margarine. Such is the simple table of our existence which brings us much fresh air and amusement & which, with a final rearrangement of beds etc & a preparatory slackening out of the ropes, ends in sweet sleep.[40]

---

38. Here and later, after he writes about his lunch "consisting of stew," Rudolf inserted a footnote to comment that "except of course what we surreptitiously cook over forbidden fires in the ditches between the tents—bacon, eggs, etc. Or an occasional custard."
39. Rudolf H. Sauter to Viola Wood, June 13, 1919, Documents.8056, Imperial War Museum.
40. Ibid.

Beyond such details of his daily life in Frith Hill Camp, Rudolf offered Viola a wider picture of his new situation as he faced it with his fellow prisoners:

> What is so interesting is to watch in what different ways the various men take this life here. [...] Some, at first miserable, soon find again the health they had lost in the stuffy air of Alexandra Palace & with it regain their spirit very quickly; Others stumble about clumsily complaining all day long. A few (to whom this sort of life is not new) were quite at home amongst their surroundings from the very first day. Some are pessimistic, most indeed—either openly or covertly and for them everything is a hardship from early morning until late at night— they do not omit to tell us so. [...] Others, whatever they may feel inside, find cause for amusement in every detail of existence. On the whole I think there is no question that we of the tower are a merrier crew than ever we were in the seclusion of our "palatial" residence on "the hill." The trouble with a certain few is that they will not see that this life is different from the one we are used to & that, here, each is very much more dependent upon his comrades (and they on HIM) for their comfort—&, failing to see this, they do not see either that a certain quantum of work is expected of each, that the whole may be complete. As first everyone, of our tents, stood round rather helplessly, shouting for food (so that those in other tents would look around at us & stare) & letting mess accumulate. (I am afraid it made some of us rather ashamed of being members of "the Tower".)

Rudolf explained further to Viola that he stood among those who were ashamed, so he took control of his own situation, while others chose to do otherwise:

> There are some who very quickly find business elsewhere when there is work to be done. It seems rather a farce, my trying to be tidy but a tent is a tent & a studio is a studio and I know that if a tent (to the ground about it) is not kept to concert pitch life is not possible in it. We are four in a tent, for which privilege we pay each of us 2/6 per week. [...] The others lie 8, poor fellows.

Amid all of these activities and arrangements, therefore, Rudolf found purpose in his own motivation and as he took his father's advice to embrace his identity as an artist. His very act of treating his space as the organized studio it had the potential to be helped him keep it to the expected "concert pitch."

Figure 2.7 Rudolf H. Sauter, untitled (Firth Hill Camp, Surrey), sepia ink wash on paper, 24.1 × 29.2 cm, private collection, photograph by Stacy Ross, © Trustees of The Estate of Rudolf H. Sauter.

Indeed, despite circumstances, he held to a distinctive artistic view of his environs:

> The other day we had our first experience of a sand-storm. The dust settled by in huge clouds all the morning, such thick clouds that they entirely obscured a tent at a distance of ten yards for as long as ¼ minute at a time. Wonderful pictures it made—with the sun coming through until the rows of tent looked like an encampment of ghostly pyramids amongst which little dark figures would scuttle & rush for shelter.

He remarked further to Viola, "I have done a few more sketches, one watercolour, but mostly I am dreadfully & abominably lazy."[41] Such self-criticism belied his productivity. He completed multiple detailed perspectives of Frith Hill Camp, including a view of its tents and the dismal conditions surrounding them (Figure 2.7).

---

41. Ibid.

Rudolf concluded his lengthy and detailed narrative to Viola: "God bless you my Darling and forgive the scrappiness of this letter which has been written in the midst of many interruptions." Curiously, based on this "scrappy" written and visual record Rudolf produced a formal survey of Frith Hill Camp itself, in color, including even greater detail and proportion, and fully absent the dismal conditions he depicted in his other works (Figure 2.8). Extant sources do not reveal why he pursued this formal survey, or how he did so with the art supplies he evidently used in this instance but not in any of his contemporary letters or other painted images of the camp. Perhaps authorities noticed his artistic talent while he was sketching and painting on camp grounds and they thought to engage him in the task of a comprehensive documentation. Nonetheless, this production alongside his many others of this period testifies measurably to his self-immersion in the ad-hoc studios of his captivity, indeed his keen ability to observe and record his internment experiences as a means to endure them.

* * *

In anticipation of his release from Frith Hill Camp, Rudolf began to plan his postwar creative life with an eye to making something of the poetry he had

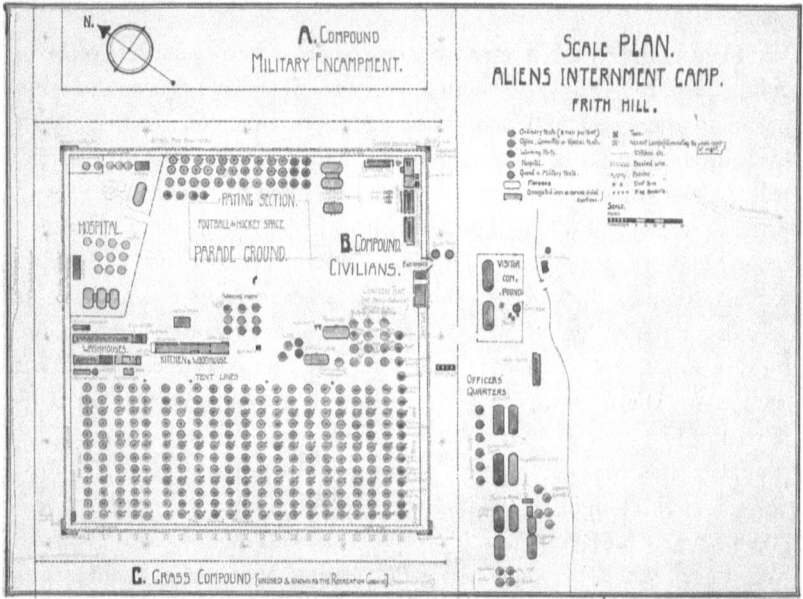

Figure 2.8 Rudolf H. Sauter, *Plan of Aliens Internment Camp, Frith Hill*, 1919, multicolored ink on paper/board, 31 × 43.8 cm, Art.IWM ART 6499, Imperial War Museum, © Trustees of The Estate of Rudolf H. Sauter.

crafted over the course of his internment. On July 13, 1919, Rudolf received a letter from his uncle offering feedback on his poems. "You are an authentic poet," Galsworthy wrote

> and when you have a little more mastered the clinch and crescendo of the short poem and are a little less vague and more objective will take very high rank. All the poems are worth while (nearly) and many have great beauty—the feeling for beauty is never absent. Something must be done with a selection from the English poems presently—the German, I'm sorry to say, I can't judge, for I can only stumble at them. I was greatly moved and touched over and over again; you have the unexpected image and turn of phrase—though you are fond of a dangerous trick of mixing the senses—talking of the smells and sound—You know what I mean. Some of them in the [Alexandra Palace] Palace [Internment Camp] are the best and deeper in feeling, which makes one rejoice that some good has come out of all this dusty dark. We are hoping for news soon.[42]

A few weeks later, Galsworthy wrote to Rudolf again, offering him more critical feedback—further to Rudolf's request—and sharing news that he had shown his work to the writer to John Masefield:

> I've been going at the poems in accordance with your wish. I've been acting barbarously towards them in every possible way, because this is the moment when you can learn—though I can't teach you. To begin with I've unstrung and re-arranged them into three sections. The first section will make a volume, perhaps reinforced by some of the second section (which I mark doubtful) and probably by others of yours which I haven't seen. The third section I reject from the *publishing* point of view. The first section contains the poems, which with a few suggested amendments or elisions really "come off." Many of them are most striking—some most beautiful and all have individual quality. I have not included in that section any vague or vapoury poems, such as it is the besetting sin of us to write when we are young. With a first book of poems one must cut ice. [to have impact or effect] I think perhaps the best of all are "You", "Lost Days," "The Ploughing," "The Storm," "The Orchid," "On the Eve," "Nocturne," "All Round" and "Why?" I showed them to Masefield; he liked many, said there was much poetic feeling, but some of them at first gave him the feeling that you lacked a subject. If I had arranged and

---

42. John Galsworthy to Rudolf H. Sauter, July 13, 1919, in Sauter, *Galsworthy the Man*, 102.

selected them he would not have had that feeling. Don't force yourself, but I expect great things from you. You are a poet.[43]

Inspired and supported by his uncle, Rudolf would indeed become a poet—albeit for a short period—as part of rebuilding his life out of the wreckage of the war and based on what he knew best from his pre-war life: his emerging artistic identity born from the nurturing and inspiration of his family and their circle of creative friends.

* * *

Concluding his wartime study of barbed wire disease, Dr. Adolf Vischer offered an "optimistic reference to the future," stating:

> To-day optimism is more vital than ever. We must wrench ourselves free from any pessimism in the contemplation of life. This would unquestionable lead to Nihilism and Bolshevism. Our prisoners in particular, deprived of social life by being driven into these camps and crushed in spirit by mistrust and anxiety, must be delivered from this dangerous state of mind. Such deliverance will not come through drugs nor through instruction and educational systems. It is above all essential that they should cast anchor again in the harbour of their own homes. The return to the family circle will prove itself the most powerful of remedies. Many prisoners who were interned in Switzerland have attested to the salutary effects of returning to their kith and kin. Family life is the solid basis of a healthy social mentality.

Vischer continued, speaking to the value prisoners of war returning to occupation on the land as a means of rehabilitating their lives. He then offered a concluding message applicable to all prisoners as they faced the prospect of freedom:

> The advantages of life on the land were long since recognised by all participators in the war. Migration to the land arises from no sentimental cry, "Back to nature," but from the elemental desire for rest, subconscious in every individual. Desire for rest lies deep in the soul of man; it will overcome that irritability and doubt, that feverish hoping and waiting, that possesses the soul of the prisoner.[44]

---

43. John Galsworthy to Rudolf H. Sauter, August 5, 1919, in Sauter, *Galsworthy the Man*, 103.
44. Vischer, *Barbed Wire Disease*, 83–84.

Vischer's words help to frame an understanding of 22-year-old Rudolf's envisioned postwar life: deep in his soul was his own desire for recovery from his experience as an enemy alien. On August 13, 1919, the authorities of Frith Hill Camp released him to pursue his desire. After an overnight stay in Grove Lodge, his uncle John's home in Admiral's Walk of Hampstead, Rudolf began his journey home to Wingstone via Waterloo Station.[45] As he made his way, he likely asked himself "Why?" as he did in his eponymous poem subtitled "1914–1919," recalling his experience of captivity, and looking to an uncertain future:

I

OH, why is man so unimagining
that he must torture every mortal thing
(as youth will prison up a little lark
to suffer humbly with its shrunken wing?)
For men aren't made like birds, which bravely fling
their purblind song against the bars of dark.
We pine instead and [...] madness is our wage.

II

A thrush is singing on the lime-tree now.
Outside is life—an earth more fair than youth.
As one comes in, the doors crash back behind
on all that was this blue and golden world,
eight long months old since fighting ceased! Within:
a wall of sudden dark which, at the touch
of sight, shrinks back into a monster hall;
a place where herds of almost human forms
creep vacantly about and stutter things
excitedly and, cringing from the light,
they blink and blink, night buzzing in their
   brains. ...
Without-the sentry tramps, the sunlight grows and
   wanes.
And everywhere is dust that chokes the light,

---

45. Lilian noted this important day in her pocket diary, writing simply "Rudo released." See Lilian Sauter, pocket diaries, JG(II)/10/1, Cadbury Library, University of Birmingham. Galsworthy noted the logistics of Rudolf's release in a letter to the superintendent of police of Moretonhampstead, Devon, August 14, 1919, JG(II)/20, Cadbury Library, University of Birmingham.

grey like the grey and tented blanket lines.
A hydra-headed din—a madhouse noise,
clatters and tramps, coughs hoarsely in the smoke;
a smoke which clusters round the gambling banks
and slinks along the half-dark, sweaty stench
of cabbage clinging by the rows of beds
(like shoddy oil between decayed sardines).
There drops of water splatch and tick the hours
down through the roof on palliasse and planks,
broad-arrowed blankets, straw, those odds and
    ends
that serve for—"home";

Men work, eat on their beds,
and sleep—*have* eaten, worked and slept; "done"
    four
dead years together, in this market-fair.
And, in the booths, there'd be … a tailor here,
or cockney German such as you might find
to do repairs and plumbing out at home.
And here a doctor; there a gutter-snipe;
this venerable Jew, a Limehouse type,
bunked next a sailor. On the other side
an artisan, professors, gamblers—men
of every age, sixteen to seventy-two [...]
and every creed: Turks, Arabs, Russians too,
all broken by the fates of war
in strangest mêlée dumped together—waste—

III

The blood too quickly clots around the sense
of him, to whom the soul of life's grown strange—
life that was full and gay, not stagnant [...] free!
For we're all mad in great or less degree,
who wait and wait and wait and ring the change
on damned uncertainty. Oh, Beauty! whence
in all thy world sprang *such* a power to hate
as that which shames the very devil's toll—
strife-sotted misery! Oh, why this crime?—
More doubly wasted than the wrack of war,
sea-offal, we, spurned on a fallow shore,
where future follows future through the slime.

Chapter 3

RECOVERY, 1919–24

Rudolf's release from Frith Hill Camp on August 13, 1919, marked the first step in his recovery from an experience that tore away his life—including his childhood home and his father—and exacerbated his mother's long-standing poor health.[1] His journey forward reflected the prevailing milieu of the generation who had survived the war, grappling with their different experiences and memories of it. Rudolf participated in this process in his own way as he faced challenges of trauma, rebuilding his life and establishing his artistic career. He returned to the fold of his family and married Viola. He also embraced the patronage of his uncle which afforded him workspaces and collaborative and independent projects that stood distinctly apart from his wartime de facto studios and related grim productions. These spaces and creations achieved therein combined to distance Rudolf physically and psychologically from his internment experience, paving the way to artistic achievement, public recognition and personal fulfillment.

Upon arriving in Wingstone from London on 14 August, Rudolf received a "touching & wonderful welcome from everyone," as Lilian documented the occasion and subsequent days in her diary.[2] The group who received

---

1. Likely adding insult to the wartime injuries sustained by Rudolf and his family was the sale of their Holland Park home shortly after the war to the artist James McBey, the Official Artist to the Egyptian Expeditionary Force, 1917–19 and known for portraits of T. E. Lawrence (of Arabia). See Historic England, "1, Holland Park Avenue," accessed June 30, 2021, https://historicengland.org.uk/listing/the-list/list-entry/1380239, and "Campden Hill Square Area," in *Survey of London: Volume 37, Northern Kensington*, ed. F. H. W Sheppard (London: London County Council, 1973), 87–100, *British History Online*, accessed June 30, 2021, http://www.british-history.ac.uk/survey-london/vol37/pp87-100. Reflecting a measure of the cultural damage done by the war and contemporary anti-German sentiment, an English Heritage blue plaque marks 1 Holland Park Avenue as being the former home of McBey, not the Sauters. See Waymarking.com, "James McBey—Notting Hill Gate, London, UK," accessed June 30, 2021, https://www.waymarking.com/waymarks/WMTWWZ_James_McBey_Notting_Hill_Gate_London_UK.
2. Lilian Sauter, pocket diary, August 14, 1919, JG(II)/10/1, Cadbury Library, University of Birmingham. Making the day even more meaningful was the fact that it was his uncle John's birthday.

him included Viola and his mother, as well as his aunt Mabel and her children, Owen and Veronica. Rudolf proceeded to spend a "wonderful evening" sleeping on the veranda as mist filled the night air. The next day he practiced Bach sonatas on his flute while Mabel took photos and his mother wrote letters. Shortly thereafter, Mabel and her family departed, and a "glorious" Sunday followed, with Rudolf, Viola and Lilian spending it together. During the next week, Rudolf and Viola practiced German, wrote letters and began to ride horses.[3] However, by the following Thursday, 21 August, Rudolf was "not v[ery] well" as he began to face traumatic symptoms stemming from his recent release. The next day he was "[in] pain" and "started stammering [*sic*]," conditions which marked the beginning of six consecutive days of illness.[4] While intermittent walks and gathering flowers filled some of this time, Rudolf spent much of it in bed.[5] Shortly thereafter he was "a little better" and "seemed much better," but soon his "symptoms of pain [were] coming on again" and he was "v[ery] depressed—& not feeling well." To help remedy his condition, Rudolf "began painting himself," once more embracing an artistic mindset as a means to cope with his circumstances.[6] The next day was a "glorious" one with Rudolf "feeling better," but "aft[er] he [was] v[ery] depressed," and Lilian walked and had "long talks with him."[7] The first of September marked her 55th birthday and the family celebrated with gift-giving, reading poems, enjoying flowers, eating cake and Lilian "lazing and walking" with her son. Rudolf spent the next two days "in bed till tea time."[8] Thereafter he felt "much better" and was "fairly well," but he was "not eating much solid" and soon became very tired."[9] He soon returned to painting—this time landscapes—and to riding during several consecutive days of "glorious weather." However, within a fortnight he was again "not well" with "pain threatening," a condition remedied with a "strict diet" of "hot fomentation with turps [turpentine] on going to bed," "Bovril and biscuits,"

---

3. Lilian Sauter, pocket diary, August 17–19, 1919, JG(II)/10/1, Cadbury Library, University of Birmingham.
4. Lilian Sauter, pocket diary, August 21–22, 1919, JG(II)/10/1, Cadbury Library, University of Birmingham.
5. Lilian Sauter, pocket diary, August 25, 1919, JG(II)/10/1, Cadbury Library, University of Birmingham.
6. Lilian Sauter, pocket diary, August 28–30, 1919, JG(II)/10/1, Cadbury Library, University of Birmingham.
7. Lilian Sauter, pocket diary, August 31, 1919, JG(II)/10/1, Cadbury Library, University of Birmingham.
8. Lilian Sauter, pocket diary, 2–3 September 1919, JG(II)/10/1, Cadbury Library, University of Birmingham.
9. Lilian Sauter, pocket diary, 5–6 September 1919, JG(II)/10/1, Cadbury Library, University of Birmingham.

Castor Oil and several days almost completely "in bed [...] feeling v[ery] bad [...] with head aches."[10] Rudolf soon felt "better," but an imminent railway strike convinced his family to return to London. There, Viola and Lilian remained "very worried & depressed" about him and decided to take him to see two doctors who examined an unspecified ailment in his leg. "Tired, & frightfully depressed," Rudolf was given "a bismuth meal" before he was "examined by X-rays 8 times," and he subsequently began "taking powders" to help improve his condition.[11] After it was determined that "nothing needs operation" and that he would "be all right with medicinal treatment," Rudolf remained at Grove Lodge, shopping regularly, seeing plays at the Court, St. James's and Old Vic theatres, as well as a film at the Kilburn Cinema and working on a portrait of Viola.[12]

Lilian, Rudolf and Viola eventually moved from Grove Lodge to "a small, uncomfortable flat, all they could afford."[13] It was an arrangement which Galsworthy ultimately found unacceptable, so he purchased a small house for them, called Freeland, in Holders Hill, Hendon.[14] This serene suburban location, which Rudolf captured in his painting *Suburban Back Gardens in Snow* (Figure 3.1), became his main studio for the next several years. It was a period of intense creativity involving independent projects and collaborations with his uncle.

Here Rudolf completed the self-portrait he had begun in Wingstone to help remedy his depression. The work represented him taking ever greater control of the trajectory of his life which had been disrupted by his internment and subsequent illness. The outcome—a stoic, Roman-nosed figure dressed in a grey coat and a blue tie—reflected his perseverance and confidence as a young artist looking to new creative horizons (Figure 3.2). It was another step on his road to recovery, indeed to his own creative awakening through a project of that very theme.

---

10. Lilian Sauter, pocket diary, September 7–20, 1919, JG(II)/10/1, Cadbury Library, University of Birmingham.
11. Lilian Sauter, pocket diary, September 21–30, 1919, JG(II)/10/1, Cadbury Library, University of Birmingham.
12. Lilian Sauter, pocket diary, October 4–18, 1919, JG(II)/10/1, Cadbury Library, University of Birmingham.
13. James Gindin, *John Galsworthy's Life and Art: An Alien's Fortress* (Ann Arbor: University of Michigan Press, 1987), 421. See also Dudley Barker, *The Man of Principle: A Biography of John Galsworthy* (New York: Stein and Day, 1969), 203.
14. Holders Hill was sold after 1924 and their trip to Africa. Eventually, both Wingstone and Grove Lodge were two small for the group of four—Rudolf and Viola, and his aunt Ada and uncle John—so Galsworthy purchased Bury House in 1926, as detailed in the next chapter. The four lived there until Galsworthy's death in 1933.

Figure 3.1 Rudolf H. Sauter, *Suburban Back Gardens in Snow*, ca. 1920, watercolor on paper, 40.5 × 58.5 cm, courtesy of Liss Llewellyn Fine Art, © Trustees of the Estate of Rudolf H. Sauter.

Figure 3.2 Rudolf H. Sauter, self-portrait, ca. 1920, oil on board, 51 × 41 cm, photograph by Richard Everett, courtesy of Alan Griffiths, © Trustees of the Estate of Rudolf H. Sauter.

Awakening

While Rudolf was recovering from his internment, his uncle was completing *In Chancery*, the second novel of his best-selling *Forsyte Saga* and planning an "interlude" between this next major installment and the previous one, *The Man of Property* (1906). The resulting short story—*Awakening*—focused on the life of 8-year-old Jon Forsyte, the child of Jolyon and Irene Forsyte, during his idyllic childhood in their home of Robin Hill as he dreamed of adventures while appreciating the beauty of his mother and the teachings of his father.[15] Galsworthy invited Rudolf to illustrate the story. The result was a cavalcade of images which effectively combined with the text to recall distinct characteristics of Rudolf himself as a child and his upbringing in Holland Park.

Opening *Awakening* to its title page, readers met Rudolf's frontispiece depicting a young Jon Forsyte, who, with his round face, full cheeks, large eyes and bushy hair, bore a distinct resemblance to the younger version of Rudolf as he had been depicted in his father's paintings, *Comrades* and *Maternity* and in contemporary photographs[16] (Figure 3.3).

The narrative of *Awakening* similarly tracked characteristics of the life of Rudolf's younger self. Just as Rudolf loved his mother dearly, evidenced by the letters he wrote from Elstree and Harrow, little Jon Forsyte loved his own mother, Irene, who "only appeared to him, as it were, in dreams, smelling delicious, smoothing his forehead just before he fell asleep and sometimes docking his hair, of a golden brown colour." More conspicuously, just as young Rudolf was close to his painter father, "with his father, too" young Jon "had special bonds of union; for [he] also meant to be a painter when he grew up—with one small difference, that his father painted pictures and little Jon intended to paint ceilings and walls, standing on a board between two step ladders, in a dirty-white apron and a lovely smell of white-wash"[17] (Figure 3.4). Additionally, while "under his father [Jon] learned to draw pleasure-pigs and other

---

15. John Galsworthy, *Awakening* (New York: Charles Scribner's Sons, 1922).
16. The resemblance between young Jon and Rudolf's younger self is undeniable even in light of the claim by Humphrey Spender (1910–2005), the British photographer, painter and designer, that he served as Rudolf's model for his illustration of Jon Forsyte. See the *Independent* (London, England), "Obituaries: Humphrey Spender, Photojournalist, Painter and Textile Designer," March 14, 2005, accessed June 30, 2021, http://www.independent.co.uk/news/obituaries/humphrey-spender-6053.html, and Humphrey Spender. Interview by Cathy Courtney, interviewee's home and British Library, October 10 and December 21, 1999, March 29 and August 9, 2000; April 10, 2001, and January 22, 2002, accessed June 30, 2021, http://sounds.bl.uk/related-content/TRANSCRIPTS/021I-C0466X0101XX-ZZZZA0.pdf.
17. John Galsworthy, *Awakening* (New York: Charles Scribner's Sons, 1920), 8.

Figure 3.3 Rudolf H. Sauter, frontispiece, in John Galsworthy, *Awakening*, illustrated by Rudolf H. Sauter (New York: Charles Scribner's Sons, 1920), © Trustees of the Estate of Rudolf H. Sauter.

animals,"[18] a school-aged Rudolf once drew a kangaroo in a letter he composed to his father. More than channeling the familial dynamic of "like father, like son," therefore, this artistic similarity was a complex matter of "like illustrator, like illustrated fictional character."

Moreover, the very atmosphere of Robin Hill—indeed the privileged world in which Jon was growing up—evoked the privilege and serenity of Rudolf's earlier life in Holland Park. "Little Jon has been born with a silver spoon in a mouth which was rather burley and large," the narrator of the story explained. "He never heard his father or his mother speak in an angry voice, either to each other, himself, or anybody else. [...] He was therefore of the opinion that the world was a place of perfect and perpetual gentility and freedom."[19] Among the many things Jon loved in his world were boats, the result of him listening to his "Auntie Jane" read her books to him when he "enjoyed a disease composed of little spots" while in "bed, honey in a spoon and [eating] many Tangerine oranges."[20]

---

18. Ibid., 10, where Rudolf depicted this scene in his illustration "Pleasure pigs and other animals."
19. Ibid., 8.
20. Ibid., 14.

Figure 3.4 Rudolf H. Sauter, "And a lovely smell of whitewash," in John Galsworthy, *Awakening* (New York: Charles Scribner's Sons, 1920), 9, © Trustees of the Estate of Rudolf H. Sauter.

When "she whisked back to London and left [the books] with in a heap," and he was better and allowed to read to himself, reading these books

> cooked his fancy, till he thought and dreamed of nothing but midshipmen and dhows, pirates, rafts, sandal-wood traders, iron horses, sharks, battles, Tartars, Red Indians, balloons, North Poles and other extravagant delights. The moment he was suffered to get up, he rigged

his bed fore and aft and set out from it in a narrow bath across green seas of carpet, to a rock, which he climbed by means of its mahogany drawer knobs, to seep the horizon with his drinking tumbler screwed to his eye, in search of rescuing sails.

Jon made a "raft out of the towel stand, the tea tray and his pillows," the result of which was his creation, "The 'Jolly Roger' under sail," depicted as such by Rudolf.[21] This image of young Jon evoked a young Rudolf who had also loved boats, talked about them with Joseph Conrad, and sketched them for his friend Curtis Dion O'Sullivan.

The gamut of these visual and textual parallels between little Jon's life and Rudolf's younger self suggests how the fictional *Awakening*—as a collaboration between beloved nephew and loving uncle—was as much autobiographical for Rudolf as it was biographical for Galsworthy. This intermixing of fiction and reality was a professional success for both of them and especially for Rudolf as it represented his first public achievement as an artist.

Awakening first appeared unillustrated in the November 1920 issue of *Scribner's Magazine*, followed by the illustrated version appearing a month later from Heinemann.[22] Advance advertisements described the volume as "an unusual and poetic study of adolescence—a little idyll of a little Forsyte; for Jon belongs to that famous family of Mr. Galsworthy's celebrated novel, 'A Man of Property,' which now comes again upon the stage in his new novel 'In Chancery.' Illustrated with delightful skill and grace in black-and-white and also in color, with full-page illustrations and marginal sketches, 'Awakening' forms one of the most attractive holiday books of the kind in many seasons."[23]

Following its publication, reviewers praised *Awakening* and particularly its illustrator. As *The Bookseller, Newsdealer and Stationer* told its readers,

> Beautifully bound in art covers, decorated and lettered in gold, a fitting and exquisite gift book is "Awakening," by John Galsworthy, with the most alluring of black-and-white and tinted illustrations by R. H. Sauter. Little "Jon," the hero of this consummately poetic study of adolescence,

---

21. Rudolf H. Sauter, *The "Jolly Roger" Under Sail*, in ibid., 16.
22. *Scribner's Magazine* 68, no. 5 (November 1920): 515–25, https://babel.hathitrust.org/cgi/pt?id=hvd.32044052973443&view=1up&seq=735&skin=2021&q1=515.
23. *The Publishers' Weekly* 98, no. 13 (September 25, 1920): 674, https://archive.org/details/sim_publishers-weekly_1920-09-25_98_13/page/674/mode/2up. See also the issue of October 9, 1920, which advertised *Awakening* alongside Galsworthy's novel *In Chancery* that was due to be published on October 22, 1920. *The Publishers' Weekly* 98, no. 15 (October 9, 1920): 1068, https://archive.org/details/sim_publishers-weekly_1920-10-09_98_15/page/1068/.

belongs to the famous family of the author's "A Man of Property" and of his recent continuation of their expression in "In Chancery," being the son of one of the principals. His feelings, sensations and emotions are recounted as only Galsworthy could do it in the perfect key and spirit of youth and the beauty of the telling is something that canot [*sic*] be described. The wide margins are filled with jolly sketches, there is a frontispiece and the lining leaves and title pages are also effectively decorated.[24]

Subsequently, *The Aberdeen Press and Journal* offered what was perhaps the greatest praise of the story and its illustrator:

> The chronicles of the Forsyte family, of which we had "In Chancery" very recently, continue to grow apace, but they may expand indefinitely if we can have, even very occasionally, such an exquisite little volume as "Awakening." This is the prettiest Christmas book we have seen this season, as it is almost as great a triumph for the illustrator, Mr. R. H. Sauter, whose happy marginal sketches of Jon's doings and imaginings are wholly in the spirit of the story.

The reviewer continued:

> Thus could one quote indefinitely, all save the talk between Jon and his mother. It is too sacred, too intimate to be quoted. For information on that particular point, see Mr Sauter's delightful illustration of a diagram of the child's heart. One section is labelled Sunlight, another nearly as large is labelled Beetles. Sir Lamorace [*sic*], Guineveres and Polar Bears have a special section. Dad is generously apportioned, while about a third of the whole, coloured bright blue, if labelled "Mum." On second thoughts a "vacant plot" is scored out and "Mum" gets the available space.

And the reviewer concluded:

> Mr Galsworthy has shown an almost uncanny sense in revealing a small boy's mind and the thoughts and feelings awakened by the realisation of the world into which destiny has placed him. No passage is sickly or

---

24. *The Bookseller, Newsdealer and Stationer* 53, no. 10 (November 15, 1920): 541, https://babel.hathitrust.org/cgi/pt?id=njp.32101065561506&view=1up&seq=547&skin=2021&q1=541.

too sentimental, but just exactly right, with the right word, tender yet restrained, in the right place and turned into perfect beauty by the additional charm of the drawings which show how absolutely Mr Sauter has entered into the feelings and spirit of Mr Galsworthy in this Forsyte Saga.[25]

Offering its own praise, the Christmas supplement of the *Bookman* shared with its readers:

If one was to apply "Awakening" the ordinary Christmas book standard, one's verdict would be that it was *the* gift-book of this season. Here is an original tale by one of the masters of the English short story: and here are illustrations of unusual promise and very considerable achievement. At times the work of Mr. Sauter recalls Mr. Heath Robinson, at times the work of M. Bosschère; but he has an ingenious fantasy of his own which makes some of his sketches the most delightful things in a book since J.F. Sullivan stopped illustrating his own fantastic fairy stories.[26]

The suggestion that Rudolf's illustrations placed him in the league of contemporary artists Jean De Bosschère (1878–1953), W. Heath Robinson (1872–1944) and J. F. Sullivan (1852–1936) was perhaps the greatest public praise he had received to date. Equally if not more meaningful was private praise from his longtime mentor Joseph Conrad, who observed that Rudolf "shows much charm in 'Awakening,' which harmonised with the charm of the text in a fascinating way."[27] Ultimately, the popularity of *Awakening* yielded its reprinting in

---

25. *The Aberdeen Press and Journal* (December 6, 1920), 2, https://www.britishnewspaperarchive.co.uk/viewer/BL/0000576/19201206/001/0002. *The Sewanee Review* echoed this review of Rudolf's work, stating that his illustrations were "made with companionable sympathy." Review of *Awakening*, by John Galsworthy (New York: Charles Scribner's Sons. 1920), 63. *The Sewanee Review* 29, no. 1 (January 1921): 127, https://books.google.com/books?id=hQEeAQAAIAAJ&vq=Awakening&pg=PA127. While it did not specifically praise Rudolf's work, the *American Hebrew & Jewish Messenger* praised *Awakening* as a "charming and entertaining biography of the boyhood of little Jon, […] [adding] another feather to Mr. Galsworthy's cap" and "transport[ing] one to the world of happy, happy childhood." *The American Hebrew & Jewish Messenger* 108, no. 12 (February 4, 1921): 372, https://books.google.com/books?id=UVxAAQAAMAAJ&vq=awakening&pg=PA372.
26. *The Bookman* 59, no. 351 (December 1920): 28, https://books.google.com/books?id=coMeAQAAMAAJ&lpg=RA1-PA28&ots=XdPoJsfjhA&dq=%22illustrating%20his%20own%20fantastic%20fairy%20stories%22&pg=RA1-PA28.
27. Joseph Conrad, Laurence Davies and J. H. Stape, eds., *The Collected Letters of Joseph Conrad Volume 7, 1920–1922* (Cambridge: Cambridge University Press, 2005), 7, 244.

several English editions, translation into German also with multiple reprintings and respectable royalties for Rudolf, the first of his burgeoning career.[28]

Domesticity

The success of *Awakening* occurred as Rudolf was facing his parents being unable to reconcile their marriage with Georg's repatriation to Germany. Although the situation yielded their permanent separation, it did not erode their mutual love and respect, or Rudolf's love and support. As Georg wrote to Rudolf from Berlin,

> My dear Rudo! The day before yesterday, I wrote to your dear mother and made some suggestions that are of utmost importance for your and her, future peace and security and I'm hoping that you'll agree to them in both your interests. I've given it a lot of thought and have come to the conclusion that, out of necessity, we have to gain our freedom and rescue what belongs to you and your dear mother in accordance with the law. I implore you, stay by her side! It hurts me deeply that, after all that she had to go through in the last five years, she'd have to suffer this misery as well and that I'm again causing her distress. It doesn't mean that our bond in spirit and in soul would break in any way—it will rather make the prospect of reuniting as close friends at a later time much more realistic and open up the world again for you and for her. A marriage like ours, torn apart arbitrarily, has legally no more value. The prospect of living together again in the coming years is so limited that all our lives would turn into relentless torture—a life in waiting stages of the most dismal kind. I can't submit you to such conditions under any circumstances.[29]

Georg continued, suggesting that this arrangement would help them navigate the rule of the British government that Lilian could only receive income—whether earned directly by her through her work or received through inheritance—as long as she lived in England:[30]

---

28. Rudolf H. Sauter, travel diary, March 23, 1924, JG(II)/9/9, Cadbury Library, University of Birmingham.
29. Georg Sauter to Rudolf H. Sauter, February 14, 1920, JG(II)/9/4 Cadbury Library, University of Birmingham.
30. Lilian Sauter to Harrison Morris, January 21, 1921, box 118, folder 4, papers of Harrison S. Morris, Princeton University Library. See also Rudolf H. Sauter, *Galsworthy the Man: An Intimate Portrait* (London: Peter Owen, 1967), 104–5.

I only blame myself for not acting any earlier and more decisively but—despite my lack in confidence in English justice—I could not believe that they would annul the last will of an Englishman and withhold the inheritance of his daughter under some pretext. The only way to reappropriate the inheritance is, in my view, the way I suggested. The future is too dark to allow for cloying sentimentality—we need to be practical now, in order to leave the muddy waters and reach the shore. I could not bear it if your dear mother would be submitted to hardship in old age, being deprived when she could have lived with you in peace and comfort. Your future will be in your interest as much as it is in mine! Your happiness will be our shared happiness.[31]

As Georg and Lilian's love for each other had survived "years of mental suffering [...] of the whole tragedy" of the war,[32] so too did the love between Rudolf and Viola, who married in late spring 1921.[33] Lilian proudly announced the occasion to her friend Ethel Fiedler:

My boy as perhaps you know is married!—to the dear girl who lived with us, & was more than a daughter to me during the war. She had been married before but very unhappily & had left her husband already when she came to stay with us. We have known her for many years & she is as good as she is beautiful. Rudo & she were deeply devoted to each other & as soon as she obtained her freedom they were married & are supremely happy It is my greatest comfort that we can all live happily together.[34]

---

31. Several months later, in a letter to his friend Harrison Morris, Georg reflected on his situation in greater detail, stating that "I will not go back to a country that [treated] me so disgracefully after I have been working there for so many years & have given my knowledge or energy in the interest of English Art, perhaps more than most Englishmen could do—their conduct was the conduct of cowards and villains not that of straight fighters. They talk pretentiously of their virtues & fair play but they act meanly [...] they practise conspiracy as a fine Art. In order to satisfy their greed they don't trouble their consciences & certainly for rendered services acknowledgement appears to them a shortcoming of their selfishness." Georg Sauter to Harrison Morris, August 12, 1920, box 118, folder 4, papers of Harrison S. Morris, Princeton University Library.
32. Georg Sauter to Harrison Morris, April 25, 1920, box 118, folder 4, papers of Harrison S. Morris, Princeton University Library.
33. Rudolf and Viola married after Viola and William Bruckman filed for divorce in the fall of 1920, claiming that she had, that summer, committed adultery with Rudolf. J 77/1704, Divorce Court File: 3018, the UK National Archives.
34. Lilian Sauter to Ethel Fiedler, December 28, 1922, MS.G/Sauter L.1, Taylor Institution Library, Oxford University.

So marked the beginning of a lifelong partnership during which Viola and Rudolf would support each other in every way, especially in making their homes, Rudolf's studios and expressing their love through his later collections of poetry.

Songs in Captivity

Following his success with *Awakening*, Rudolf opened another chapter in his emerging artistic career by closing a chapter of his previous life: he returned to his wartime poetry, seeking to publish it as his uncle had been encouraging him to do. Galsworthy even suggested a title for the collection—*Songs in Captivity*—and likely also encouraged the Heinemann publishing house to take on the project, which it did.[35]

Rudolf included 50 poems in *Songs in Captivity*. Among them was "Gedanke" (Thought), which he had originally composed in German shortly before his internment, as well as the aforementioned "Time," "Sleepless," "Doing Time," "Night in the Big Hall," "Barbed Wire All Around" and "Barbed Wire." He also included poems entitled "Lost Days," "Fragments of Memory," "Years of Captivity," "Waste," "Foreboding," "Why?," "Despair," "Under Canvas—On the Eve of Peace" and "Dawn Over Camp," all of which vividly conveyed his state of mind and the scenes of his internment which he had painted and sketched in his ad hoc studios. Among the most poignant compositions he included in the collection was "The Before and After: A Confession," which simultaneously captured his past sense of uncertainty and present hope for the future.

I

MY God! How I loved the great sky;
the big wind, running across the stars;
foam of dark leaves, floating the darkness
and breaking over the trees [...] !
The light of suns tossed on the sea;
and stillness, too,
that holds the tides up from a depth,
where no man's ever been:
These and a thousand other things
were full of childish wonder for me yesterday
　—and through the flocks of yesterdays,

---

35. Rudolf H. Sauter, *Galsworthy the Man: An Intimate Portrait* (London: Peter Owen, 1967). 101–3.

migrating fatefully.
Under the shadow of the mountains, too,
was I content to be a grain of darkness; there
to worship silently, in solitude,
the sweet soul of the earth, still undefiled.

II

Out of the sky tumbling-raucous death!
and very vileness, stinking on the wind!
Where mountains reel, even the night is deaf
with sudden tumult […] !
Seas, agape to let dark terrors slip
in over the land
(like clammy monsters, feeding on the hour,
until the soul is foul).
The eyes that used to peer along the shore
at night
—sparks from the same anvil as the stars—
pricked out and scummed
with hideous nastiness!
Death's in the world, aping the form of Man,
who, terribly, gave birth to this mad child.
Am I that Man? For, that I am a man,
—O God!—
1 helped to bring about this awful thing!

III

But after it! […] What then? Can there be light?
Will there be Song of birds and will the sight
of loveliness return to man again,
after he's felt the savagery of pain?
Is there forgiveness for this awful dearth
of Love?
Or do I dream there's beauty in the earth
above
this Present? […] Surely, as to-morrows come
out of days, when beauty was not dumb!
Has Man yet killed the wind, or made the corn
grow back into the seed, when once it's born?
Or caused one song to be unsung in spring,
or broken the soul of any living thing?

Such things go on; whatever man has done,
there *must* be beauty and who says there's none,
has bound his eye and cannot find the knot.
Forgive me, God!—
I, too, have seen it and perceived it not.

Songs in Captivity appeared in January 1922, as a slim and unassuming volume with promotion by its publisher which did not reference the main subject of the book: the war. "With singular freshness and poignancy these poems deal with the moods of the spirit of captivity," Heinemann's List of Spring Books announced.[36] Similarly, *The Publishers' Circular and Booksellers' Record* and *The Scotsman* advertised *Songs* as a "book of poems" by an "author, a young painter [who] has expressed in these poems with a beautiful freshness and poignancy the moods and feelings of the spirit in captivity."[37] Similarly, *The Spectator* conveyed that "these poems by a young painter embody to the highest and most poignant degree the spirit of the soul in captivity."[38] *The Pall Mall Gazette* offered a more critical observation alongside an excerpt from the book:

Cud of captivity must be bitter in the chewing; so there is bitter-sweetness in "Songs in Captivity," by R. H. Sauter. [...] Unpretentious they have yet distinction of their own. Metrical arrangement has not, as often happens, superseded underlying thoughts. The poems are slight. This of the slightest is prettily as well as concisely expressed:

    The Opal
I held God's palette in my hand,
And watched the colours drip and burn
In it, where He has mixed the sky.
The sea, blue hills and sunrise land.
The master brushwork of His wand
Grew blinding as I held it high.

---

36. *The Bookman* 61, no. 366 (March 1922): 277.
37. The *Publishers' Circular and Booksellers' Record* 116 (1922): 179, https://books.google.com/books?id=ZGxNAAAAYAAJ&focus=searchwithinvolume&q=179, and the *Scotsman* (Edinburgh, Scotland), February 23, 1922), 2, https://www1.britishnewspaperarchive.co.uk/viewer/BL/0000540/19220223/141/0002.
38. The *Spectator* (London, England), February 18, 1922, 30, http://archive.spectator.co.uk/page/18th-february-1922/30. The *Yorkshire Post and Leeds Intelligencer* also promoted the book but by name only. See "New Books Received," *Yorkshire Post and Leeds Intelligencer* (Leeds, England), February 27, 1922, 10, https://www.britishnewspaperarchive.co.uk/viewer/BL/0000687/19220227/202/0010.

This opal. Of, that I might learn
To prentice art where He had planned.[39]

Ultimately, despite such attention—or very likely due to it revealing that the subject of the book involved a wartime experience—*Songs in Captivity* was largely overlooked by a reading public that was tired of war stories, or it was quickly set aside by those who did read it. Its fate was comparable to many other war-related books published at the end of the period 1919–22 when memory of the war was fresh enough to allow stories about it to be told and before public distaste for such accounts became widespread and did not rebound until the end of the decade.[40] However, Rudolf likely neither expected his book to be a success nor aspired to achieve success through the project, because it was, fundamentally, a personal initiative intended to help him achieve closure to his wartime experience and move on in his professional life. As he explained to the American poet Robert Haven Schauffler to whom, in 1922, he sent a copy of *Songs*, writing:

> I enclose you herewith in some trepidation my little book of verses, as I promised to do. I've worked so hard on them that I want to spell the title
>
> "Songs In CKaptivity'
>
> Because I am, by now, so heartily SICK of these lines. So, if you feel inclined, immediately to rise up and smite something, don't be afraid of hurting, because I'd really like to know what you think and am prepared for the worst anyhow.[41]

While Schauffler's thoughts on the book are unknown, it is evident that, whether due to lack of confidence or simply a desire to move on from the project and the memories it held, Rudolf himself evidently wanted to forget *Songs* almost as soon as it appeared and despite the hard work he dedicated to realizing the project. And he did forget it, at least publicly until the 1960s when he chose to revisit and reshape the material to give it new meaning.

---

39. "The Book Lover," *Pall Mall Gazette* (London, England), March 9, 1922, 7, https://www.britishnewspaperarchive.co.uk/viewer/BL/0001947/19220309/129/0007.
40. Ian Isherwood, *Remembering the Great War: Writing and Publishing the Experiences of World War I* (London: Bloomsbury, 2017); and Mary Hammond and Shafquat Towheed, eds., *Publishing in the First World War: Essays in Book History* (London: Palgrave Macmillan, 2007).
41. Rudolf H. Sauter to Robert Haven Schauffler, February 24, 1922, TXRC96-A17, box 5, folder 3, Harry Ransom Humanities Research Center, University of Texas at Austin.

Illustrations for Galsworthy's Manaton Edition

Another career-defining project undertaken by Rudolf during his recovery from internment involved the Manaton edition of his uncle's collected works, published starting in 1923.[42] Galsworthy intended this project professionally as a means to ensure remembrance of his literary career and personally as a means to forget the painful memories of his own war experiences as a volunteer helping disabled soldiers and as a loving brother-in-law and uncle whose family was unfairly treated and forever broken.[43] As he observed shortly before his death, the war "killed a terrible lot of—I don't know what to call it—self-importance, faith, idealism, in me."[44] However, while the Manaton edition was largely a project of closure for Galsworthy, it was the opposite for Rudolf as it functioned along with other projects of the period to help him establish his reputation as a visual artist.

The Manaton edition contained nearly two dozen illustrations by Rudolf, all of which appeared as frontispiece photogravure plates. They depicted a variety of individuals and scenes, from figures, situations and landscapes of the Forsyte Saga to the homes which Rudolf shared with his uncle, aunt and Viola, including Grove Lodge, Wingstone and, later, Bury House, as well as the many dogs who lived with them. More significantly, the illustrations by Rudolf included notable stage actors who brought Galsworthy's plays to life—including Leon Lion, Norman McKinnel, Ernest Milton, Stephen More and Ernest Thesiger—as well as writers to whom Galsworthy dedicated the volumes, including J. M. Barrie, C. S. Evans, Thomas Hardy and John Masefield. These notables very likely saw their images as created by Rudolf, boosting his reputation as a new artist on the scene. This was especially the case for Masefield.[45]

Masefield and Sauter

In 1923, Masefield sat for Sauter, who drew him in charcoal. The outcome was an expressive and thoughtful image that was emblematic of their lifelong friendship (Figure 3.5).

---

42. John Galsworthy, *The Works of John Galsworthy. Manaton Edition. With Plates, Including Portraits* (London: William Heinemann, 1923–36). Charles Scribner's Sons published this collection in the United States, also beginning in 1923.
43. Jeffrey S. Reznick, *John Galsworthy and Disabled Soldiers of the Great War: With an Illustrated Selection of His Writings* (Manchester: Manchester University Press, 2009).
44. Galsworthy to Gilbert Murray, March 6, 1932, as quoted in Marrot, *Life and Letters*, 803. See also Reznick, *John Galsworthy and Disabled Soldiers of the Great War*, 280.
45. Galsworthy also dedicated specific volumes to Ada, Rudolf and Lilian.

Figure 3.5 Rudolf H. Sauter, *The Poet, John Masefield*, 1923, charcoal, 62.5 × 45 cm, courtesy of Liss Llewellyn Fine Art, © Trustees of the Estate of Rudolf H. Sauter.

A decade later, Masefield wrote to Rudolf, asking if he would undertake a commission for his new book, *The Taking of the Gry*, which took place in the fictional Latin American country of Santa Barbara. "I greatly admired your maps & drawings in the Rio journal," Masefield explained "and I sadly need a map for my new tale. [...] Will you let me have a word about it & tell me your charges if you care to undertake it?"[46] Rudolf humbly accepted the opportunity to contribute a map of Santa Barbara. Masefield offered a sketch of the image he envisioned, and Rudolf responded with a number of questions about its expected detail, design and layout as a planned wrapper or endpaper of the book. As to Masefield's question about cost, Rudolf replied, "About the price? I don't quite know; but would between five and ten guineas be about right, according to the amount of work required? If this seems suitable, please don't let that stand in the way because I'd love you to have a shot at it anyway." Masefield agreed and the two then corresponded extensively about the details of the project as they pertained to Masefield's vision, Rudolf's approach and style and the narrative of the story. The result was an

---

46. John Masefield to Rudolf H. Sauter, undated, likely 1932 or 1933, 821 M396 Is-T, Archives & Special Collections, Phillips Exeter Academy. To what specific journal Masefield was referring is unknown, but when it could be this detail would open another window onto Rudolf's creative life and work.

Figure 3.6 Rudolf H. Sauter, *Map of the Story*, 1934, pen and black ink with turquoise and pink wash on paper, 25 × 34 cm, courtesy of Richard Kay, © Trustees of the Estate of Rudolf H. Sauter.

image that Masefield described to Rudolf as being an "enchanting design," "delightful" and one "which pleases us & the publisher, too."[47] Heineman's C. S. Evans agreed, explaining to Masefield, "I think Rudo's drawing for the wrapper and endpapers is splendid. I think he has surpassed himself. I will see that his reproduction instructions are carried out to the letter."[48] Thanking Rudolf for his "thought & care," Masefield sent him a check for nine guineas. Rudolf's final work illustrated the inside cover of the 1934 American first edition of Masefield's *The Taking of the Gry*. It is an exquisite further example of his diagrammatic skill, keen sense of place and space, and ability to bring a narrative alive (Figure 3.6).

---

47. Correspondence between John Masefield to Rudolf H. Sauter, undated, likely 1932 or 1933, 821 M396 Is-R, Phillips Exeter Academy Archives and Special Collections.
48. William Heinemann, Ltd./C. S. Evans to Masefield, August 13, 1934, MS-02702, Harry Ransom Humanities Research Center, University of Texas at Austin.

Rudolf and Masefield remained close friends. In 1958, Rudolf and Viola visited Masefield on the occasion of his 80th birthday, and in 1966, Masefield presented Sauter with a copy of his book *Grace before Ploughing*.[49]

* * *

For Rudolf, the half dozen years following the Great War were formative ones, marked by independent and collaborative opportunity, success and recognition of his emerging identity and skills as a sensitive artist. During the decade to come, he would seize his expanding creative world with gusto despite the persistent issue of his citizenship.

---

49. John Masefield, *Grace before Ploughing* (London: William Heinemann, 1966), copy inscribed by Masefield to "Rudo," accessed June 30, 2021, https://www.rarebookhub.com/book_sellers/194/books/2074968?id=2074968. Rudolf H. Sauter, "A Visit to John Masefield on His 80th Birthday: Celebrated 1st June 1958," undated typescript, 821 M396 Is-U, Phillips Exeter Academy Archives and Special Collections.

Chapter 4

ARTISTRY I, 1924–39

Lilian died on October 27, 1924, at the age of 60, falling victim to her long-standing poor health made worse by the "countless anxieties and sufferings" of the war years and likely also by the stress of her postwar marital separation.[1] "My dear mother passed away quite suddenly and very peacefully yesterday morning," 29-year-old Rudolf wrote to Hermann Fiedler. "It was most unexpected although she had been ill for some time, but her passing was just as quiet as one could have wished—she slept."[2] Apropos of her death, Rudolf reprinted her 1910 poem "The Pause" and distributed copies to friends and family who attended her funeral:

> Surely our life, in essence, is concrete,
> Eternal verity and death
> Only the pause in the incessant beat
> Of many-pulsing life, the breath
> Indrawn, the wave receding, that returns?
>
> Not the eternal dark which severeth,
> Not quenching of the light that burns.
> Only a moment's holding of the breath
> A moment's darkening of the sight,
> A hush, a step, the unknown, openeth ...
> On the alternate wave-beat of the light? ...

---

1. Georg Sauter to Harrison Morris, December 9, 1919, box 118, folder 4, papers of Harrison S. Morris, Princeton University. Suggesting the extent of her ill health during the immediate postwar period, Lilian wrote to her friend Ethel Fiedler in late 1922. "I was very ill all last winter & spring, & in June had to have a serious operation, after which travelling was impossible." Lilian Sauter to Ethel Fiedler, December 28, 1922, MS.G/Sauter L.1, Taylor Institution Library, Oxford University.
2. Rudolf H. Sauter to Hermann Georg Fiedler, October 28, 1924, MS.G/SAUTER R.1, Taylor Institution Library, Oxford University.

Responding to Lilian's death the *Nottingham Evening Post* informed its readers not only that she was "the wife of Professor Sauter, the painter [...] [and] John Galsworthy's sister" but also that "Professor [Georg] and Mrs. Sauter's house in Holland Park avenue was a rendezvous of literary and artistic London before the war, for Mrs. Sauter was a poetess of achievement, a frail little woman whose gentle personality was far-reaching in its personal influence."[3] As the paper concluded that "her son is pursuing art like his father," a contemporary portrait of Rudolf, drawn by Georg in his German realistic style, depicted the young man facing new creative horizons.[4] Here was a profile of a confident emerging artist whose creative mind was informed and inspired by his upbringing in Holland Park, by overcoming his war experience and by the love and support of his family. Now, after several years of retreating into literary landscapes, Rudolf sought to explore the wider world, but not before he faced a persistent challenge to his identity which echoed his wartime experience.

Legally speaking, Rudolf was a stateless individual, the result of being born in Germany, raised in Britain and never having become a British citizen. He could not hold a British passport, and by choice he declined to hold a German one because he did not wish to identify himself as a German citizen. In order to travel abroad, therefore, he needed to possess the proper documentation, namely a Nansen passport, the first legal instrument used for the international protection of refugees.[5] As a practical measure after obtaining this documentation, Rudolf transcribed it for safekeeping as his "Document of Identity

---

3. "Mr. Galsworthy's Loss," *Nottingham Evening Post*, November 3, 1924, 4, https://www.britishnewspaperarchive.co.uk/viewer/BL/0000321/19241103/017/0004. Notably, years later Rudolf recalled his mother in a similar light, being "a person of great selflessness, to come into contact with whom was like crossing the frontier into another world, in which the values of currency had been mysteriously transmuted into something other than those negotiable in ordinary life. Everybody loved her, with her slight figure which any wind might blow away, her halo of grey hair, her serious smile, her beautiful grey eyes and her loving nature, small and delicate, she was able to unlock most hearts." Rudolf H. Sauter, *Galsworthy the Man: An Intimate Portrait* (London: Peter Owen, 1967), 35.
4. Georg Sauter, portrait of Rudolf H. Sauter, 1924, charcoal, 35.5 × 22.8 cm, private collection.
5. The namesake of the Nansen passport was Fridtjof Nansen, the Norwegian polar explorer and the first head of the League of Nations Office of the High Commissioner for Refugees. He recognized that one of the main problems refugees faced was their lack of internationally recognized identification papers, which in turn complicated their request for asylum. Marit Fosse and John Fox, *Nansen: Explorer and Humanitarian* (Lanham, MD: Rowman & Littlefield, 2015). See also Cara Giamo, "The Little-Known Passport That Protected 450,000 Refugees," AtlasObscura, accessed February 7, 2017, https://www.atlasobscura.com/articles/nansen-passport-refugees.

issued to an Applicant who cannot obtain a National Passport."[6] More than a legal measure, his possession of this passport symbolized how the nation in which he grew up—and with which he identified so closely—still rejected him.

Despite this circumstance and in the same vein as he had embraced his creative identity as a means to cope with his wartime internment, Rudolf used his Nansen passport extensively over the next three years, traveling to Italy, North Africa, Spain and France. Along the way, he drew and painted a variety of landmarks and scenes of daily life, including The Puente Nuevo in the southern Spanish city of Ronda (Figure 4.1), boats off the coast of Palermo, the Cisterns of La Malga (Carthage) near Tunis, solider ants in the Algerian town of Béni Ounif and mosquito nets in the Moroccan city of Oujda.[7] Through all of these travels, Rudolf advanced his skills as a sensitive English artist, fueled his creative output and grew his professional reputation. These visits also strengthened his bonds with his regular traveling companions—namely Viola and his aunt Ada and uncle John—as well as his father, with whom he spent several months in Italy during the spring of 1924. Indeed, among all of Rudolf's travels during this period, his time in Italy with Georg was the most significant in shaping his creative identity and outlook.

Italy

Rudolf's tour of Italy was extensive. He arrived in Sestri, traveled south to Carrara and then to Pisa where, upon walking through its Piazza del Duomo, he declared in his travel diary, "here real Italy begins."[8] Following a visit to "The Drunken Tower" and spending time studying the frescos and stained glass in the Campo Santo, he proceeded to Florence and the Uffizi Gallery and subsequently to Bologna, Padua and Venice.

---

6. Rudolf H. Sauter, undated notes in travel diary for 1924 to which he added, for himself, "No. 50118/2. Rudolf Hellmut Sauter, holding registration Certificate 139018. Freeland. Holders Hill. Hendon. Registered as of German nationality. Endorsed for Italy, France, Switzerland, Egypt, Algeria, Tunic, Tangiers, Spain, Austria and Morocco. Age 29. Height 5 ft. 7 ½ in. Eyes blue. Hair dark. Date Nov 4, 1924," and for Viola, "Ditto. No. 50118/1—Viola Ada Emily Sauter. Certificate 39019. Age 39. Height with boots 5 ft. 6 in. Eyes Brown Hair dark brown. Date 4 November 1924. Illegible signature of H.M. Chief Inspector. Aliens Branch. Hone Office. London. S.W.1." JG(II)/9/9, Cadbury Library, University of Birmingham.
7. Rudolf H. Sauter, "Sketch Books. Sicily & N. Africa," 1925, private collection.
8. Rudolf H. Sauter, travel diary, January 28, 1924, JG(II)/9/9, Cadbury Library, University of Birmingham.

Figure 4.1 Rudolf H. Sauter, untitled (The Puente Nuevo), ca. 1925, drypoint etching, 25 cm × 17.5 cm, private collection, © Trustees of the Estate of Rudolf H. Sauter.

The art that Rudolf and Georg experienced in all of these locations—as they painted together in galleries, rented studios and en plain air—became background against which Georg consistently—and sometimes relentlessly—criticized Rudolf's impressionistic style and technique. Being a staunch realist in the German tradition and wanting his son to know it and to embrace a similar approach, Georg persisted with his well-intentioned advice and criticism as Rudolf frequently became frustrated and even angry hearing it while holding fast to his identity as a sensitive English artist.

An especially notable day for Rudolf was February 23, 1924, after he painted all morning and Georg "came and criticized" his image of the Italian cruiser *San Giorgio*, "saying that steamer was in wrong place, competing too much with the church in distance."⁹ Rudolf took his father's advice, noting to himself "*there must not be two centres in a picture*; otherwise neither is effective & the whole thing is spoilt—cf. Giotto." Later that day, he sought comfort in a "long talk with Viola about all sorts of things," a "v[ery] enjoyable]" conversation, as he described it in a Shakespearean fashion:

> If one could only see life from a high window (only one story or two) always, he would find the thick brambles become, what they really are, but little rose bushed, & see that the mountains are but mole-hills. [...] To live every moment as if it were, or might be, one's last: that is to say, keeping the ideal always before one like the Roman kept a skull. For no one would like to die unworthy of the best he could achieve [...] worry, anger, "nerves"; a question of perspective of proportion! [...] V. says the engine goes round too fast and one is too self conscious: "after all" she says: "what does it all matter: if one person does good work or another; whether you leave behind you wonderful pictures or not? The only thing which is of account is *the trying*. Don't worry so! Don't think so much of self (as much as to say: 'I can't do this; I'm no good at it; I haven't experience; I can't remember that) What does it all matter!? If you don't think so much about those things you'll be more natural and, what is more, more *individual* too." [...] Anything which drives one back on self-tending to self-consciousness, cramps individuality.¹⁰

With such solace, Rudolf tried his best to handle his father's relentless advice and criticism. Three days later, he "worked all day" and faced "criticism early," his father explaining,

> A picture must not only be a representation, but it must *sing*. Of course Nature is, also, sometimes, "dead," and then it is difficult. [...] One must work all the time, in fact, far more than one is *not* painting. The outing onto a canvas is a thing to itself and will come in time, perhaps—*But one must first learn to see*. In two or three months you will probably see these houses opposite, the sky and the water quite differently from the way you see them now. And you must *feel* them. In any case you must see to it that, in the picture, they sing. The picture

---

9. Rudolf H. Sauter, travel diary, February 23, 1924, JG(II)/9/9, Cadbury Library, University of Birmingham.
10. Rudolf H. Sauter, travel diary, February 23, 1924, JG(II)/9/9, Cadbury Library, University of Birmingham.

must be a summing-up of a subject, the spirit—not the external form only."[11]

Recognizing the difference, indeed the tension, between his impressionism and his father's realism, Rudolf noted to himself the next day that, in his own mind, he "must think of each failure as something learnt, then won't get so depressed & hopeless when F.[ather] says a thing is no use."[12] A few weeks later, Rudolf reflected on his sketches of fishing boats being, in his own view, "rotten & again rotten" even as Georg Brandes, the contemporary German artist, "came to see the drawings" and "seemed interested" in them.[13] After Rudolf "began composition for [an] afternoon picture" he noted that "sometimes one gets so mad one wants to smash-on the paint. But it is all no use. Patience! & study; study; study! F.[ather] says: 'at first one only looks *at* a thing but after a time one begins to *see* it from inside.' Not till then can one make a fine work."[14] Later that day, Rudolf, recalled that his father was "v[ery] dear about my drawings" and suggested that Rudolf should, "if an opportunity occurs, show them somewhere in London [...] in a good place" and "go on in your own way; never mind what people say; you will always have difficulties; but, keep fresh."[15] Shortly thereafter, Georg shared with his friend Harrison Morris how very proud he was of Rudolf, who "was working very hard & doing rather exceptional things."[16] Georg wrote further that "it is a tremendous delight to watch the keenness of a young spirit in its development for me in particular as I have been separated from him for so many years & allas [*sic*] will be again, heaven knows for how long. It is a cruel business!"

Several weeks later, during his stay in Venice and despite all he had learned and the increasing encouragement and support his father had expressed, Rudolf continued to doubt himself, remarking "somehow there's always something which prevents my seeing things on a large scale. Why?! If only I could grip onto the real facts & come to some true conclusions instead of

---

11. Rudolf H. Sauter, travel diary, February 26, 1924, JG(II)/9/9, Cadbury Library, University of Birmingham.
12. Rudolf H. Sauter, travel diary, February 27, 1924, JG(II)/9/9, Cadbury Library, University of Birmingham.
13. Rudolf H. Sauter, travel diary, March 19, 1924, JG(II)/9/9, Cadbury Library, University of Birmingham.
14. Rudolf H. Sauter, travel diary, March 19, 1924, JG(II)/9/9, Cadbury Library, University of Birmingham.
15. Rudolf H. Sauter, travel diary, March 19, 1924, JG(II)/9/9, Cadbury Library, University of Birmingham.
16. Georg Sauter to Harrison Morris, March 24, 1924, box 118, folder 4, papers of Harrison S. Morris, Princeton University Library.

this uncertainty. F.[ather] says he has always been a fighter but never fought. I'm not made that way."[17] In the wake of such persistent self-doubt, Rudolf again turned to Viola for support—albeit from a distance as she had returned to England—writing to her about one's purpose and perspective when facing challenge while experiencing a "lovely day":

> But if we keep our spirit at the open window—it will overlook all the trifles & by keeping the mind on that distant, wonderful view, leave no spot open for the senses to climb those four steep flights of stairs—when we are tired. But it is just then that we most need that breadth of vision & that sense of perspective which height alone can give.[18]

Georg's criticism continued, as did Rudolf's effort to learn from it. "F.[ather] criticised my paintings, v[ery] dearly, carefully & for a long time. He picked out 5 or 6 [...] and said: 'That is the way you must follow up; you see what progress you have made—let me see the first one you did here [...] you see! How dull it is. Always compare; then you will see how you progress. Now you must go on in your own way (and this is just the right time of year). Always watch the whole picture & the light which falls on a thing. [...] And then, do not let yourself be too much carried away by the effect of the movement, keep an individuality, try and get a certain style like you get in your drawings."[19] Emblematic of Rudolf embracing his self-confidence along with his father's guidance was a self-portrait he completed around this time, his youthful face half shaded as his eyes stared directly at the viewer.[20]

Such was the dynamic between Rudolf and Georg through the remainder of their first tour of Italy together through the spring of 1924. Their second tour began that autumn, and shortly before they reconnected Rudolf had a "long talk with V[iola] re. F[ather].," concluding "to hurt wisely—and not mind; that is what I have to learn and to do it kindly. May I learn to see things in proportion. Proportion! Not to be carried away by the moment."[21] A day before the two parted company in early January 1925, following their

---

17. Rudolf H. Sauter, travel diary, April 15, 1924, JG(II)//9/9, Cadbury Library, University of Birmingham.
18. Rudolf H. Sauter, travel diary, April 15, 1924, JG(II)/9/9, Cadbury Library, University of Birmingham.
19. Rudolf H. Sauter, travel diary, April 28, 1924, JG(II)/9/9, Cadbury Library, University of Birmingham.
20. Rudolf H. Sauter, self-portrait, 1924, pencil on paper, 63.5 × 43 cm. Janette McCaffrey to the author, "Sauter," e-mail dated October 27, 2020.
21. Rudolf H. Sauter, travel diary, November 28, 1924, JG(II)/9/9, Cadbury Library, University of Birmingham.

travels from northern to southern Italy, Rudolf helped Georg pack his bag in Palermo, where they had dinner together with Viola. "Sad but a little closer," Rudolf noted in his diary and "felt for the first time for a long time as if M[other] was quite near looking on at us. F[ather]'s cold worse; put him to bed with hot drink."[22] The next day, Rudolf "saw F[ather] off to Taormina. v[ery] sad."[23]

Interlude: Georg's Future and Passing

During the autumn of 1926, Georg returned to London to marry Valda Broad, a native of the city who he had met on a train during his "homelessness and wandering life" in Italy.[24] Georg and Valda woke early on September 14, bought flowers in Covent Garden and traveled to Highgate Cemetery where they placed several on Lilian's grave.[25] Their marriage ceremony took place later that morning with Rudolf and Viola in attendance along with John and Ada Galsworthy and Georg's best man, John Lavery, the Irish painter.[26] A few days later, Georg and Valda departed London to visit friends in the Netherlands and Germany. They lived in Italy for a period and eventually settled in Brannenburg. Rudolf and Georg remained close and corresponded regularly about personal and professional matters. On at least one occasion, during the summer of 1937, Rudolf and Viola visited Georg and Valda at their home in Jena, Germany.[27]

Georg died in December 1937 at the age of 71.[28] The following day, shortly after he drew his father's portrait and as he had done following his mother's

---

22. Rudolf H. Sauter, travel diary, January 11, 1925, JG(II)/9/9, Cadbury Library, University of Birmingham.
23. Rudolf H. Sauter, travel diary, January 12, 1925, JG(II)/9/9, Cadbury Library, University of Birmingham.
24. Georg Sauter to Rudolf H. Sauter, May 3, 1926, MS.G/SAUTER G.15, Taylor Institution Library, Oxford University.
25. Memoirs of Valda Sauter, unpublished typescript, private collection.
26. Georg Sauter to Hermann Georg Fiedler, November 4, 1926, MS.G/SAUTER G.14, Taylor Institution, Oxford University. See also Sauter, *Galsworthy the Man*, 35.
27. Memoirs of Valda Sauter, unpublished typescript, private collection.
28. Notably, the British press covered Georg's passing, one article explaining that "after the war broke out" he "declined to become a naturalised Englishman," and that he was "interned" and eventually returned to Germany, after which he "visited London 1924," but it did not explain the reason for this visit, which was to marry Valda. See "Death of Well-Known Painter," *Western Daily Press and Bristol Mirror*, December 29, 1937, 9, https://www.britishnewspaperarchive.co.uk/viewer/BL/0000513/19371229/102/0009. See also "Portrait Painter: Death of Prof. Sauter in Jena," *Western Morning News and Daily Gazette*, December 29, 1937, 7, https://www.britishnewspaperarchive.co.uk/viewer/BL/0000329/19371229/041/0007.

passing 13 years earlier, Rudolf read her poem "The Pause" to family and friends who had gathered to pay their respects.[29] Such was Rudolf's public tribute to both of his parents before his father's memorial service in early January 1938.[30] His private tribute to his father, written after the service, conveyed the meaning of Georg's life, his accomplishments as a respected artist and Rudolf's appreciation of his love and mentorship:

> So passed back into the ground the body, which for a time had been the instrument by which the spirit had achieved its purpose on earth. It had seemed so fitting, so natural and so right, that one for whom Nature meant so much should thus be laid away. And, returning to the house, it seemed impossible that he who had done so much was there no longer; that all these flights of imagination should survive the hand which had given them their life.[31]

The passing of his father, along with memories of his mother and his childhood influenced heavily by both of his parents, perhaps inspired Rudolf, in 1938, to paint the playful winter scene of his childhood home in Holland Park, depicting a half dozen men shoveling snow alongside a frolicking dog.[32] As far away as he was from that formative site, he recalled it as fondly and held those memories dear as he did also the lessons and creative legacies of his parents.

Citizenship

Although Rudolf's time in Italy reinforced the Englishness of his artistic outlook, if not his English identity itself, he still faced public scrutiny for being stateless and labeled as such by holding a Nansen passport. An August 1926 article in the *Dundee Evening Telegraph* exemplified such attention, pointedly describing him as a "man without a nationality [...] a nephew of Mr John Galsworthy [...] an artist and poet," and making it known that he had "applied to the Home Secretary for naturalization as a British subject." The article went on to quote Rudolf on the fact of his German birth, his undeniable

---

29. Memoirs of Valda Sauter, unpublished typescript, private collection.
30. Europeana Collections, "Brief von Valda Sauter, Rudolf Helmut Sauter und Viola Sauter an Gerhart Hauptmann, Danksagung für Anteilnahme am Tod von Georg Sauter," accessed June 30, 2021, https://www.europeana.eu/en/item/2048611/data_item_sbb_kpe_DE_1a_8535_DE_611_HS_1988131.
31. Rudolf H. Sauter, "The Passing of Georg Sauter, 1937, Christmas, St. Margarethen," 5, unpublished typescript, 1, JG(II)/9/5, Cadbury Library, University of Birmingham.
32. Rudolf H. Sauter, untitled (winter scene in Holland Park), 1938, watercolor, 57 × 39 cm, private collection.

Englishness by association with his famous uncle and his unspecified "personal experience" that informed his published poetry. "There has been doubt about my nationality for some years," his statement began, continuing:

> In the circumstances, I am seeking to become a regularized British subject, a change which is purely formal, for I have lived uninterruptedly in Britain since I was 12 months old. I was born in Germany and I came here as an infant. All my work has been quite British and I have illustrated some of the books of Mr. Galsworthy, including a limited edition of his and his book "Awakening." I have also done oil portraits of both Mr and Mrs Galsworthy and a good deal of landscape work in Italy and Morocco, publishing series of lithographs of them. I have exhibited at the Royal Academy, the Royal Scottish Academy and the Liverpool Gallery. I published a book of poems entitled "Songs in Captivity," based to some extent upon personal experiences.[33]

As this testimony reflected Rudolf's artistic achievements and aspirations rooted in his English upbringing, it revealed how he faced a persistent challenge of the state that once imprisoned him and remained infused with anti-German sentiment. Ultimately, Rudolf prevailed, becoming a naturalized British citizen in November 1926.[34] With this accomplishment, he very likely felt vindicated, embracing anew the only national identity he had ever held, which had informed his upbringing, his education and his lineage. Moreover, upon his naturalization Rudolf seized the opportunity to continue his overseas travel. From 1926 to 1931, he returned to France and toured the United States, South Africa, South America and Portugal, again painting en plain air and in multiple rented studios, now unfettered by any issue pertaining to his origins, outlook and intentions.

America

In the early spring of 1926, Rudolf traveled to America, accompanied by Viola and his aunt Ada and uncle John. Together, they crisscrossed the country, visiting California, Arizona, New Mexico, Illinois, Indiana, Ohio,

---

33. "An Artist without a Nationality: Nephew of John Galsworthy Asks for Naturalisation Papers." *Dundee Evening Telegraph* (London, England), August 6, 1926, 14, https://www.britishnewspaperarchive.co.uk/viewer/bl/0000563/19260806/130/0014.
34. Certificate of Naturalization, wherein Rudolf self-identified as being "Of No Nationality," and related correspondence and notes, HO144/5759, C681523, the UK National Archives.

Maryland and New York.[35] As Rudolf recounted to his friends Michael and Elizabeth Harrison, with whom the group had stayed during their visit to northern Arizona, they

> stopped off at Santa Fe for a day or two; at Chicago for 3 hours to see friends and the art Gallery only; at Indianapolis for 1 night to see the performance of a play by Mr. Galsworthy; at Mentor (some 30 miles from Cincinnati) to stay with a friend of Mr. Galsworthy's for 2 nights [...] at Baltimore, 1 night where we saw "The Vanishing American" and marvelled at the lack of humour, which allowed people to crowd along to see a "picture" like that without seeing its inner significance; at New York, for six most hectic days and nights before sailing from U.S.A. on the *Acquitania* and arriving in London—April 21st.[36]

Rudolf explained further that:

> Altogether our stay in America was a great and appreciated experience not only on account of the wonderful scenery with which the whole country is so marvellously endowed but especially because of the great kindness and hospitality which were showered upon us everywhere—and the thing quite new to us in England's frigid climate, which makes it difficult for people to show even such feelings as they have.[37]

The "wonderful scenery" to which Rudolf referred meant especially the Grand Canyon, which he experienced firsthand through the knowledge and

---

35. Sauter, *Galsworthy the Man*, 164–65.
36. Rudolf H. Sauter to Michael and Elizabeth Harrison, June 1926, BANC MSS 89/72z, The Bancroft Library, University of California, Berkeley. Michael Harrison was an employee of the National Park Service with a deep appreciation of the desert southwest and the Navajo and Hopi tribes. He had worked at the Grand Canyon since 1922, leading tours of the area for visiting VIPs. Harrison's marriage to Elizabeth ended in 1928. He left his public service at the Grand Canyon in 1931 to manage the Big Bear Lake Lodge in California's San Bernardino Mountains. A year later, he met and married his second wife, Margaret. University of California, Davis, Library, "Archives and Special Collections: About Michael and Margaret B. Harrison," accessed June 30, 2021, https://www.library.ucdavis.edu/archives-and-special-collections/michael-margaret-b-harrison-western-research-center-collection/michael-margaret-b-harrison/. Don Lago, "Haunted by Time: British Writers Discover the Grand Canyon," *Ol' Pioneer: The Magazine of the Grand Canyon Historical Society* 25, no. 2 (Spring 2014): 6–15, https://grandcanyonhistory.org/uploads/3/4/4/2/34422134/top_2014_2.pdf.
37. Rudolf H. Sauter to Michael and Elizabeth Harrison, June 1926, BANC MSS 89/72z, The Bancroft Library, University of California, Berkeley.

hospitality of the Harrisons. He was deeply inspired by this natural wonder, painting it repeatedly from various vantage points along the canyon rim. He also appreciated the culture of the site through a gift of the region which he and Viola had received from the Harrisons: a Kachina doll. The figure represented the likeness of a masked impersonator of a supernatural being who appeared in the kivas and plazas of the Hopi nation.[38] Rudolf became captivated by this artifact. As he conveyed to the Harrisons from the Bishop's Lodge in Santa Fe, New Mexico, "our delightful Cachina doll [sic], at present so unfortunately packed away in our luggage, will adorn the studio/workspace in London (where he will feel quite at home) and bring us good luck and remind us of you."[39] Indeed, the doll adorned Rudolf's workspace in Freeland, he captured it in a contemporary still life (Figure 4.2), and he treasured it for decades not only as a material reminder of visiting the Grand Canyon and the recurring inspiration of that natural wonder of the world, but also as a symbol of the far horizons to which he and Viola had traveled and which had helped him expand his artistic creativity. As Rudolf wrote in a subsequent letter to the Harrisons,

> Since our return I have been working hard on a large picture of the Cañon [sic], compiled from one of my small canvases and the assistance of others. Though it is extremely difficult to keep in mind that fine clarity of atmosphere which keeps the colour of the rock so clean and yet soft, while we are surrounded by damp and misty wrappings of cloud—usually described in the journals under the heading: "visibility poor." I have also painted a small "flower piece," of carnations in which, standing by the side of the vase I have utilized the little Cachina doll [sic] with which you so kindly sped us on our way: "for luck." It stands always in the studio/workspace, sometimes here, sometimes there and excites universal interest, which is always increased when we explain how we came by the 'little charmer' and what he stands for[40]

Rudolf's appreciation of his Kachina doll and visit to the Grand Canyon would remain with him for decades to come, inspiring him to recall and find new meaning in the beauty of northern Arizona as he reflected on the arc of his creative life.

---

38. Harold S. Colton, *Hopi Kachina Dolls with a Key to Their Identification* (Albuquerque: University of New Mexico Press, 1959), 2.
39. Rudolf H. Sauter to Michael and Margaret Harrison, April 1, 1926, BANC MSS 89/72z, The Bancroft Library, University of California, Berkeley.
40. Rudolf H. Sauter to Michael and Elizabeth Harrison, June 1926, BANC MSS 89/72z, The Bancroft Library, University of California, Berkeley.

Figure 4.2 Rudolf H. Sauter, *Carnations in a Glass Vase*, 1926, oil on canvas, 61 × 43.2 cm, courtesy of Liss Llewellyn Fine Art, © Trustees of the Estate of Rudolf H. Sauter.

Bury House

In the spring of 1926, shortly after Rudolf and company returned from America, his uncle began to look for a new home that could accommodate everyone. A local housing agent pointed him to a residence in Bury, Sussex, a few miles south of Pulborough. Despite Rudolf's expression of horror at the £69,000 price of the 12-acre property, known as Bury House, Galsworthy purchased it.[41] Situated among "boxwood hedges carefully trimmed and rounded" and a peaceful "rich landscape rolling in chequers of arable and pasture,"[42] the site became Rudolf's new base from which he would substantially grow his artistic career by planning exhibitions of his work at internationally renowned galleries, winning praise from contemporaries and establishing his own studio. Emblematic of his success during this period was Rudolf's photographic portrait by Emil Otto Hoppé, Britain's most famous and influential photographer

---

41. "Mr. Galsworthy's Sussex House," *West Sussex County Times and Standard*, May 4, 1931, 2, https://www.britishnewspaperarchive.co.uk/viewer/bl/0001925/19340504/026/0002.
42. Pierre Quiroule, "John Galsworthy at Home: Creator of the Forstye Saga: A Country Retreat," *Register News-Pictorial* (Adelaide, South Africa), August 24, 1929, 21,

of the day. The image depicted a contemplative and confident young man, chin in hand, as he considered his future as an artist approaching pinnacle of his career.[43]

Rudolf's initial efforts in Bury House included proposing an exhibition of his work to the recently established Lefevre Gallery, in London's King Street. He also corresponded with John Francis Kraushaar about an exhibition in his esteemed New York galleries, which had been regularly mounting innovative shows that mixed European and American work.[44] In a letter to Kraushaar, Rudolf mentioned his contact with the Lefevre Gallery as well as the thoughtful support of his artist cousin Frank.[45] "As you may have heard from Mr. Lefevre," Rudolf wrote, "I have been trying to arrange with him a show of some of my things before sending them on to you. [...] A distant cousin of mine, Mr. Frank Galsworthy, a flower painter, is sailing shortly and will be sure to call and see you in N.Y. and show you some reproductions which will—not!—give you some idea of the work I have been doing in South Africa."[46] Kraushaar responded supportively:

> I hope you are able to arrange with Mr. Lefevre for an exhibition in his galleries, as I think today they are unquestionably one of the best galleries in London to show in. I have placed your exhibition for April but if you should prefer to send it over for the Fall, it will be perfectly satisfactory to me and you can let me know regarding it. As soon as you have decided you could let me know. I will be very glad to meet your cousin Mr. Frank Galsworthy when he calls and also to see the reproductions of the work you have been doing in South Africa.[47]

---

https://trove.nla.gov.au/newspaper/article/53477727?browse=ndp%3Abrowse%2Ftitle%2FR%2Ftitle%2F90%2F1929%2F08%2F24%2Fpage%2F4577565%2Farticle%2F53477727.

43. This photographic portrait illustrates the cover of this book. Rudolf sat for Hoppé in 1928, according to Hoppé's photographic log. Graham Howe to the author, "Re: Follow-Up ~ Permission to use Hoppé photograph of Rudolf Sauter," e-mail dated September 22, 2020.
44. Artist Biographies, "LeFevre Gallery," accessed June 30, 2021, https://www.artbiogs.co.uk/2/galleries/lefevre-gallery.
45. Frank Galsworthy was the son of John Galsworthy's cousin Sir Edwin Galsworthy.
46. Rudolf H. Sauter to John Francis Kraushaar, November 6, 1927, Kraushaar Galleries Records, 1885–2006, box 1, folder 28, Smithsonian Archives of American Art.
47. John Francis Kraushaar to Rudolf H. Sauter, November 16, 1927, Kraushaar Galleries Records, 1885–2006, box 1, folder 28, Smithsonian Archives of American Art.

Rudolf's networking paid off. The LeFevre Gallery opened its exhibition of his work in April 1928.[48] The artist William Palmer Robins praised the show, writing in the *Bookman's Journal and Print Collector* that

> the war, of course, interrupted [Sauter's] career, but its termination found the young artist eager to express his individuality and to draw on his long gathered impressions and ideas. [...] Throughout [the past several years] he has been fortunate in having the indefatigable interest and criticism of his wife; nor can one suppose that the revelation of Galsworthian appreciation of art, as may be happily instanced in the Forsyte Saga, has been without its effect. Much may be expected of a young artist who is not yet thirty; and we may expect to see him developing along his sound lines from his present promise to the complete expression of his ideas and personality.[49]

Rudolf was humbled by the positive reception of his exhibited work, by the presentation of it in the journal and by the mistake in the review. "I have just read with interest Mr. Robbin's [*sic*] article about my work," he wrote to the editor Wilfred Partington:

> It seems to me that, especially considering that I've done practically no etching, he has taken considerable pains and been extremely kind to my endeavours. One slip I must call attention to: that he has put me down as 'under thirty'—well, I have to admit to another five years—But there, again, he's been very kind.

Rudolf concluded, "The reproductions, of which you have chosen a nice lot, have come out excellently & I'm very pleased with them indeed. It's such a pleasure not to have one's stuff served up in an unrecognizable salad of Printer's Ink or dressed with all kinds of smears & blots."[50]

Rudolf sent John Francis Kraushaar a copy of the LeFevre Gallery catalogue, hoping it would entice his interest.[51] It did and three months later the

---

48. C. W. Kraushaar Art Galleries, *Exhibition of Paintings and Lithographs by R.H. Sauter, April 14–30, 1928* (New York: C. W. Kraushaar art Galleries, 1928).
49. *The Bookman's Journal* 17, no. 10 (1929): 83. See also "Art Notes," *West Sussex Gazette*, January 19, 1928, 2, https://www.britishnewspaperarchive.co.uk/viewer/BL/0002166/19280119/020/0002.
50. Rudolf H. Sauter to Wilfred Partington, September 3, 1929, mssPAR 1120, The Huntington Library.
51. Rudolf H. Sauter to John Francis Kraushaar, February 1, 1928, box 2, folder 29, Kraushaar Galleries Records, 1885–2006, Smithsonian Archives of American Art.

Kraushaar Galleries opened its exhibition of Rudolf's work.[52] The show consisted of a variety of paintings and lithographs completed during the course of his recent international travels, including scenes of the Grand Canyon, Italy, Morocco, South Africa and the United Kingdom, as well as an intimate portrait of his aunt Ada featured on the cover of the exhibition catalogue.

Return to America

Rudolf traveled to America again in 1930–31, once more accompanied by Viola, and his aunt Ada and uncle John. The group returned to Arizona, California and Ohio, and for the first time they visited Pennsylvania and Utah. In San Francisco, Rudolf exhibited "water colors, lithographs and drawings" in the gallery of Vickery, Atkins and Torrey, including a drawing of the San Francisco financial district featuring the Francis Drake Hotel.[53] While visiting the city, he and Viola were guests of Rudolf's childhood friend Curtis O'Sullivan, to whom Rudolf had sent one of his earliest landscape drawings.[54] Rudolf had drawn Curtis in charcoal in early 1926, offering the piece to him and his wife Helen with "happy mem[ories]." He drew Curtis again in 1955.[55] The pair remained close until Curtis's passing in 1967.

In Cincinnati, Rudolf exhibited in the Closson Galleries, thanks to W. T. H. (William Thomas Hildrup) Howe, vice president of the American Book Company, who had generously arranged the week-long show after the pair crossed paths in Arizona a month earlier. Howe's interest in supporting Rudolf set off what was likely a frenzied change of plan to Rudolf's upcoming show in the Kraushaar Galleries. Rudolf wrote to Kraushaar asking that he send to Howe a selection of works so they could appear in Cincinnati.[56] Kraushaar

---

52. C. W. Kraushaar Art Galleries, *Exhibition of Paintings by R.H. Sauter, April 14–30, 1928*, Smithsonian Archives of American Art.
53. *The San Franciscan* 5, nos. 4–6 (February, March and April 1931): 20, 21 and 11, respectively, https://archive.org/details/sanfranciscan19301931sanf/page/n537/mode/2up; https://archive.org/details/sanfranciscan19301931sanf/page/n571/mode/2up; https://archive.org/details/sanfranciscan19301931sanf/page/n595/mode/2up.
54. ill. 1–5, above. John Francis Kraushaar to Rudolf H. Sauter, c/o O'Sullivan, March 6, 1931, box 4, folder 11, Kraushaar Galleries Records, 1885–2006, Smithsonian Archives of American Art. See also James Karman, *The Collected Letters of Robinson Jeffers, with Selected Letters of Una Jeffers: Volume Two, 1931–1939* (Stanford, CA: Stanford University Press, 2011), 18.
55. Rudolf H. Sauter, *Curtis O'Sullivan*, 1926, charcoal, 38 × 26.6 cm and 1955, charcoal, 53 × 35.5, private collection.
56. Rudolf H. Sauter to John Francis Kraushaar, February 21, 1931, box 14, folder 4, Kraushaar Galleries Records, 1885–2006, Smithsonian Archives of American Art.

obliged, yielding the Closson exhibition of Rudolf's oils, etchings and charcoal drawings. The *Cincinnati Enquirer* covered the show, pointing out to its readers that "as a portraitist the work of Mr. Sauter has particular appeal to those interested in modern English literature."[57]

A month later, after the Closson Galleries had returned the works it had exhibited, the Kraushaar Galleries opened its second exhibition of Rudolf's work. Like his first show three years earlier, this one consisted of paintings and etchings completed during his international travels, including scenes of Brazil, Italy, Spain and the Grand Canyon and other parts of the American southwest. It also included scenes of Bury and other areas of southern England and portraits of his aunt and uncle. The cover of the exhibition brochure featured his landscape *Little Towers of Terreno*.[58] *New York Times* art critic Ruth Green Harris offered a positive and thought-provoking review of the show, observing that

> A sprint of reality is sometimes created by stressing the little asides you yourself might indulge in were you looking at that scene. This makes the picture warmly your own. For you it is real. Rudolf H. Sauter, at the Kraushaar Galleries, paints a "Lowering Storm, Sussex" and scoops out the famous white cliffs; they look like beautiful shells along the coast. Then you remember that chalk cliffs have always looked like shells. In "Sunflowers" the brown centre of a flower is placed almost in the middle of the canvas. There is a green bird in one of the branches; a black cat, almost licking its chops, looks at a bird. It is a circus scene. You remember that the ragged petals of a sunflower have always reminded you of a paper-covered hoop after the clown has pushed through his head. "Rio de Janeiro Harbour at Dawn" is like a blue landscape seen through a Florentine window. "Vigo Bay" is like—well, perhaps we are pushing our imagination too far. But it is because our imaginations have been stimulated that we like these paintings so much.[59]

The Brooklyn Daily Eagle also covered Rudolf's second exhibition in the Kraushaar Galleries, describing him as the impressionistic artist he was

---

57. "Sauter Visit," *Cincinnati Enquirer*, March 14, 1931, 10, https://www.newspapers.com/image/103208948.
58. C. W. Kraushaar Art Galleries, *Paintings, Drawings and Etchings by Rudolf H. Sauter, 30 March to 11 April, 1931* (New York: C. W. Kraushaar Art Galleries, 1931).
59. R. G. H., "Exhibitions; Work Now on View—Art Notes: Sauter and Others," *New York Times*, April 5, 1931, 113, https://timesmachine.nytimes.com/timesmachine/1931/04/05/issue.html.

Figure 4.3 Rudolf H. Sauter, *New York from South End of Central Park*, 1931, pastel on buff paper, 36.8 × 57.2 cm, courtesy of Liss Llewellyn Fine Art, © Trustees of the Estate of Rudolf H. Sauter.

striving to be, "a painter whose sensitive talent is dedicated to recording the storied places of the earth." The reviewer explained further that

> his exhibition is a species of pictorial traveler's log were it not that his pictures are carefully painted, with nothing of the casual freshness of a sketch. They have the quality of deeply felt but pondered emotion. The places recorded extend from Arizona to Brazil and from Mallorca to Johannisberg [*sic*] and Sussex.[60]

A "deeply felt but pondered emotion" characterized Rudolf's time in New York itself, the *Green Bay Press Gazette* reported, adding that he stayed at St. Moriz On-The-Park, located on the south end of Central Park.[61] From this vantage point, Rudolf captured the iconic cityscape, including the Chrysler Building and the Empire State Building (Figure 4.3).

---

60. *The Brooklyn Daily Eagle*, April 5, 1931, 62, https://www.newspapers.com/image/57550684/.
61. "Artist Prefers to Paint Skyline of New York at Dawn," *Green Bay Press-Gazette*, April 1 1931, 5, https://www.newspapers.com/image/186489958/.

Rudolf completed this pastel "in his pajamas," and because he was determined to "[get] New York in the proper light," he awoke "at 5am without waiting to dress" in order to "[catch] the first rays of the sun (if any) as they struck the towers." As the *Green Bay Press-Gazette* reported further about his impressionistic work,

> There is a proper light effect to be had also at sunset, so Mr. Sauter catches it again in the last rays of the sun. Mr. Sauter's particular interest is the mid-town skyline and he was amused at the thought that comparatively few New Yorkers see it as he does—most of them being in bed when the dawn illuminates it in the proper way and dashing for subways when the evening light is right. The Empire State is his favorite building on the skyline. He hopes they never hitch a dirigible to the tip of it. New York is a wonderful city for landscapes, but somewhat too fast and too exciting to live in, said the painter. He finds its daytime air cleaner than London's, its night sky quite similar. He prefers his home in Sussex to either.[62]

Rudolf and Viola did return to Sussex shortly after his exhibition in the Kraushaar Galleries closed on April 11, 1931. Once they settled back into Bury House, they embarked together on a remarkable project: designing a new studio. Infused with Rudolf's long-standing appreciation of studios as he had first experienced them, in his father's of Holland Park and as he later conceived them by necessity during his wartime internment and by choice during his postwar travels, the space he and Viola envisioned would stand well part from anything he had occupied previously. It would be his own in every sense of the word, a creative center achieved at the pinnacle of his career.

Bury Studio

"We were not abroad at all last winter," Rudolf wrote to the Harrisons in December 1932, "but I was busy designing in every detail and building with local labour and personally doing some of the decorating of a studio in the country down here. Last year it was in the making, this year we are installed."[63] Here was Bury Studio, the bespoke design, construction and decoration of which Rudolf paid for himself through his "accumulated reserves from good

---

62. Ibid.
63. Rudolf H. Sauter to Michael Harrison, December 14, 1932, BANC MSS 89/72z, The Bancroft Library, University of California, Berkeley.

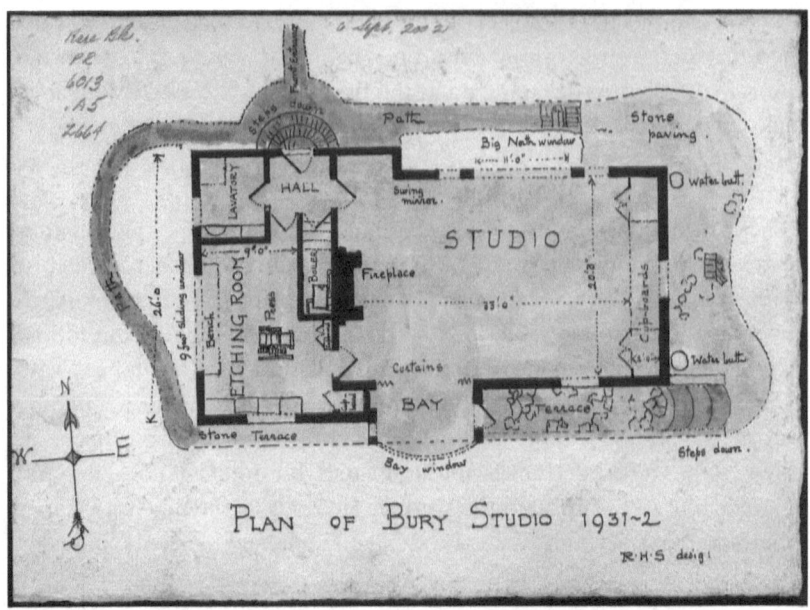

Figure 4.4 Rudolf H. Sauter, *Plan of Bury Studio 1931–32*, captioned "Designed and devised by R. H. Sauter with the connivance and assistance of V. Sauter who made all the curtains and covers and all sorts of jolly decorations," in Rudolf and Viola Sauter, *Book of the Studio: Contrived by R. et V. Sauter for Mr. W. T. H. Howe Whose Generous Interest Is as the Gentle Rain from Heaven and Bringeth Forth Even Studios* (privately compiled, 1931–32), n.p., Rauner Special Collections Library, Dartmouth College, © Trustees of the Estate of Rudolf H. Sauter.

[investment] years."[64] More than this, he and Viola painstakingly recorded every detail of its creation and development in a bespoke volume they compiled, called *Book of the Studio*. This production was as remarkable as the space it documented.

Dedicated to W. T. H. Howe who had helped Rudolf achieve his exhibition in Cincinnati's Closson Galleries, *Book of the Studio* contained nearly three dozen photographs along with highly detailed drawings that recalled the style of his depictions of the Alexandra Palace and Frith Hill Camp (Figure 4.4).

Together, these photographs and drawings revealed Bury Studio from conception to creation: wooden model to detailed layout, multiperspective land survey to multiphased construction, monogrammed decoration to relaxed and artistically productive habitation. Beyond its exquisite documentation, *Book*

---

64. Rudolf H. Sauter to Ada Galsworthy, January 3, 1934, JG(II)/8/8/3, Cadbury Library, University of Birmingham.

of the Studio presaged Rudolf's later interest in printing as a medium through which he would creatively and effectively share his visual and literary creations. Indeed, this book itself was a unique work of art, or nearly so: Rudolf and Viola created only two copies. They kept one for themselves, and they gifted the other to their friend W. T. H. Howe.[65]

Rudolf and Viola's careful documentation of their bespoke studio directly informed their contemporary and custom holiday greeting cards. His card for Christmas 1932 reproduced a version of his *Book of the Studio* drawing of Bury Studio as a "skeleton out of the cupboard" (Figure 4.5). Here was the exterior of Bury Studio under construction. It was the same image that appeared in *Book of the Studio* but without Rudolf's detailed marginal notes, which labeled the "apple trees" surrounding the structure, "elm boards" used in the construction, "the fire screen" monogrammed with the couple's initials, "the plan" and "the model" that appeared on other pages of *Book of the Studio* and, curiously, "old pan tiles from Seigfried Sassoon's old family property at Walton." Rudolf's card for Christmas 1933 reproduced a photograph of the interior of Bury Studio, which also appeared in *Book of the Studio*. Significantly, Rudolf drew all of these holiday cards in Bury Studio itself. Moreover, he produced them partly in its etching room, a location he depicted in *Book of the Studio* with a photograph of himself clad in his printer's apron, one hand on his press and the other holding an etching plate (Figure 4.6).

The interplay between *Book of the Studio* and these holiday cards reflected Rudolf and Viola's joint, deep and proud investment in Bury Studio simultaneously as their home—complete with their beloved sheepdog Colin—and as Rudolf's center of artistic achievement, complete with the inspirational Kachina Doll gifted to the couple by the Harrisons in 1926.[66] Unfortunately, despite their enthusiastic dedication to creating, building and documenting this unique space, their occupation and enjoyment of it would be short-lived.

Responsibility and Roots

As Rudolf emerged as an artist on his own terms during the decade following the Great War, he remained like a son to his aunt Ada and uncle John. When Galsworthy died in 1933, Rudolf became a trustee of his estate in cooperation with Ada. Together, the pair created *Ex Libris: John Galsworthy*, a posthumous

---

65. Rudolf H. Sauter and Viola Sauter, *Book of the Studio: Contrived by R. et V. Sauter for Mr. W. T. H. Howe Whose Generous Interest Is as the Gentle Rain from Heaven and Bringeth Forth Even Studios*, privately compiled, 1931–32. Dartmouth College Library holds one copy of this work, while the other is in private hands.
66. Rudolf H. Sauter to Michael and Margaret Harrison, January 27, 1927, BANC MSS 89/72z, The Bancroft Library, University of California, Berkeley.

Figure 4.5 Rudolf H. Sauter, holiday greeting card for 1932, BANC MSS 89/72z, The Bancroft Library, University of California, Berkeley, © Trustees of the Estate of Rudolf H. Sauter.

collection of Galsworthy's quotations and thoughts. Ada edited the volume and Rudolf contributed to it "enlivening and beautiful decorations,"[67] the effort behind which, he explained to her, was "purely out of love for you, really, without any thought of profit."[68] Rudolf's work appeared throughout the collection and

---

67. Ada Galsworthy, foreword to *Ex Libris: John Galsworthy* (London: Heinemann, 1933).
68. Rudolf H. Sauter to Ada Galsworthy, March 3, 1934, JG(II)/8/8/32, Cadbury Library, University of Birmingham. Rudolf conveyed this sentiment to Ada in response to learning that Heinemann was offering him a £25 royalty payment, which he was reluctant to accept because he did not want her to receive that amount less in her own royalties. More thoughtfully, he explained further to her: "You see it's a little difficult for me to write of these things being as I am in the double capacity both of Trustee & beneficially interested so to speak under the suggestion you make in your own letter [that I should accept such royalty] which is all but awkward & complicated."

Figure 4.6 Photograph, "The Etching Room," from Rudolf and Viola Sauter, *Book of the Studio: Contrived by R. et V. Sauter for Mr. W. T. H. Howe Whose Generous Interest Is as the Gentle Rain from Heaven and Bringeth Forth Even Studios* (privately compiled, 1931–32), n.p., Rauner Special Collections Library, Dartmouth College, © Trustees of the Estate of Rudolf H. Sauter.

adorning the cover was the bookplate he had designed for his uncle, depicting one of the many dogs belonging to the family, a cocker spaniel bringing its master a book. With equal thoughtfulness a few years later Rudolf designed a bookplate for Ada, depicting the musical notes of A, D and A, above two rows of windpipes and two of the family's beloved dogs.[69] Around the same period, he designed and produced matching bookplates, for himself and Viola, reflecting their loving partnership. While his depicted a painter's palette, her's depicted a violet (Figure 4.7).

While Rudolf's creation of these bookplates reflected his familial connectedness, it paled in comparison to his contemporary illustration of an elaborate family tree based on notes collected by his uncle.[70] This outsized work—measuring

---

69. Rudolf H. Sauter, bookplate designed for Ada Galsworthy, accompanied by the note that it was "rough so please make suggestions & be ruthless," Rudolf H. Sauter to Ada Galsworthy, JG(II)/8/9/111a, Cadbury Library, University of Birmingham. So beloved were the dogs depicted in these bookplates, and in Rudolf and Viola's custom holiday cards, that John Galsworthy published a book about them, illustrated by Maud Earl—*Memories* (New York: Charles Scribner's Sons, 1918)—as did Ada, shortly after her husband's passing in 1933—*The Dear Dogs* (London: William Heinemann, 1935).
70. Rudolf H. Sauter, family tree, ca. 1934; updated ca. 1960, 121.9 × 213.3 cm, JG(II)/30, Cadbury Library, University of Birmingham.

more than four feet tall and seven feet wide—served to ground Rudolf following the loss of his uncle, a reminder of his roots as he was becoming known as an accomplished artist with his own style and talents.[71] Two decades later, after Ada's passing and when he became the primary representative of his uncle's literary legacy, Rudolf updated this family tree not merely for accuracy but as an act of appreciating his family—his uncle and aunt, as well as his mother and father—and all they had taught him and inspired him in his artistic talents.

Rudolf's inheritance from his uncle provided him with a regular income for the remainder of his life. However, it was not enough to enable him to keep and maintain his beloved Bury Studio, so he and Viola needed to look for a new home.[72] As he explained this situation to Ada, "the crux of all accommodation for me is either 'the' Studio or 'a' Studio & for Vi smallness of running & upkeep."[73] Their "house hunting" initially led them to the Cotswolds, but when the opportunity of a cottage there fell through, they found what they were looking for in Kent, "at Wittersham, about 4½ miles inland from Rye." There, standing "about 200 ft. above the marshes, which it nearly, but not quite overlooks […] is quite the best thing we've seen for our requirements."[74] The property was called The Stocks. It was a mill dating from the 1780s which most recently had been owned by the actor Norman Forbes-Robertson, restored as a playhouse, but still dilapidated due to age and lack of upkeep.[75] To improve the site and make it his own, Rudolf intended to "build on to [it] a sort of loft above the garage to make a Studio," a renovation he began to plan even before the couple completed their purchase of the property.[76]

Rudolf depicted the couple's move from Sussex to Wittersham in a whimsical change-of-address card depicting their caravan journey across the English countryside (Figure 4.8). For their 1934–35 holiday greeting card Rudolf drew their new abode itself. The scene included their longtime companion Colin, their new companions "Mr. and Mrs. Owl who lived on the top floor," and

---

71. Rudolf H. Sauter, Family Tree, ca. 1934; updated ca. 1960, 121.9 × 213.3 cm, JG(II)/30, Cadbury Library, University of Birmingham.
72. Nor could Ada afford to remain in Bury House, so she moved to Torquay, where she lived until her passing in 1956. Rudolf H. Sauter to Ada Galsworthy, January 24, and February 1, 1934, JG(II)/8/8/20 and 21, Cadbury Library, University of Birmingham.
73. Rudolf H. Sauter to Ada Galsworthy, February 1, 1934, JG(II)/8/8/21, Cadbury Library, University of Birmingham.
74. Rudolf H. Sauter to Ada Galsworthy, April 15 and 22, 1934, JG(II)/8/8/50 and 56, Cadbury Library, University of Birmingham.
75. *A Guide to Stocks Mill, Wittersham, Kent* (Wittersham, Kent: Friends of Stocks Mill, 1995), 2.
76. Rudolf H. Sauter to Ada Galsworthy, April 22, 1934, JG(II)/8/8/56, Cadbury Library, University of Birmingham.

Figure 4.7 Clockwise from top: Rudolf H. Sauter, bookplates designed for Viola Sauter and himself, private collection; for his aunt Ada Galsworthy, JG(II)/8/9/111a, Cadbury Library, University of Birmingham, and for his uncle John Galsworthy, cover illustration of John Galsworthy, *Ex Libris: John Galsworthy* (London: Heinemann, 1933), all © Trustees of the Estate of Rudolf H. Sauter.

Rudolf's studio located on the first floor, wherein he proudly displayed the Kachina doll gift from Michael Harrison, a continued artistic inspiration and reminder of America (Figure 4.9).

As Rudolf wrote to Harrison, "the Indian mascot figure you gave us at the Grand Canon has been in the place of honour in each of my Studio/

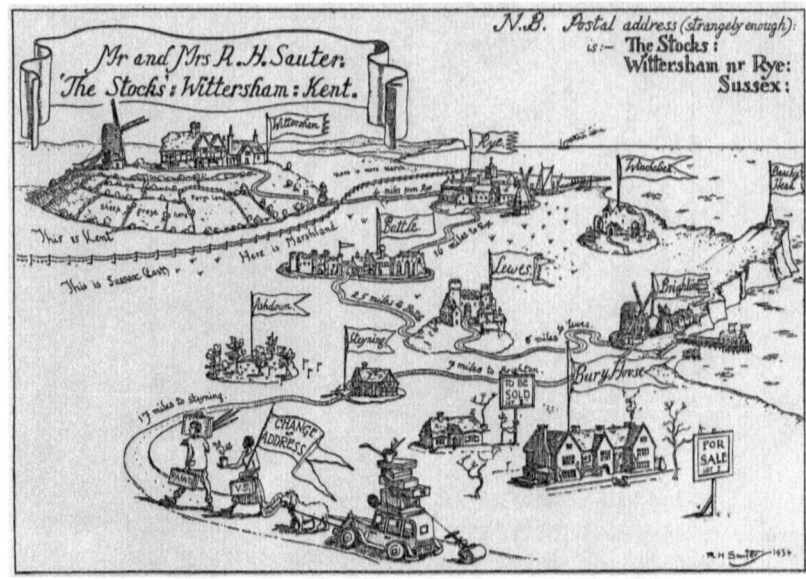

Figure 4.8 Rudolf H. Sauter, change-of-address card, 1934, BANC MSS 89/72z, The Bancroft Library, University of California, Berkeley, © Trustees of the Estate of Rudolf H. Sauter.

workspaces ever since and now reposes, much faded but still game to bring us good fortune, in a niche of the brickwork at the side of our great single fireplace in our present dining room."[77] Rudolf found his new home and studio to be "very charming, being very old, but full of a kindly atmosphere with low ceilings and big open fireplaces in which at this moment we burn very large logs of wood. The garden too is very full of flowers and very charmingly laid out."[78]

---

77. Rudolf H. Sauter to Michael Harrison, February 4, 1936, BANC MSS 89/72z, The Bancroft Library, University of California, Berkeley.
78. Rudolf H. Sauter to Michael Harrison, February 4, 1936, BANC MSS 89/72z, The Bancroft Library, University of California, Berkeley. Rudolf's description overlooked serious problems with the integrity of the structure which was "one of the finest post mills extant" but had been "attacked and seriously damaged by the death watch beetle larva." The framework was "riddled in many places with the pest," crumbling to the touch, even as both the core of the oak timbers and the centre-post remained sound. Rudolf therefore had the restoration project cut out for him when he contracted the local firm H.C. Paine to carry out the work. "Wittersham Landmark: Restoration of the Stocks Mill," *Sussex Agricultural Express*, August 12, 1938, 15, https://www.britishn ewspaperarchive.co.uk/viewer/BL/0000655/19380812/347/0015.

Figure 4.9 Rudolf H. Sauter, holiday greeting card for 1935, BANC MSS 89/72z, The Bancroft Library, University of California, Berkeley, © Trustees of the Estate of Rudolf H. Sauter.

Proud of the site in which he and Viola had found and began to make their own, he repeatedly painted the structure and its surrounds (Figure 4.10).[79]

Rudolf's drawing of the intricate renovation of the Stocks graced the couple's holiday greeting card for 1939, suggesting how they embraced their envisioning of this space with as much enthusiasm as they had done with Bury

---

79. See also *A Windmill [The Stocks, Wittersham]*, ca. 1940, oil on board, 51 × 61 cm, and *Sails Ride the Summer Storm*, ca. 1940, oil on board, 35 × 43 cm, accessed June 30, 2021,

Studio.[80] The couple would live here for the next ten years, its studio and environs being where Rudolf would produce some of his most impactful art influenced directly by the Second World War.

Revealing his state of mind and creativity during this period and his tempered hopes to travel overseas once more, Rudolf wrote to Michael Harrison:

> Oh yes, the itch [to visit] is upon us all right, but while you never know what may happen, the prospects of a visit aren't too grand at present. Nor is the world outlook, very grand, either. Everything seems to run to madness on these days. Gas masked figures, the gleaming knife-edge of swooping planes, caught in a searchlight, the grey shadow of great bombers, the red daubed, steel crucifix of girders on which youth is crucified haunted my dreams for 18 months, till it had to be flung on canvas—three big pictures—a modern Triptych. Now it is finished and about to be shown in London in March.[81]

The exhibition to which Rudolf referred was "NEVER MORE…! (a modern Triptych) and other paintings" at the Arlington Gallery in Old Bond Street.[82] Consisting of nearly fifty works, it showcased his landscape and portraiture work in charcoal and oil punctuated by an anti-war triptych (Figure 4.11) and this associated poem in the exhibition catalogue:[83]

> Man has unleashed his falcons in the night
> His metal-bodies falcons in the day,
> Taloned with steel to swoop about their prey.
> Man's voice is swift about the earth as light;
> His knowledge, bloated till its burst its cage,

---

https://www.easyliveauction.com/catalogue/lot/694e0c09b89690d8212bd968e5381078/0af8d24542e81eb9357e7ef448a6646f/pictures-books-automobilia-antiques-interiors-lot-11/ and https://www.easyliveauction.com/catalogue/lot/79d0cc4148ce92a9deb6a6e07147d044/0af8d24542e81eb9357e7ef448a6646f/pictures-books-automobilia-antiques-interiors-lot-29/, respectively.

80. Rudolf H. Sauter, holiday greeting card for 1939, BANC MSS 89/72z, The Bancroft Library, University of California, Berkeley.
81. Rudolf H. Sauter to Michael Harrison, February 4, 1936, BANC MSS 89/72z, The Bancroft Library, University of California, Berkeley. The craft to which Rudolf referred was bookbinding.
82. Artist Biographies, "Arlington Gallery," https://www.artbiogs.co.uk/2/galleries/arlington-gallery.
83. *"Never more-!", a Modern Triptych and Other Paintings by R.H. Sauter. Dealers' Catalogue, published to accompany an exhibition held at Arlington Gallery, London, 3rd–13th March, 1936* (London: Arlington Gallery, 1936).

Figure 4.10 Rudolf H. Sauter, *Windmill*, oil on board, ca. 1940, 71 × 58.5 cm, private collection, © Trustees of the Estate of Rudolf H. Sauter.

Has built him wintry skeletons of steel
To serve each fancy of the teasing wheel
Of change. When shall be the heritage
Bequeathed of this achieving? That his sons
Become a race of masked and stunted apes
Crouched before Destruction's swooping shapes,
To grasp till Death more mercifully stuns?
That were too much! God, let this no more be!
Else man were beast, no beast more beast than he.

Underscoring the anti-war messages of Rudolf's visual and written work was the journalist Sir Philip Gibbs, who was also a member of the Royal Commission on the Manufacture of and Trade in Armaments Commission. He opened the exhibition with an "impassioned outburst against war," speaking as he stood in the section of the show entitled "Mad New World,"

Figure 4.11 Rudolf H. Sauter, *NEVER MORE...! (a modern Triptych)*, 1936, oil on panels, unknown dimensions, reproduced in *"Never more-!", a modern triptych and other paintings by R.H. Sauter. Dealers' catalogue, published to accompany an exhibition held at Arlington Gallery, London, 3rd-13th March, 1936* (London: Arlington Gallery, 1936), Victoria & Albert Museum, London, © Trustees of the Estate of Rudolf H. Sauter.

and specifically in front of the center section of Rudolf's triptych, entitled "The Reaping." Its scene depicted "a young workman, in dungarees, crucified on a cross of steel girders at the foot of which gas-masks figures bartered his life for gold." To Gibbs's right was the panel entitled "The Sowing," depicting "youth and childhood in fresh-ploughed fields and the shadow of a bomber with factories in the background," which Gibbs observed were "working double shift manufacturing death in gas and high-explosive shells." To Gibbs's left was the panel entitled "The Harvest," depicting "the bombers swooping on a desolate countryside where Death walked alone." Gibbs concluded his remarks with the declaration that war "will be, the end of all things, but an ideal is more powerful than brute force—we must reach across frontiers [to prevent it]."[84]

Over the next three years, Rudolf achieved several more exhibitions. However, none would be as timely and significant as the one in the Arlington Gallery, and none reflected so vividly the fatalism of his public triptych or the similar outlook he and Viola had communicated privately to their friends through their holiday greeting card for 1936 (Figure 4.12).

---

84. "Arms Commissioner Denounces War." *Daily Harold* (London, England), March 4, 1936, 9, https://www.britishnewspaperarchive.co.uk/viewer/bl/0000681/19360304/124/0009. See also Frank Swinnerton, "Authors Talk for Opening of Art

Figure 4.12 Rudolf H. Sauter, holiday greeting card for 1936, BANC MSS 89/72z, The Bancroft Library, University of California, Berkeley, © Trustees of the Estate of Rudolf H. Sauter.

* * *

In the years ahead, Rudolf would largely set aside peacetime subjects in favor of the themes of these productions.[85] Indeed, these works anticipated the hallmarks of his body of work to come, images that would be directly inspired by and reflect events of the Second World War and, in so doing, stand in stark contrast to anything he had previously created.

Exhibitions: Crush Greets H.G. Wells at London Show," *Chicago Daily Tribune*, April 4, 1936, 18.

85. One significant exception would be in the Ferens Art Gallery, where he displayed "Somewhere in England," which the curators at the Royal Academy for their permanent collection. "Hull Buys Royal Academy Pictures." *Daily Mail* (London, England), May 28, 1940, 6.

Chapter 5

ARTISTRY II, 1939–50

For Rudolf and Viola, the Second World War was a period of "intense anxiety and fear" as they lived in Kent under Doodlebug Alley "with German buzz bombs flying overhead daily [...] dogfights [...] over their heads" and Viola never knowing if Rudolf would return after she kissed him goodbye each morning.[1] Significantly, where Rudolf regularly set out reflected his naturalized citizenship of the state that had previously labeled and imprisoned him as an enemy alien, but which he now chose to serve as it faced another war. He had enlisted as a Local Army Welfare Officer in the Eastern Command, covering East Anglia and the Central Midland Counties. His duties across this region allowed him to continue painting. His resulting work, which focused on a variety of subjects symbolizing the realities and physical force of the nation at war, stood in stark contrast to the images of captivity he created during the previous war. Although he was never an official war artist, Rudolf documented Britain at war as accurately and meaningfully as the productions of these contemporaries.[2]

1939–40

Rudolf's earliest wartime works included *Homo Sapiens: MCMXL* (Figure 5.1), a related piece depicting the same figure holding a gas mask,[3] *After the Raid* (Figure 5.2) depicting a gas mask hanging from a crossbeam of bombed-out building and *Not to be Removed* (Figure 5.3), showing lines of barbed wire and concrete bollards along a coastline. The individual and collective grimness

---

1. Inglis Fletcher, *The Story of My Life: Pay, Pack and Follow* (New York: Henry Holt, 1959), 263–64.
2. Stamps indicating "passed censor" appear on the reverse of many but not all of the works Rudolf completed following his enlistment on November 24, 1941, retroactive from 21 August of the same year, suggesting that his service as an army welfare officer required him to submit his artwork to military censors. No such stamps appear on the reverse of his work completed before his enlistment.
3. Rudolf H. Sauter, *Soldier Holding a Gas Mask*, 1939, pencil and watercolor on paper 78.5 × 56.5 cm. Liss Llewellyn Fine Art. This work was possibly a self-portrait.

126   WAR AND PEACE IN THE WORLDS OF RUDOLF H. SAUTER

Figure 5.1 Rudolf H. Sauter, *Homo Sapiens: MCMXL*, 1940, unknown medium, unknown dimensions; "British Art Scans War While Official Painters Prepare Record Other Express Personal Reactions," *New York Times*, July 7, 1940, X12, https://timesmachine.nytimes.com/timesmachine/1940/07/07/issue.html, © Trustees of The Estate of Rudolf H. Sauter.

of these works—no less their subjects of civil defense, gas warfare and protective masks—echoed the themes of his earlier triptych and holiday cards. Rudolf knew then what was unfolding, and he was now in the throes of living it daily and capturing it through his art, particularly the aforementioned *Homo Sapiens: MCMXL*.

Homo Sapiens: MCMXL

Rudolf submitted *Homo Sapiens: MCMXL* for display in the 1940 United Artists Exhibition in Burlington House, supporting the Lord Mayor's Red Cross and St. John Fund and the Artists' General Benevolent Institution.[4]

---

4. Rudolf submitted works to the second (1942) and third (1943) United Artists' Exhibitions in aid of H.R.H. The Duke of Gloucester's Red Cross and St. John Fund and the Artists' General Benevolent Institution. Rudolf's *The Three Graces* appeared in the first of these subsequent exhibitions and two of his works—*Old Southwark* and *Rose Chrysanthemums*—appeared in the second. See *The Second United Artists' Exhibition in Aid of H.R.H. The Duke of Gloucester's Red Cross and St. John Fund [and the Artists' General Benevolent Institution]* (London: Royal Academy of Arts, 1942), 24. *The Third United Artists' Exhibition in Aid of H.R.H. The Duke of Gloucester's Red Cross and St. John Fund [and the Artists' General Benevolent Institution]* (London: Royal Academy of Arts, 1943), 24.

Figure 5.2 Rudolf H. Sauter, *After the Raid*, ca. 1940, watercolor on paper, 49.5 × 60 cm, courtesy of Liss Llewellyn Fine Art, © Trustees of The Estate of Rudolf H. Sauter.

Spearheaded by the Royal Academy of Arts and inspired by its similar effort of 1914–15, the exhibition involved "the willing and energetic collaboration of twenty-four Art Societies" presenting "the great variety of styles and tendencies in contemporary art, and which, besides reminding the public of the importance of the fine arts and professional artists to our civilisation, affords an opportunity of giving much-needed assistance to the two funds in aid of sufferers in the fighting forces and artists and their families who are in distress."[5] The exhibition itself was "a bold experiment," being "the first time in its history it has invited all the opposing schools of contemporary British art to co-operate and they have really done so [...] [for this] charitable appeal."[6] The placement of Rudolf's *Homo Sapiens: MCMXL* in the Large South Room of the exhibition—between Alexander J. C. Bryce's *The Old Town, Menton* and Albert E. Berbank's *Old Barns, Chalfont St. Peter*—exemplified the convergence of opposing schools while reminding observers about the

---

5. Edwin L. Lutyens, Preface, United Artists' Exhibition in Aid of the Lord Mayor's Red Cross and St. John Fund and the Artists' General Benevolent Institution (London: Royal Academy of Arts, 1940), iii.
6. "R.A.s and Surrealists Unite: All Schools of Art Represented at the Academy," *Yorkshire Post and Leeds Intelligencer*, January 5, 1940, 6, https://www.britishnewspaperarchive.co.uk/viewer/BL/0000687/19400105/263/0006.

Figure 5.3 Rudolf H. Sauter, *Not to Be Removed*, ca. 1940, watercolor, 39 × 58 cm, courtesy of Liss Llewellyn Fine Art, © Trustees of The Estate of Rudolf H. Sauter.

war.[7] As the *Daily Colonist* reported with specific reference to the location of Rudolf's work, "there are over 2,000 exhibits crowded into the rooms, most of them reminiscent of happier days. Reminders of the war are not lacking, however. Between two landscapes is Rudolf H. Sauter's 'Homo Sapiens: MCMXL,' an air raid warden in gas mask and anti-gas suit."[8]

Several other newspapers featured this massive exhibition and Rudolf's distinctive contribution to it. "Side by side you will find the work of the most staid academicians, the bolder impressionists and the wildest spirits of the London Group," reported the art critic of the *Yorkshire Post and Leeds Intelligencer*, who continued:

> the result is immensely interesting, enlightening and diverting and the "rebels" against tradition have not got the best of the encounter by any

---

7. *United Artists' Exhibition in Aid of the Lord Mayor's Red Cross and St. John Fund and the Artists' General Benevolent Institution* (London: Royal Academy of Arts, 1940), 23.
8. "Art Exhibition Raises Funds to Aid Red Cross Work: War's Reminders," *Daily Colonist* (Victoria, British Columbia), March 3, 1940, 2, https://archive.org/details/dailycolonist0340uvic_1/page/n23/mode/2up?q=exhibition.

means. "Death" (a trio of sepulchral figures), "Cosmic Cradle," and a few others are examples the meaning and significance of which I shall not attempt to interpret. On the other hand, such symbolic paintings as C. R. W. Nevinson's "The Twentieth Century," and Rudolf Sauter's "Homo Sapiens, 1940" are strong and definite impressions of the artist's ideas. Mr. Nevinson depicts the century as a grim titanic figure of a man in deep thought, surrounded by all the destructive implements of war and seeks to illustrate "the conflict between human thought and man's predatory instincts." Mr. Sauter's figure is a man in gas mask, steel helmet and trench coat against a background of corrugated iron.[9]

Moreover, in its coverage of the exhibition the *Evening Telegraph* noted that "several pictures will be talked about. One is 'Homo Sapiens MCMXL.' It is a gruesome picture by Rudolf H. Sauter. The subject is an air warden. He stands in gas mask and overalls against a background of corrugated iron."[10] *The Ottawa Journal* also noted Sauter's contribution as being among "the most striking" of the "warlike subjects" on display, as it depicted "a man complete covered in gas mask and decontamination outfit of pilskin [oilskin] clothing and mitts."[11]

Several weeks after the United Artists Exhibition, Rudolf became one of the "notable" and "well-known and rising artists" who exhibited in "The War As I See it" at the British Art Centre, Stafford Galleries, St. James Place.[12] The guidance to the contributing artists involved working "deliberately to the theme," giving "something for their imaginations to bite on and [...] not merely following free fancy." Rudolf embraced this guidance to the letter, as well as the currency of what was then his most notable work, and contributed to the exhibition his provocative *Homo Sapiens: MCMXL*.

---

9. "R. A.s and Surrealists Unite: All Schools of Art Represented at the Academy," *Yorkshire Post and Leeds Intelligencer*, January 5, 1940, 6, https://www.britishnewspaperarchive.co.uk/viewer/BL/0000687/19400105/263/0006.
10. "Angus Artists in Royal Academy," *Evening Telegraph* (Dundee, Scotland), January 5, 1940, 3, https://www.britishnewspaperarchive.co.uk/viewer/BL/0000563/19400105/031/0003.
11. Guy Rhoades, "Royal Academy Art Exhibit Most Peaceful in Many Years: Scarcely a Dozen Pictures Deal with Warlike Subjects, among 2,219 Subjects Shown," *Ottawa Journal*, February 2, 1940, 4, https://www.newspapers.com/image/48429019.
12. "War Fancies in Paint," *Liverpool Daily Post*, April 16, 1940, 6, https://www.britishnewspaperarchive.co.uk/viewer/BL/0000650/19400416/142/0006. Others included Raymond Coxon, Dora Crockett, Mariette Lysis, Michael Rothenstein, Feliks Topolski and Kenneth Wood. See also "Stafford Gallery: 'The War As I See It,'" *Times* (London, England), April 21, 1940, 4.

Enlistment

Rudolf enlisted in the Army Welfare Service on November 24, 1941, "without pay & allowance," with his service being retroactive from 21 August of the same year.[13] His enlistment took place during the period of the war when "Army Welfare was serving a useful purpose in providing a form of 'Military Service' for certain individuals of military age"[14] as well as those British citizens who were, like 46-year-old Rudolf, "too old to be called up."[15] The resulting "lists of those who [had] joined [the Army Welfare effort] showed the democratic character of the service," which was to "effect a proper liaison between the Army and the civil population and to settle amicably the numerous misunderstandings which occur in war-time."[16] Herein was the most important aspect of Welfare Officer work, namely "the respect and confidence he should command, with a view to becoming a personal friend to each and every man in the unit" as they fight "inactivity and monotony."[17] With his own background as a former enemy alien turned naturalized citizen and as an accomplished artist, Rudolf in his own way became a representative of the "democratic character" of the Local Army Welfare Officers and their effort to make a positive difference in the war effort. As he recalled his duties, they afforded him, yet again, "occasion to see what misery war can bring."

> In the first war it had been to families divided by national cleavages, in the second to those separated by war from those on active service. It was my job [...] to visit the personnel of remote ack-ack [anti-aircraft guns] and searchlight sites clustered round the south coast and to become involved in their welfare and that of their families. I shared their anxieties as the fleets of German bombers growled overhead on their way to London. I visited the wives and children of those from my

---

13. "Rudolf H. Sauter, Army Form B199A," Historical Disclosures, Support Division, the UK Army Personnel Centre.
14. "Six Years of Army Welfare," *Journal of the Royal United Services Institution* 91, no. 561 (1946): 52–55, https://www.tandfonline.com/doi/pdf/10.1080/03071844609433898.
15. Rudolf H. Sauter, "Enemy Alien," in *While They Fought: An Anthology of Prose and Verse Exploring the Lives of Those Who Did Not Fight, but Who Had to Endure the Second World War*, ed. Michael Marland and Robin Willcox (London: Longman, 1980), 87.
16. "Six Years of Army Welfare," *Journal of the Royal United Services Institution* 91, no. 561 (1946): 52–55, https://www.tandfonline.com/doi/pdf/10.1080/03071844609433898.
17. "The Army Welfare Officer," *Spectator* (London, England), December 12, 1941, 14, http://archive.spectator.co.uk/article/12th-december-1941/14/the-army-welfare-officer.

area who were sent overseas and whose concern about them sometimes required compassionate leave. It was my turn now to try and heal the wounds which separation brings. These were men cut off from life—not prisoners—human beings isolated from the experience of life and thrust bewildered into the experience of war.[18]

As a result of such experience, Rudolf began to feel that he and everyone "live in such times that 'Time' seems no longer to bear any relation to reality and days go by and seem like a few hours and hours go by and seem like days."[19] His own days as a local army welfare officer involved assisting injured soldiers in returning home and reconnecting with their loved ones, as well as organizing sporting events and activities for the Salute the Soldier Week campaign held during the spring of 1944.[20]

Through his combined experiences of military service and living in Kent, where doodlebugs "sometimes shower out of the sky like the proverbial plague of frogs," Rudolf produced more iconic scenes of the militarized home front, and a great many focused on aviation. These works included four *Studies of Contrails*, and one specifically entitled *Sky Battle*, completed in 1940.[21] The following year, he completed *Searchlights along the Thames Estuary* (Figure 5.4), capturing the ominous night landscape along the south coast of England. In 1943–44, he turned his attention to depicting Spitfires and Republic Thunderbolts, completing a number of works, including *Into Battle: Thunderbolts Supporting a Bomber Sweep at Dawn*,[22] *The Sinister Insect: The Dragon Fly*,[23] *Phantom Eye—Phantasy*,[24] *Return at Dawn: Spitfires on Patrol*,[25] *Out of the Dawn: Thunderbolt*

---

18. Rudolf H. Sauter, "Enemy Alien," in Marland and Willcox, *While They Fought*, 89–90.
19. Rudolf H. Sauter to Ada Galsworthy, June 17, 1944, JG(II)/8/9/192, Cadbury Library, University of Birmingham.
20. Rudolf H. Sauter to Ada Galsworthy, June 17, 1944, and August 8, 1944, JG(II)/8/9/192 and 194, respectively, Cadbury Library, University of Birmingham.
21. Rudolf H. Sauter, *Studies of Contrails*, 1940, watercolor on paper and chalk on paper, 45.7 × 58 cm, FA00172, and *Sky Battle*, October 15, 1940, watercolor on paper, 40 × 57.5 cm, FA00171, Royal Air Force Museum.
22. Rudolf H. Sauter, *Into Battle: Thunderbolts Supporting a Bomber Sweep at Dawn*, July 10, 1943, watercolor on paper, 45.7 × 58 cm, FA00170, Royal Air Force Museum.
23. Rudolf H. Sauter, *The Sinister Insect: The Dragon Fly*, ca. 1940, watercolor on paper, 27.7 × 39.5 cm, in *WW2 – War Pictures by British Artists*, ed. Sacha Llewellyn and Paul Liss (London: Zenith Media, 2016), 89.
24. Ibid., 91.
25. Rudolf H. Sauter, *Return at Dawn: Spitfires on Patrol*, September 30, 1943, watercolor on paper, 40 × 58.5 cm, with stamp on verso indicating "passed censor," FA00173, Royal Air Force Museum.

Figure 5.4 Rudolf H. Sauter, *Searchlights along the Thames Estuary*, October 1940, gouache and pastel, 59.5 × 38 cm, courtesy of Liss Llewellyn Fine Art, © Trustees of The Estate of Rudolf H. Sauter.

about to Take Off,[26] and *Paths in the Moonlight—Bombers Going Out Over the Channel* (Figure 5.5).

Closer to home—through works he called *Doodlebug Alley—Death on the Way* (Figure 5.6) and *Doodlebug Alley—The Crooked Cross*[27]—Rudolf captured the terrifying dogfights he and Viola witnessed over their heads while living in Wittersham. Complementing these scenes, Rudolf composed, illustrated and published, in July 1944, a pair of related poems. "Ode to the Doodle-Bug" was "a little "broadsheet" he wrote upon "returning from a short absence" and for the benefit of the Red Cross and St. John Prisoner of War

---

26. Rudolf H. Sauter, *Out of the Dawn: Thunderbolt about to Take Off*, 1944, watercolor, gouache and pencil on paper, 39 × 56.6 cm, with stamp on verso indicating "passed censor," FA00175 Royal Air Force Museum.
27. *The Crooked Cross*, 1944, watercolor on pencil, 26 × 37 cm, with stamp on verso indicating "passed censor," in *WW2—War Pictures by British Artists*, ed. Sacha Llewellyn and Paul Liss (London: Zenith Media, 2016), 92.

Figure 5.5 Rudolf H. Sauter, *Paths in the Moonlight—Bombers Going Out Over the Channel*, October 16, 1944, watercolor on paper, 29 × 40 cm, courtesy of Liss Llewellyn Fine Art, © Trustees of The Estate of Rudolf H. Sauter.

Figure 5.6 Rudolf H. Sauter, *Doodlebug Alley—Death on the Way*, 1944, watercolor over pencil on paper 25 × 35 cm, courtesy of Liss Llewellyn Fine Art, © Trustees of The Estate of Rudolf H. Sauter.

Fund.[28] Featuring his drawing of a Doodlebug on the cover, and another of their home inside the broadsheet, the poem began "STANDS Wittersham, still," and continued:

> Looking over to France,
> Beneath the Flying Bomb
> On the nape of a hill?
> Stands Wittersham where
> This morning she stood
> When I rose and set out
> And departed from there?
>
> *For the hunt was up at the break of day*
> *Over Sussex and Kent, towards London way.*
> *Where the evil, black fox goes streaking away*
> *To the sound of the Siren's warning.*
>
> Is the house still cream
>   And rufous and grey?
>   Still crinkled the rood,
>   And weathered the beam?
>   With a friendly gleam
>   In the ancient eye
>   For the many things
>   Which so lovely seem?
>
> For I've seen the whole pack of them hunting at noon
> Spitfire, Mosquito—Mustang, Typhoon;
> Tempest and Thunderbolt, hot to the tune
> And the baying of the guns in the morning.

Rudolf's related poem—dedicated to Viola and including his pen-and-ink illustration of a bomb blast captioned with "FINIS"—offered a more personal perspective on their wartime life together:

> Over Sussex and Kent
> The Wittershams stand—
> Though many's the home
> Lies blasted and bent;

---

28. Rudolf H. Sauter to Ada Galsworthy, August 8, 1944, JG(II)/8/9/194, Cadbury Library, University of Birmingham.

On Down and Weald
From Town to the sea
Will be rubble this night.

If you ken the grim Fox with his coat so black
And his fiery brush cocked over his back.
You will ken the heart beat with the run of that pack,
And the life of the heart at returning.[29]

Alongside Rudolf's many paintings of the period, these poems reflected the direct impact of the war on his life and how he leveraged his experiences to creative inspiration in his own artistic style. Later in the war, these experiences included witnessing the construction of Mulberry harbor spud piers as they were being prepared for the D-Day landings.[30] Combined with his contemporary scenes of preparedness and actual battle, these works conveyed how very far Rudolf had come—existentially and creatively—from his state of captivity during the final days of the Great War. This former enemy alien once imprisoned by Britain, now a naturalized citizen having served meaningfully in its military ranks, had come full circle to embrace his nation soon to be victorious in the Second World War.

Finding Peace

In June 1944, Rudolf and Viola decided they could not remain in the Stocks after the war "even if it was spared" from bombings, "partly on account of the labour and partly because of upkeep."[31] Their search for a new residence took them London's Highgate West Hill, where 5 Holly Terrace offered a

---

29. Rudolf H. Sauter, untitled poem "for V," printed by Adams & Son, Printers, Rye, JG(II) 7/3/7, Cadbury Library, University of Birmingham.
30. Rudolf H. Sauter, *Three Spud Piers Being Prepared for the D-Day Normandy Landings*, ca. 1944, with stamp on verso indicating "Passed for publication, 24 May 1945, Ministry of Information," watercolor over pencil, 25.5 × 37.5 cm. https://www.modernbritishartgallery.com/img-8579__A_116.htm; *Two Spud Piers Being Prepared for the D-Day Normandy Landings*, ca. 1944, watercolor, 26 × 37.8 cm. https://www.modernbritishartgallery.com/img-8568__A_116.htm; *Spud Piers with Dazzle Camouflage Being Prepared for the D-Day Normandy Landings*, 1945, with stamp on verso indicating "Passed for publication, 24 May 1945, Ministry of Information," gouache, 39.5 × 57.8 cm, https://www.modernbritishartgallery.com/img-8567-A_116.htm. See also Sauter, *Architectural View of the Mulberry Harbour Construction*, 1945, watercolor, 2000-05-22, National Army Museum.
31. Rudolf H. Sauter to Ada Galsworthy, June 17, 1944, JG(II)/8/9/192, Cadbury Library, University of Birmingham.

magnificent view from its top floor and an ideal location for Rudolf's new studio while the semi-basement served well as his picture store.[32] Although they found this location "more be-doodled" than they had been led to believe, with "water pouring in and windows and sashes (and slates) in a precarious condition," they moved in and made it their own as they had done with their previous residences.[33] Here they remained for the next few years before moving again to Coddington, Herefordshire, just north of the market town of Ledbury, near the Malvern Hills. During this period—specifically on December 24, 1946—Rudolf relinquished his military commission and shortly thereafter authorities granted him the honorable rank of captain.[34]

As he did following the Great War, but this time without personal trauma and a sense of tragic loss, Rudolf immediately began to take up new artistic projects to move beyond the war, regain peace of mind and grow his creativity. Emblematic of this effort was his collaboration with Henrietta Leslie, a longtime family friend, to illustrate her new book, *Go as You Please: Memories of People and Places*, with whimsical drawings of the alphabetized subjects in its pages, from "Apple-Cart" to "Motor Boat" to "Zeppelin."[35] Critics received the book warmly, and especially its illustrations. The *Western Mail* described it as "entertaining" and "made more attractive by many pleasing drawings and paintings in line and colours by R.H. Sauter."[36] Notably, around the same

---

32. Ibid.
33. Rudolf H. Sauter to Ada Galsworthy, November 18, 1944, JG(II)/8/9/196, Cadbury Library, University of Birmingham.
34. His decommission was retroactive to August 11, 1945. "Rudolf H. Sauter, Army Form B199A," Historical Disclosures, Support Division, the UK Army Personnel Centre.
35. Henrietta Leslie, *Go as You Please: Memories of People and Places* (London: Macdonald, 1946). Born Gladys Henrietta Raphael Schütze, Leslie very likely knew Rudolf through his uncle, who contributed the provocative and poignant foreword to her bestselling novel *Mrs. Fischer's War*, about experiences of the Great War "as it seemed to an English wife marries to a German husband, with an English-born son." Leslie, Galsworthy wrote, "has treated her subject with an intimacy, a moving sincerity of feeling and a comprehension that are wholly remarkable. I was deeply impressed; the more so, that, knowing much on this subject, I am not thereon easily deluded. One cannot exaggerate the poignancy and carking nature of the prolonged misery which many poor women went through during the war and after, because of being married to 'alien enemies.' [...] This novel is to be welcomed and commended. Human and interesting from page to page; broad, just and tolerant; above all, warm and breathing, it makes you think. Yes, it makes you think." Galsworthy in Leslie *Mrs. Fischer's War* (New York: Book League of America, 1931), foreword.
36. "Memories of Odd Places," *Western Mail* (Perth, Australia), August 28, 1947, 24, https://trove.nla.gov.au/newspaper/article/52179042?browse=ndp%3Abrowse%2Ftitle%2FW%2Ftitle%2F101%2F1947%2F08%2F28%2Fpage%2F3654812%2Farticle%2F52179042

Figure 5.7 Rudolf H. Sauter, *Plants Springing from a Barren Landscape*, ca. 1947, oil on board, 51 × 61 cm, courtesy of Simon Rayner of Simon Rayner Fine Art, © Trustees of The Estate of Rudolf H. Sauter.

time Rudolf embarked on this project, he finished work on *Plants Springing from a Barren Landscape* (Figure 5.7) which, through its depiction of humanlike sprouts, represented his hope for society during the postwar era and his new creative beginning and escape with Viola to a more peaceful life.[37]

In Coddington, Rudolf and Viola took up residence in Coddington Court, a red brick mansion dating from the late eighteenth century and surrounded by farmland.[38] Rudolf painted en plain air across the region, in town and around the countryside.[39] He displayed examples of his work in a pair of "two-man exhibitions," one in Malvern, with fellow artist C. W. Edwards and

---

37. See also Rudolf H. Sauter, *Out of Barren Rock*, 1947, oil on board, 76 × 62 cm, Ann Hambley. This contemporary painting depicts an octopus-like plant emerging from the base of a rocky cliff.
38. Herefordshire Past, "Moorfields/Coddington Court History," accessed June 30, 2021, https://herefordshirepast.co.uk/buildings/moorfieldscoddington-court/.
39. See Rudolf H. Sauter, "The Artist Sketching in the Malvern Hills," watercolor, 39 × 54 cm, accessed June 30, 2021, https://lissllewellyn.com/show-8540-A_116__k.htm;%20lissllewellyn.com/show-8563-w_Artist-Rudolf-Sauter__A_116__r.htm; "The Retreat Pub Ledbury," watercolor, 53.2 × 39 cm, accessed June 30, 2021, https://www.lissllewellyn.com/show-8563-A_116.htm, and "The Market Hall at Ledbury," watercolor, 39.3 × 53 cm, accessed June 30, 2021, https://www.lissllewellyn.com/show-8558-w_Artist-Rudolf-Sauter__A_116__r.htm.

another in Worcester. The former included over forty of his works, from still lives to domestic and overseas landscapes to several wartime works, including *British Camp, The Scorched Hill; British Camp from Evendine; British Camp, The Hot Summer; British Camp in Mist;* and *British Camp, The Bare Figure*.[40]

* * *

As Rudolf remained artistically productive in Coddington, he and Viola remained socially active, hosting many longtime friends in Coddington Court and inspiring them in their own creative work. Among them was Inglis Fletcher who recalled her visit while she was completing research on the Cromwellian period for her next book, *Bennett's Welcome*:

> In the morning, I went downstairs, exalted by my experience [of learning about the area of Coddington during the Cromwellian period]. "I have my story!" I exclaimed. "I have the folk who lived here at the time of Cromwell! I know everything about them, all but their names." Rudi said, "I think I can help you there." He brought out old documents and maps. "Here is the first deed to Richard Monington, Lord of Coddington Manor." As Rudi read the dozen names signed to the deed, I again saw people rising from the past, each one bending over the table to affix his signature. These were real people, flesh and blood people, not only did I see them, I heard them speak, I knew what was in their minds.[41]

Fletcher continued, explaining how her time with the Sauters inspired her further research and ultimately the outcome of her efforts:

> I have never had an experience to equal this one at Coddington Manor. I not only saw the past, I was part of it, even when the hero escaped from England, after the capture of the king and sought safety in the young Colony of Virginia. I wrote the whole book under the inspiration of my experience at Coddington Manor. I have never written any other book in which I have not had breaks in the story line or trouble with the characters, trying to fit them into history. I had no trouble with *Bennett's Welcome*. I went back to London, still in a state of excitement and began rereading history. There was a wealth of material available. For the

---

40. *Pictures by C. W. Edwards, R.B.A., R.I. and R.H. Sauter, R.B.A., R.I., Malvern Public Library, 1–22 April 1950,* JG(II)/7/3/7, Cadbury Library, University of Birmingham.

41. Fletcher, *The Story of My Life*, 272–73. During their visit to San Francisco, the Sauters stayed with Fletcher and her husband John, and the Fletcher themselves had visited the Galsworthys in Sussex.

Quaker section, I visited the Euston Street Meeting Society of Friends; for details on furnishings, I went to the Victoria and Albert Museum [...] I was able, in *Bennett's Welcome*, to follow through the discovery I had made in research for Roanoke Hundred—that many of the names of the folk who were in the First Colony on Roanoke Island appeared again in the Jamestown Colony. This proves, I believe, that Jamestown was really a continuation of Roanoke, the colonies that failed.

Published in 1950 and translated into a number of other languages, *Bennett's Welcome* became one of Fletcher's most popular and critically acclaimed books, its success stemming from her friendship with Rudolf that was itself as part of his expansive creative network, including Henrietta Leslie, C. W. Edwards and others. Despite the feeling he expressed to Inglis Fletcher that "both in painting and poetry" his "personal tastes" did not "seem to march with the times" [42]—or perhaps due to his lifelong dedication to being an artist—Rudolf would expand his creative network considerably over the last two and a half decades of his life, consistently experimenting with new media to reflect on his experiences in two world wars and existential concerns of modern times.

---

42. Rudolf H. Sauter to Inglis Fletcher, May 7, 1950, collection no. 21, Joyner Library, East Carolina University.

Chapter 6

REFLECTIONS, 1950–77

In August 1950, Rudolf authored a posthumous appreciation of the artist George Graham and his creation paintings, a collection of deeply spiritual images which reflected Graham's search for meaning and truth while provoking viewers to embark on a similar journey.[1] "George Graham, as I knew him," Rudolf began:

> was one of the finest men it has ever been my privilege to meet, one of the sanest and most practical and perhaps the greatest visionary. That these two usually opposing trends were so harmoniously blended in him may have had to do with the character of the work here exhibited. For no one who had any contact with the mind behind these paintings, can fail to have been moved by the transparent sincerity, the deep artistic integrity and the philosophic outlook, in which they were conceived and which, one might almost say, compelled their execution.

He continued:

> But his was not the cold philosophy of abstractionism. On the contrary, there was a warm humanity about George Graham which infused everything he did with a sort of urgency, very refreshing to the mind and a broadness of outlook which enabled him not only to overcome physical disability in himself, but to turn it to good and profitable account. He had those qualities of greatness, which cause everything in their neighbourhood to grow and expand, as distinct from the qualities which make for success, under whose branching shade art all too easily dwindles away, So, in his presence, you became a greater man; and from that rugged, honest personality you came away feeling that life was just

---

1. Hastings Online Times, "George Graham: The Creation Paintings," January 6, 2017, https://hastingsonlinetimes.co.uk/arts-culture/arts-news/george-graham-the-creation-paintings.

that little but more worth while and, above all, art was something which really mattered.[2]

While this tribute was a reflection on the characteristics of a contemporary who thought deeply about existential concerns, it anticipated these very characteristics becoming hallmarks of Rudolf's own later life. During this period, he and Viola lived in Stroud, Gloucestershire. They moved there from Coddington at the encouragement of friends to appreciate the growing local arts scene, particularly the Stroud Festival for Religious Drama and the Arts. For £9,500 they purchased Fort William, a mid-nineteenth-century property located high atop the town at the end of its Rodborough Common.[3] Reflecting on his new home and studio, Rudolf wrote to Inglis Fletcher that "as time goes on and we live in the house and become accustomed to its ways, we get more and more attached to it, like it the more and feel more at home in it." He explained further that

> It is of course, quite unlike Coddington, but much more manageable and 'liveable' and suits our present needs and conditions better. I wish very much that you could visit us and see our view, which has been quite spectacular all this winter, with the mists crawling and creeping about the valley which we overlook and the low-slanting rays of the sun sliding their spears between the trees till they are laid low in shadows along the contours of the hills of the opposite side and the smokes of the factories and houses congregating at certain times and flowing into the upper air like thick flocks of unearthly birds. Of course this a very different beauty from what we imagine surrounding you in your own peaceful retreat, but it is a beauty of its own, always changing, seldom dull and never uninteresting."[4]

Rudolf concluded his letter to Fletcher by emphasizing that he was "painting pretty hard on and off" and was "very excited" about the "new terrain" in

---

2. Rudolf H. Sauter, "George Graham and His Creation Paintings: An Appreciation," in *George Graham and His Creation Paintings: Appreciations and Extracts from His Letters* (London: W. P. Griffith and Sons, 1952), 3. This publication appeared in conjunction with a posthumous exhibition of Graham's paintings at the Royal Society of British Artists.
3. G. G. Hoare, "Delius Slept Here?," *Delius Society Journal* 54 (January 1977): 5–7, https://www.delius.org.uk/delius-society/publications/delius-society-journals/journals-newsletters-1970-1979-dsj43-65-newsletters-26-42/#gallery-24. Robert Oldmeadow, interview by the author, September 9–10, 2018.
4. Rudolf H. Sauter to Jack and Inglis Fletcher, January 24, 1952, collection no. 21, Joyner Library, East Carolina University.

Figure 6.1 Rudolf H. Sauter, *Our Time and Age*, ca. 1957, oil on canvas, 71 × 58.5 cm, private collection courtesy of Sarah Colegrave Fine Art, © Trustees of the Estate of Rudolf H. Sauter.

and around Stroud, "which is so very different from the landscape round the Malverns [that] it requires quite a different approach and technique." Rudolf captured his new environs through a number of contemporary paintings, including *Our Time and Age*, which depicted Viola looking from Fort William onto the Golden Valley as it stretched from Stroud to Chalford, including the River Frome and the Cotswold canal as it paralleled the Cheltenham to London railway (Figure 6.1).

Rudolf completed other works during this period which he displayed in the Royal Academy Summer Exhibition, continuing his long and continuous profile in this venue, dating from 1922.[5] At the same time, creative frontiers

---

5. Following his 1922 debut at the Royal Academy Summer Exhibition, Sauter exhibited there in 1924–25, 1931, 1933, 1936, 1938–39, 1946–50, 1952–54 and 1958. See Paul Mellon Centre for Studies in British Art, "The Royal Academy Summer Exhibition: A Chronicle, 1769–2018," accessed June 30, 2021, https://chronicle250.com/. See also "The Royal Academy. Nine Old Harrovians Are Exhibiting at the Royal Academy This Year," *Harrovian* 65, no. 25 (May 28, 1952): 95, which documents Sauter exhibiting an unidentified work with his fellow graduates Lord Alexander, R. J. Burn, L. Byng, Winston S. Churchill, R. A. Hignett, E. Hodgkin, B. Jonzen, E. Le Bas. See also Stephen Bone, "Sixteen Painters: Exhibition at R.B.A. Galleries," *Guardian*, September

beckoned closer to his new home and studio. Rudolf, now in his 50s, responded to their call.

Stroud Festival

Soon after he settled in Stroud, Rudolf joined like-minded residents to support and expand the annual Stroud Festival of Religious Drama and the Arts, which had been established in 1947 by local arts patrons Margaret and Netlam Bigg.[6] Rudolf participated in festival poetry readings and competitions, one of the most notable being in 1959 when he joined the poet Laurie Lee in a reading entitled "The Seekers," arranged by Maurice Broadbent, one of the directors of the festival.[7] In 1963, Rudolf and Viola were subscribers to the festival and two years later he read his poem "The Day the World Went Backwards" to attending audiences.[8] In 1971, he debuted the creative "experience" of a theatrical work entitled *The Fifth Hunger*, and in 1972, with the poets Peter Hearn and Shirley Toulson, he judged the festival's junior poetry competition.[9] Involving himself in the Stroud Festival in all of these ways and likely others, placed Rudolf at the center of the artistic life of the region. It helped him to expand his established professional network to include new colleagues and friends with whom he cooperated on several multimedia projects, the first of which was *Four Hungers: A Dramatic Poem*.

Four Hungers (1960)

Encompassing spoken words, music and singing, sound effects and lighting, *Four Hungers* addressed the "FOUR GREAT HUNGERS"—emphasis being Rudolf's own as he explained in the event program—which "consume the Human Race," including "HUNGER of the body, beyond all creed or

---

16, 1953, 5, which documents Sauter exhibiting *Little Mills of the Frome*. "The Royal Academy: Seven Old Harrovians Are Exhibiting at the Royal Academy," *Harrovian* 66, no. 30 (July 1, 1953), 122, documents Sauter exhibiting his work *Winter Valley* alongside works by Lord Alexander, R. J. Burn, Sir Winston S. Churchill, Hignett, E. Hodgkin, B. Jonzen, E. Le Bas. "The landscapes are full of personality and often of dramatic force," wrote one critic, "as in [...] R. H. Sauter's powerful 'Winter in Rodborough.'"

6. John Gardiner, *The World of Netlam Bigg: A Centenary Celebration* (Stroud, Gloucestershire: J. F. Gardiner, 1999).
7. Ibid., 76.
8. *Souvenir Programme. Stroud Festival. 20–27 October 1963*, 4. Rudolf's "The Day the World Went Backwards" subsequently appeared in *Crie du Coeur*, his 1968 self-published volume of poetry, with a note that he had read it at the 1965 Stroud Festival.
9. Eric Walter White, *Silver Jubilee Stroud Festival, 10–24 October 1971*. (Stroud: Stroud Festival, 1971); Gardiner, *The World of Netlam Bigg*, 114.

Nation; HUNGER of the Spirit, that lights the human face; HUNGER for destruction and HUNGER of creation." To convey the meaning and origins of the project, Rudolf revisited some of his earlier work giving it new meaning in a new era. The inside of the program included his 1936 work *NEVER MORE...! (a modern Triptych)* along with an extensive narrative of its scenes which dated from the period when Rudolf, in the 1930s, wrote the first scene of *Four Hungers*. That scene, he explained, took place "between Christmas, 1936 and Mid-summer, 1938, (that is: well before the War) at a time when we were still in a state of so called 'peace,' though the possibility of another conflagration was becoming increasingly apparent."

In these days past, Rudolf explained further from his vantage point of the early 1960s:

> "'The Welfare State" was a dream in the imagination of the few; and, for ordinary mortals, the ATOM was still snuggling up to Newton, comfortably undivided; Hydrogen was an ingredient more commonly associated with synthetic Blondes; and Sir John [Cockcroft] had not yet projected his JET into a molten world.[10]

As for the original context of *Four Hungers*, he explained:

> Inevitably, parts are no longer so applicable, today; but, apart from large excisions, some revision of language and the adaptation of the whole for the present purpose, the main theme is substantially as written. [...] The "Pictures" which appear, framed in their setting during the course of the performance, are to be regarded as images passing behind the eye. They are an integral part of the whole and form an illuminated commentary on the spoken word.

Scene two, Rudolf explained further in the program, takes place "in a bombed crypt" when

---

10. "Sir John" referred to Sir John Cockcroft, recipient of the 1951 Nobel Prize in Physics, with Ernest Thomas Sinton Walton, "for their pioneer work on the transmutation of atomic nuclei by artificially accelerated atomic particles." JET referred to Joint European Torus, the largest and most successful fusion experiment in the world, located in the Culham Centre for Fusion Energy, Oxfordshire, and based upon the achievements of Cockcroft and Walton. The Nobel Prize, "The Nobel Prize in Physics 1951," accessed June 30, 2021, https://www.nobelprize.org/prizes/physics/1951/summary/. See also Jonathan Hogg, *British Nuclear Culture: Official and Unofficial Narratives in the Long 20th Century* (London: Bloomsbury, 2016), 24, 38.

the foreshadowed WAR is more or less over and in this part, you are to imagine the return to a world of uneasy peace, after the conflagration. The year is 1946 and perhaps you will bear in mind how greatly times have changed since then and try and imagine yourselves back in the atmosphere of those days:—their frustrations, shortages, rationings, restrictions and "Utility"—the aftermath of a War just over. The scene is a bombed Site and the figures speak against a background of smoke, coiling continually within itself. The visual commentary of pictures continues, framed in a ragged window.

Moreover, Rudolf included on the cover of the program an illustration of the wartime sky over Wittersham, where he and Viola had lived, with doodlebug trails high above as a pair of hands reached up to suggest mercy and hope for relief from the noise and threat of destruction (Figure 6.2).[11] Directly recalling tumultuous yet hopeful years of the Second World War as he did in *Four Hungers* itself, this image was an iteration of his painting *Annunciation*, which he had displayed in 1938 at the Royal Scottish Academy (Figure 6.3).

Complete with incidental music composed by Rudolf himself, *Four Hungers* premiered in Stroud's Cotswold Playhouse in May 1960 as a benefit for the World Refugee Fund, a cause that Rudolf held dear as it supported the World Refugee Year (1959–60).[12] Produced by Maurice Broadbent and John Evans, both directors of the Stroud Festival, the premiere consisted of three evening performances and one matinee. None involved the Cotswold Players per se, but several members of the group participated, including Robert Bashford, Rachael Blundell, June Dodsworth, Jeanette Luker, Michael Bishop and, on the stage crew, Charles Hunt and Ronald Knee.[13]

Four Hungers received critical acclaim from the *Stroud News and Journal*, its theatre critic observing,

---

11. "Royal Scottish Academy: Exhibition Pictures Sold," *Scotsman*, June 1, 1938, 15. Contemporary to *Annunciation* was an untitled work depicting a cloaked individual releasing a dove into the sky adjacent to a tree without leaves shaped like a praying mantis. The background of multicolored farmland was likely a scene of the Malvern Hills where Sauter was living during this period. Rudolf H. Sauter, untitled, ca. 1940s, gouache on paper, 38 × 53 cm, Ellie Jones, Andelli Art, accessed June 30, 2021, http://www.andelliart.com/rudolf-helmut-sauter-1895-1977/.
12. "New Literary Work at Stroud," *Gloucestershire Countryside* (Leamington Spa, England), April–June 1960, 9.
13. Theatrical program for *Four Hungers*, May 1960, kindly made available to the author by Terry Clifford. The program also notes that the performances were recorded. The locations of these recordings, if extant, are unknown.

Figure 6.2 Rudolf H. Sauter, untitled illustration on the cover of the theatrical program for *Four Hungers*, May 1960, unknown medium and dimensions, courtesy of Terry Clifford, © Trustees of the Estate of Rudolf H. Sauter.

Figure 6.3 Rudolf H. Sauter, *Annunciation*, ca. 1940s, tempera on board, 50 × 62.5 cm, courtesy of Andelli Art, © Trustees of the Estate of Rudolf H. Sauter.

> Local poet and author, Rudolf Sauter, has not restricted himself to a narrow canvas, nor is he content to express his histrionic themes in one medium only. For verse, drama, music and the visual image are together utilised in this unique production, each being employed to supplement the other. And it is Mr. Sauter who is a poet, composer and artist. In fact, this can be regarded as a revealing experiment in dramatic expression. As the theme unfolds, expounded powerfully by Maurice Broadbent, it is backed up by recorded music and by black and white drawings projected on to a background panel. This latter arrangement is ingenious—but, one wonders, does it contribute anything which is not already contained in Mr. Sauter's moving verse? Alas, one feels that the pictures—many of which I found indistinct viewed from the balcony—could have been dropped, without any loss of force. The verses and music are adequate. This is not an easy work to follow, but the man of sensitivity will find it a rewarding one. The characters—"narrative," "soliloquy (the inner thought)" and so on—are purely symbolic, yet the words they utter are pregnant with meaning for us all.

The critic continued, noting the currency of the production in light of the recent failure of diplomatic discussions, held in Paris, between the United States and Soviet Union regarding the future of Berlin:

> Though the emotions are conceived by the author are eternal, many seem peculiarly poignant in the light of the summit disappointments of the past few days. This play is running for the rest of the week. It will serve two good causes—first, the Refugee Year Appeal and secondly, that of showing Stroud's more discriminating playgoers to what use the stage can be put as an instrument of a mind so versatile and inventive as Mr. Sauter's.[14]

In 1967, the governing board of the Cotswold Players invited Rudolf to become president of the theatre. The year happened to be the centenary of the birth of his uncle, and the Players were planning to mark the occasion with a production of Galsworthy's play *The Skin Game*. While this familial association certainly contributed to Rudolf being offered the theatre presidency, his own reputation as the versatile and inventive mind behind the *Four Hungers* was likely influential. Rudolf remained a presence with the Cotswold Players for

---

14. "Experiment in Drama," *Stroud News and Journal*, n.d., n.p. This article is lodged with a copy of the theatrical program for *Four Hungers*, dated May 1960, kindly made available to the author by Terry Clifford.

many years to come, and to this day the theatre holds a pastel portrait of him by the renowned Gloucestershire artist Edward Payne.[15]

The Fifth Hunger (1971)

The success of Rudolf's multimedia *Four Hungers*—and the supportive community environment in which he produced it—prompted him to pursue *The Fifth Hunger*, which debuted at the 1971 Stroud Festival. As he explained in the festival program, it was "not a play, in the ordinary sense, nor entertainment as such. It is the presentation, in an unusual form—through the 'THEATRE OF THE MIND'—of an experience in which we are all involved and which can be shared and lived through together. It is concerned with fundamental relationships and their bearing on the present and future of Mankind." Rudolf explained further:

> The Basic theme has been with me for many years, finding expression in poems (some of them dating back to the 1914–18 war) and a play entitled "FOUR HUNGERS". The present and changing condition of the world points to increasing awareness of a need for the FIFTH HUNGER which is the subject of the present work.

Rudolf then offered a window onto his creative focus and determination to complete this sequel in his Fort William studio:

> Since it was begun, I have lived it night and day; whenever anyone is present it is seldom possible to avoid discussion of the issues involved. It has taken over 17 months to develop, growing all the time—re-written and re-recorded four more times, it has changed in the process beyond recognition. In this version, five voices and a singer are recorded and it is introduced "live" from the platform. "Sound" and music amplify the meaning, light effects evoke perception.

---

15. Payne presented this portrait to the Cotswold Players in November 1977, following Rudolf's passing in June of that year. Steve Goodwin to the author, "RE: Cotswold Playhouse Website Message" and "RE: Greetings & quick question re Sauter portrait held by Cotswold Playhouse," e-mails dated July 18, 2014 and June 15, 2021, respectively. Around the same time as Payne worked on his portrait, Rudolf's cousin Jocelyn Galsworthy, the noted portrait painter and sporting artist, also completed a portrait of him, which captured him with his still chistled features and grey hair grown to the base of his neck and just over his ears. See "Rudo Sauter," pastel, 1976, in Jocelyn Galsworthy, *White Hats and Cricket Bats: My Painting life* (Shrewsbury, England: Swan Hill Press, 2000), 25.

More specifically, Rudolf explained, observers would expect to see that

> In imagination "MAN" is divided and his two halves (here exemplified by MAN and WOMAN) seek each other. Their hungers become personified, their dreams more and more grotesque, their dilemmas apparently insoluble [...] UNLESS ...! Through the acquisition of knowledge beyond the capacity to understand, men have assumed the role of "Undergods" in a situation they are no longer able to control.—"Angry" passions are at war in us, we grow increasingly apart and do not know to get together again. What are we to do? [...] That is the question. This "experience" takes place through a series of episodes—MAN and WOMAN attempt to solve the problem in their own way, but are continually acted upon by the "media" and environment (personified by the grotesque character known as "G") which surround them. In the end? [...] But that is what this is all about.

Working again with Rudolf to realize the production were Maurice Broadbent, who offered its introduction, John Evans, who contributed his voice to the recorded narrative and Rachael Blundell who played the "Woman" and "other female voices." Rudolf himself played "Man, the character 'G,'" and other male voices and his acknowledgement which appeared in the program conveyed how deeply he appreciated the support, collaboration and patience of his friends and colleagues during his creative process:

> Warm and grateful thanks are extended to all those who have lived through and discussed this experience as it developed and whose comments have been invaluable; to those who have loaned valuable equipment and assisted in other ways; and in particular to Ken Loynes for his untiring and imaginative manipulation of recording equipment (under conditions which would have appalled a specialist) to produce on tape the sounds without which this performance would have been impossible; and last but not least to those who have allowed their voices to be borrowed and distorted for the purpose of this recording.[16]

Regarding that recording and the overall planning of *The Fifth Hunger*, Rudolf revealed that it involved his home studio becoming

---

16. Eric Walter White, *Silver Jubilee Stroud Festival. 10–24 October 1971*. "The Fifth Hunger's First public performance of a new work, by Rudolf H. Sauter" (Stroud: Stroud Festival, 1971), n.p.

impregnated with the adjuncts of production: tape-recorders in the bedroom, petrol tines on the stairs, typewriter, instruments, a model theatre, figures and lighting equipment have converted the whole house into a workshop in which it is quite difficult to move about in comfort. Whenever anyone is present, it is seldom possible for long to avoid discussion of the issues involved. So it has already become a means of communication, which it is hoped may extend still further.[17]

His work on *The Fifth Hunger* did extend as he had hoped, into 1972, when he completed a revision of the piece in June of that year. In 1976, he self-published his final version of the work in a limited edition run of 30 copies, a "version intended for reading as well as playing—and the reader is the player who plays the whole himself."[18]

Erda (1972)

Inspired by his pair of works which addressed hungers "that consume the Human Race," and by a short period of unspecified illness, Rudolf completed *Erda: Poem for the Earth, The Trial of Man: A Masque for 1972*, in which he addressed the human race consuming itself and the world.[19] The "argument" of this new project was that

"ERDA," the ancient Goddess-of-the-EARTH, has been brutally murdered by her children—Humankind—and in the process they, too, have perished. THE SUN and the Earth's childless brothers and sisters, the Planets, are assembled to hold an autopsy. They summon the "GHOST-OF-MAN" to answer for his actions. Each puts his or her point of view, MARS is the guise of the accuser, VENUS speaking in defence. The SUN sums up, delivers his verdict and pronounces sentence.

Likely using some if not all of the same audiovisual equipment in his home studio, which he had dedicated to realizing *The Fifth Hunger*, Rudolf recorded a version of *Erda* encompassing 13½ minutes of narration by him with "accompanying 'sound.'"[20]

---

17. Rudolf H. Sauter, *The Fifth Hunger*, self-published, 1971. Rudolf's recordings associated with *The Fifth Hunger*, if extant, are unknown.
18. Rudolf H. Sauter, *The Fifth Hunger*, self-published, 1976.
19. Rudolf H. Sauter, *Erda: Poem for the Earth, The Trial of Man: A Masque for 1972*, self-published, 1972.
20. Ibid., 7. Like the recordings of *Four Hungers* and *The Fifth Hunger*, the location of this recording, if extant, is unknown.

Recalling the Great War: 1964–68

As an active and engaged member of his local creative community who was in tune with global concerns, Rudolf publicly embraced the subject of the Great War during its 50th anniversary, composing new work inspired by the occasion and revisiting and reshaping work he completed during his internment experience. These activities were a prelude to further reflections on the Great War period he would soon undertake, recalling his earlier work and recasting it to give it new personal meaning, artistic currency and contemporary relevance.[21]

In the fall of 1964, Rudolf heard a radio broadcast of Benjamin Britten's *War Requiem* performed in the Basilica of Ottobeuren in Bavaria. It was his fifth such listening after he had heard performances transmitted from Coventry, York, Worcester and the 1964 Promenade Concert.[22] The experience of the Ottobeuren performance inspired him to compose "The Three Trees," a "meditation" on the theme of Britten's work. As he explained in the introductory note of the work that "though the reception was poor, the impact was particularly poignant owing to the circumstances of the production and the poem began to grow out of the music as it progressed—hanging, so to speak, in the air." Rudolf elaborated on his creative process, noting that "parts were already written down before the performance came to an end; but in the following weeks the poem became almost an obsession and continued to expand and work strongly for some months," and that "in addition to the music and Wilfrid [*sic*] Owen's words, the contemporary war paintings of Paul Nash, Nevinson and other War Artists may be recalled in connection with certain passages." In offering this context, nowhere did Rudolf mention his own artwork of period, or even suggest that he had painted during this time. Nonetheless, his opening lines channeled the hallmarks of his earlier experience that had torn away the life he knew:

The music folds about us like a dream
Out of the thin, long air

---

21. The existence of an unpublished draft volume entitled *Moods, Cameos and Impressions, a Manuscript of Poems 1918–1957* suggests that Rudolf was thinking about a collection of his work during the late 1950s. This material was auctioned by Chorley's on March 19, 2009. See Invaluable, "Chorley's, Lot 29: Books: Sauter (R H) *Moods, Cameos and Impressions*," accessed June 30, 2021, https://www.invaluable.com/auction-lot/books-sauter-r-h-moods-cameos-and-impressions-29-c-D36BB5B191.
22. Rudolf H. Sauter, introductory note, "The Three Trees: A Meditation on the Theme of Benjamin Britten's War Requiem," enclosed with his letter to Benjamin Britten, December 13, 1964, GB 1111 BBA/SAUTER, Britten Pears Arts.

And the aching years
And the pool of tears
Through the thinning Tree
And the falling lives
And the new-born Soul, crying anew:
"From hate deliver me!"

Rudolf concluded his work with another direct reference to the music that so moved him:

This music, moving through us like a stream
To its appointed union with the heart,
Wearing away the stony agony,
Nourishes in each of us his dream,
His living tree from which these ghosts can choir
Their pleas to Heaven for celestial fire...!
    ...OUR trees on which the fruit, "TOMORROW" grows
    Be it through us the sap of Pity flows![23]

Rudolf eventually sent a copy of "The Three Trees" to Benjamin Britten, thinking that he "might be interested to hear the effect of [his] *War Requiem* on one member of the audience," and noting that the piece was "little enough to show [...] but the rejected versions and notes alone make a bundle over a half and inch thick." Rudolf explained further to Britten that

> my wife [...] is over 80 and I nearly 70, so that we remember not only the occasion for which your work was composed, but with equal vividness the circumstances under which Wilfred Owen's words were written. This being so, it is perhaps natural that we found the performance from Ottobeuren (from which we happen to know) of very special significance.[24]

Herein Rudolf was recalling—yet withholding details about—his own life-changing experience of the war, as well as that of his father. Equally, his

---

23. Rudolf H. Sauter, "The Three Trees," 1964, typescript included with his correspondence to Benjamin Britten, December 13, 1964, GB 1111 BBA/SAUTER, Britten Pears Arts.
24. Rudolf H. Sauter to Benjamin Britten, December 13, 1964, GB 1111 BBA/SAUTER, Britten Pears Arts.

reference to the "special significance" of Ottobeuren was in connection with his Bavarian roots.

Hand in hand with remembering the war through Britten's *Requiem*, Rudolf did the same through the lens of his own work, specifically his poem "Barbed Wire." He granted permission to the historian Brian Gardner to use the piece in a new collection of wartime poetry, including poems by Edmund Blunden, Rupert Brooke, Robert Graves and Siegfried Sassoon.[25] A decade later, the literary scholar Paul Fussell included "Barbed Wire" in his seminal study of wartime poetry, but without attention to the original context of the poem and therefore incorrectly associating it with the Western Front.[26] More than a dozen years after the publication of Fussell's study, the author Edward Hudson included "Barbed Wire" in his own collection of Great War poetry, with its preface by the noted literary scholar Jon Stallworthy. Hudson illustrated the poem with a photograph of barbed wire between the lines of the Western Front and included a biographical endnote suggesting the proper context of the poem—that it originated from Rudolf being "interned in Britain"—but incorrectly stating that he was in captivity "for four years;" in fact, the duration of Rudolf's internment was approximately 17 months, from March 1918 until August 1919.[27] Despite the inaccuracies and incompleteness of these works— or rather due to these shortfalls—they presented Rudolf's "Barbed Wire" as part of the canon of First World War poetry, therefore giving him his own place in the modern memory of that war and designating him to be—however contentiously due to his lack of experiencing the front—affiliated with the "generation of 1914."

Crie du Coeur (1968)

The first artist's book Rudolf produced was *Crie du Coeur* (1968) (Figure 6.4). In seeking a publisher for the volume he had in mind, Rudolf visited Stroud Typewriting, Rotaprinting and Duplicating Service, operated by Patricia Scrivens and her son John. He discussed his project with them, focusing on the level of customization he sought to achieve through offset lithography, an increasingly popular printing process among artists, in order to yield a book

---

25. Brian Gardner, ed., *Up the Line to Death: The War Poets, 1914–1918* (London: Methuen, 2007). A revised edition was first published in 1976, reissued with corrected biographies in 1986, and reissued again in 2007 with a new cover and updated biographies. Rudolf's "Barbed Wire" has appeared in every edition.
26. Paul Fussell, *The Great War and Modern Memory* (Oxford: Oxford University Press, 1975), 248, as noted by James Gindin, *John Galsworthy's Life and Art: An Alien's Fortress* (Ann Arbor: University of Michigan Press, 1987), 376.
27. Edward Hudson, ed., *Poetry of the First World War* (London: Wayland, 1989), 118, 126.

that could creatively pair his texts and images. As Rudolf described the book he envisioned, John became more and more excited about it, welcoming the challenge and opportunity to work with an artist with such a sense of creativity and since his usual printing work had involved ordinary commercial projects with no customization.

The pair embarked on their collaboration. Over the course of several months, Rudolf visited the shop regularly, sometimes for entire days, discussing with John the custom plates to be designed for the book. Each color required a different plate and printing ink, so if a single page had multiple colors, multiple plates were needed. As John later recalled, Rudolf was "meticulous and especially with the colors he expected in the book. Sometimes he would take three, four, five goes at just mixing the color [...] getting [it] just exactly how he wanted. He supervised every color print of every page of every copy of the book." Rudolf also chose the paper used for the book, John recalled.

> He picked that as well, [and] we ordered it. [...] It was everything that he wanted. [...] So if he wanted it that way, that's the way it was going to be. And if it took him a week, he would take a week. [...] He did things [for the book] as he went along [...] [like] an artist painting bit by bit until you get the finished product. If he didn't like the color he would change it until he got it right. [...] So I think he treated this more like an oil painting than a book [...] going with it as it rolled along. [...] Anything that wasn't as he wanted it he would just keep on going until he had it exactly right. He was so precise. [...] We would [sometimes] take nearly a whole day to print one page [...] [and] spend hours and hours, sometimes the whole day [together, to get what he wanted].[28]

The result of Rudolf's meticulous collaboration with John Scrivens was a unique volume of poems and words printed in multiple fonts and directions—diagonally, horizontally and vertically—along with multicolored and block-printed illustrations. This collection of words and images combined to be, as Rudolf explained in his introduction,

> an informal communication between people, in which hand and eye may be more involved than on the cold, white pages of a printed book. It has been prepared as much by hand as possible consistent with duplication. The cover and illuminations designed to enhance the mood rather than to illustrate individual poems, are from blocks by the author and

---

28. John Oldmeadow, interview by the author, September 9–10, 2018.

Figure 6.4 Rudolf H. Sauter, *Crie du Coeur* (Stroud, Gloucestershire: Stroud Typewriting, Rotaprinting and Duplicating Services, 1968), private collection, © Trustees of the Estate of Rudolf H. Sauter.

the poems themselves have been carefully selected and arranged as a sequence.[29]

He explained further,

> If any further justification were needed for the nature of some of these poems, it lies with the age in which we live and in which we have to make our contributions and communications, an age which differs in a number of respects from any other period in history.

More specifically, Rudolf referred to:

> Potential nuclear destruction, racial tension, which has become global, the "population explosion," danger of world famine, aerosol warfare and the problem of genetic mutation are only some of the hazards which combine to produce a human situation demanding toleration, under-standing, co-operation and goodwill all over the world on an unprecedented scale if mankind is to survive.

---

29. Rudolf H. Sauter, *Crie du Coeur*, preface, dated Easter, 1968, 1.

Therefore, he concluded, "it is with our dilemma in face of such condition that the present volume is largely concerned."[30]

Rudolf dedicated *Crie du Coeur* to Viola, on the occasion of their 50th wedding anniversary. The book encompassed more than seventy pages and dozens of poems ranging from deeply personal reflections on their long and strong relationship to commentary resounding with contemporary cultural relevance. Among his most poignant personal poems was "The Circle," dated 1960:

I hold my loved-one by the hand,
My left hand in her right,
Our hearts are mingled where they meet—
My life flows through hers, hers through mine;
But still our world is incomplete.
I lift my right hand to the sun,
And she her left hand to the night—
The groping circle is complete,
The current flows through us like wine
And we are one![31]

Rudolf's contemporary commentary included his best-known poem, "Barbed Wire," reprinted fully under the heading "I: 1919" and then refashioned as "Barbed: Wire," under the heading "II: 1968," therefore giving the piece a new life for the modern era:

```
           1968
       BARBED: WIRE
    WIRE        BARB
    IRE         BARB
    DIRE        BARBS

    B  E  W  A  R  E

    BARBED      AIR
    BARBED      IRE![32]
```

"The Intruder," dated 1968, was equally if not more provocative as it explicitly engaged readers through an asterisked prompt to "insert here whatever happens to be the current war or latest evidence of violence."

---

30. Ibid.
31. Ibid., 33.
32. Ibid., 14.

The day came bleeding
up over the hill
dripping Vietnam
all over my valley—
a day with all its ancestry
limping into my valley
from Sinai and Vietnam   (*)
from New Jersey and Illinois
from Prague and Biafra
into the seclusion of my valley.
my private valley

As I said: "GET OUT!
  "you are trespassing
  "I want nothing of you
  "in the valley
  "of my seclusion!"

But the day limped on—
And the blood
was in my valley
and in yours.[33]

"The Intruder" joined several other poems in *Crie du Coeur* that had poignant currency—from "Night-Watchman" wherein Rudolf acknowledged "children lie in the streets, dead in the streets of Saigon," to "Stepping-Stones," a poem "to be spoken freely by two voices alternately to the following accompaniment [of] tick-tock, tick-tock" and in which he asked "from one generation to another who can see eye to eye?" All of these works testified to Rudolf's deep concern about—and existential connection to—the wider world beyond Stroud.

Following its print run of 500 copies, *Crie du Coeur* joined a constellation of artists' books which had recently been produced in and around Gloucestershire.[34] Rudolf arranged a sale of his book through the Stroud

---

33. Ibid., 10. Rudolf noted at the end of this poem that he had read it on the BBC as part of its Midland Poets series.
34. This constellation included a series of eight books produced by John Furnival's Openings Press, involving the work of Louis Zukofsky, Augusto De Campos, Ian Hamilton Finlay, Melvin Clay, Franciszka and Stefan Themerson, Dom Slyvester Houédard, Ronald Johnson and Hansjörg Mayer. See http://www.worldcat.org/oclc/79545329 and http://artistsbooksandmultiples.blogspot.com/2013/01/the-openings-press.html.

Festival bookstall, and he mailed copies to selected individuals, including Benjamin Britten, as a "small token" of "personal appreciation and gratitude" for "something so unique and moving, especially in times such as those in which we live and have our being," namely "the unforgettable experience" of hearing Britten's opera *Prodigal Son* at Gloucestershire Cathedral.[35] Rudolf also sent a copy of *Cri du Coeur* to the poet Leonard Clark, explaining that his new "little book" was

> the result and final pruning of many years and has been produced in its present form because I find it increasingly difficult to get warmth from the cold, white pages of a mechanically printed book—especially when a number of poems are assembled there, page after page. I also feel nowadays, all the arts run into each other and coalesce more than they have ever done in the past—and that this is a good thing and increases the range of perception in all directions. This little volume is an attempt to put into practice these ideas.[36]

Similarly, Rudolf wrote to Margaret Turnbull that his book "(after more frustrations and difficulties than I care to mention) is at least out—on the Stroud Festival Book-stall" and "not quite the ordinary conventional 'book.'" He added that he was also

> working hard on an extension in yet another dimension of one of the poems, which has resulted in a sort of free-standing semi-flying object, surrounded by eight block-prints, which has been invited to and stands in the centre of the main gallery of the Festival Exhibition. [...] The poem in question is the "Meditation" at the beginning of the book which I think you will see could easily demand more expansion than the book can give it.[37]

Rudolf sought a wider audience for his poems, but at least with regard to PEN, he was unsuccessful. "I am so sorry to have to tell you that I have drawn a blank about your poems," wrote its secretary David Carver.

---

35. Rudolf H. Sauter to Benjamin Britten, October 26, 1968, GB 1111 BBA/SAUTER, Britten Pears Arts. With this letter and copy of *Crie du Coeur*, Rudolf enclosed "3 more recent poems," all custom printed, illustrated with block prints, and signed with Christmas greetings, including a copy of "The Day the World Went Backwards," which he had read at the 1965 Stroud Festival.
36. Rudolf H. Sauter to Leonard Clark, October 8, 1968, private collection.
37. Rudolf H. Sauter to Margaret Turnbull, October 14, 1968, private collection. The location of the "object" Rudolf described here, if extant, is unknown.

I have found them most moving and very remarkable in their way and I congratulate you on them most warmly. But my colleagues on the Poetry Committee find them elusive as to meaning and do not seem to have any ideas about getting them reproduced anywhere. I am so sorry about this, but as a writer of somewhat esoteric poetry and prose you must be used to this rather philistine reaction.[38]

Regardless of such reaction, Rudolf persisted in combining his poetry with the book arts, producing two more volumes, both of which, like *Crie du Coeur*, appeared in limited quantities and which he intended to be read completely, from cover to cover, in the order of their carefully curated contents.

A Soothing Wind *(1969)*

Rudolf's second artist's book, *A Soothing Wind*, was much like *Crie du Coeur* both physically and thematically. It was also printed in cooperation with John Scrivens, with its texts in multiple fonts and directions and illustrated with block prints. Moreover, it was another "tribute to V.S." but as such a more deeply personal "collection of love-poems," which Rudolf hoped "will have some relevance to our profoundly disturbed world." The arrangement of the contents, he explained with emphasis in his foreword, "is more or less chronological and *intended to be read in sequence*, bearing in mind the general period of stress and romantic feeling in which the earlier ones were written."[39]

The volume opened with "1968," specifically "on the seventeen thousand, one hundred and sixty-seventh day" of Rudolf and Viola's marriage. He then spoke directly to her:

with my eyes I can perceive you
with my finger-tips I read you
with my lips I plead you—

through my ears I heed you
in my sense I receive you

---

38. David Carver to Rudolf H. Sauter, February 13, 1969, PEN Archive, 1932–83, 1984.004.71.76, Department of Special Collections and University Archives, University of Tulsa. Carver's handwritten note on an earlier letter from his assistant to Sauter prefigured this reply: "Cannot help. Poems too esoteric for general public." Elizabeth Warner to Rudolf H. Sauter, December 11, 1968, PEN Archive, 1932–83, 1984.004.71.75, Department of Special Collections and University Archives, University of Tulsa.
39. Rudolf H. Sauter, *A Soothing Wind* (Stroud, Gloucestershire: Stroud Typewriting and Duplicating Services, 1969).

and with all my being
>   need you.⁴⁰

Following this introduction, Rudolf transported readers back to 1918 when he had conveyed to Viola words from which he derived the title of the volume:

> When you are near—beauty fills my veins
> to hear you speak is like a soothing wind
> your hair is like the night and in your breath
> such tenderness as even death
> might lose himself in.
> the stars themselves
> hang deeply in your eyes
> to prove the darkness nothing!⁴¹

Following this piece, he included poems to Viola dating from his internment alongside a reproduction of untitled handwritten verse by Viola herself, dating from 1929, wherein she observed a:

> Pale green hill
> all ringed with trees
> a summer scent
> The hum of bees
> a sky so clear
> a heart so free
> a song of love
> Sweeps over me.⁴²

Rudolf then explained to his readers in an autobiographical note, with emphasis through all capital letters and a simple pen-and-ink illustration of an airplane diving from the sky, that

> AFTER A BRIEF PERIOD OF SEPARATION DURING 1918 AND 1919 IN WHICH MOST OF THE PRECEDING POEMS WERE WRITTEN, THERE FOLLOWED AN INTENSIVE TIME OF TRAVEL, PAINTING AND ACTIVE LIFE TOGETHER and WITH OTHERS. THEN IN THE THIRTIES, GROWING TENSIONS &

---

40. Ibid., 7.
41. Ibid., 9.
42. Ibid., 12.

> THREATS OF WAR PRODUCED A CRITICAL ATMOSPHERE IN WHICH THE NEED FOR POETIC EXPRESSION AGAIN BECAME URGENT.[43]

Herein Rudolf was referring to *Four Hungers*, and in the two facing pages that followed he revisited that project through differently angled text printed in multiple fonts above a block-printed black war-torn landscape and a single black circle representing the darkness of war (Figures 6.5a and 6.5b).

A large yellow sun greeted readers on the following page. In the progression of the book, this image signaled the new chapter of their lives which began after 1945, first in Coddington Court—where they "dwell[ed] together—finding grace"—and in then Stroud.[44]

Rudolf began to conclude his volume as he had started it, by stating that

> With my eyes I still perceive you
> With my finger-tips I read you
> With my lips I hold you near,
>
> through my ears I heed you, Dear.
> in my very heart
>
> > I need you.[45]

The final page of *A Soothing Wind*—opposite a gold-toned block print of two aged facial side silhouettes, Viola's inside Rudolf's—revealed to readers the poignancy of the narrative they were about to complete because they had followed Rudolf's instruction to read the contents "in sequence." A printed handwritten note shared the news that "on the 8th May, 1969—before the printing of this tribute was completed—Viola died—at the age of 85 years."[46]

The Loving Cup (1977)

Rudolf's third and final volume of poetry, *The Loving Cup*,[47] was a traditionally printed book, by Stroud's Downfield Press, and therefore not an artist's book like his previous works. He organized the contents of *The Loving Cup* under

---

43. Ibid., 15.
44. Ibid., 23.
45. Ibid., 41.
46. Ibid., 45. See also "Viola Ada Emily Sauter. Close Links with the Galsworthy Family," *Stroud News and Journal*, May 22, 1969, n.p.
47. Rudolf H. Sauter, *The Loving Cup* (Stroud: Downfield Press, 1977).

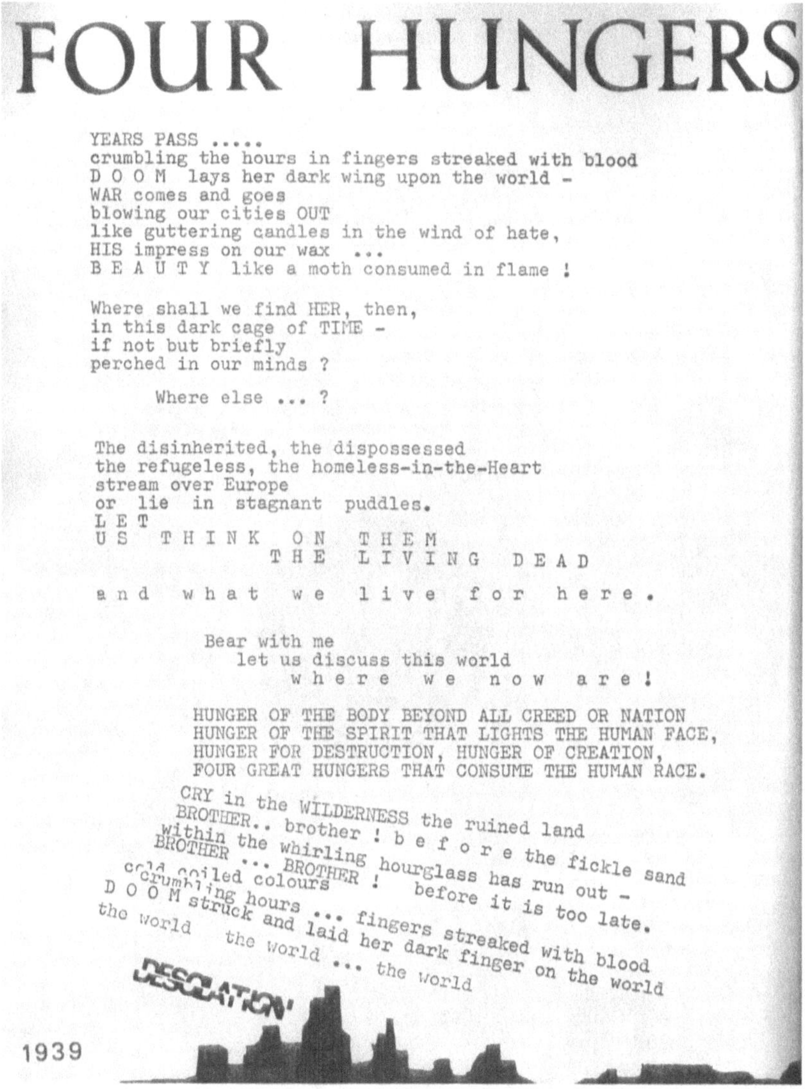

FOUR HUNGERS

```
YEARS PASS .....
crumbling the hours in fingers streaked with blood
D O O M  lays her dark wing upon the world -
WAR comes and goes
blowing our cities OUT
like guttering candles in the wind of hate,
HIS impress on our wax ...
B E A U T Y  like a moth consumed in flame !

Where shall we find HER, then,
in this dark cage of TIME -
if not but briefly
perched in our minds ?

          Where else ... ?


The disinherited, the dispossessed
the refugeless, the homeless-in-the-Heart
stream over Europe
or lie in stagnant  puddles.
L E T
U S    T H I N K    O N    T H E M
                    T H E    L I V I N G    D E A D

a n d    w h a t    w e    l i v e    f o r    h e r e .

               Bear with me
                  let us discuss this world
                     w h e r e    w e    n o w    a r e !

               HUNGER OF THE BODY BEYOND ALL CREED OR NATION
               HUNGER OF THE SPIRIT THAT LIGHTS THE HUMAN FACE,
               HUNGER FOR DESTRUCTION, HUNGER OF CREATION,
               FOUR GREAT HUNGERS THAT CONSUME THE HUMAN RACE.
```

CRY in the WILDERNESS the ruined land
BROTHER.. brother ! b e f o r e the fickle sand
within the whirling hourglass has run out -
BROTHER ... BROTHER ! before it is too late.
cold coiled colours
Crumbling hours ... fingers streaked with blood
D O O M struck and laid her dark finger on the world
the world   the world ... the world

DESOLATION

1939

Figure 6.5a and 6.5b (*Continued*)

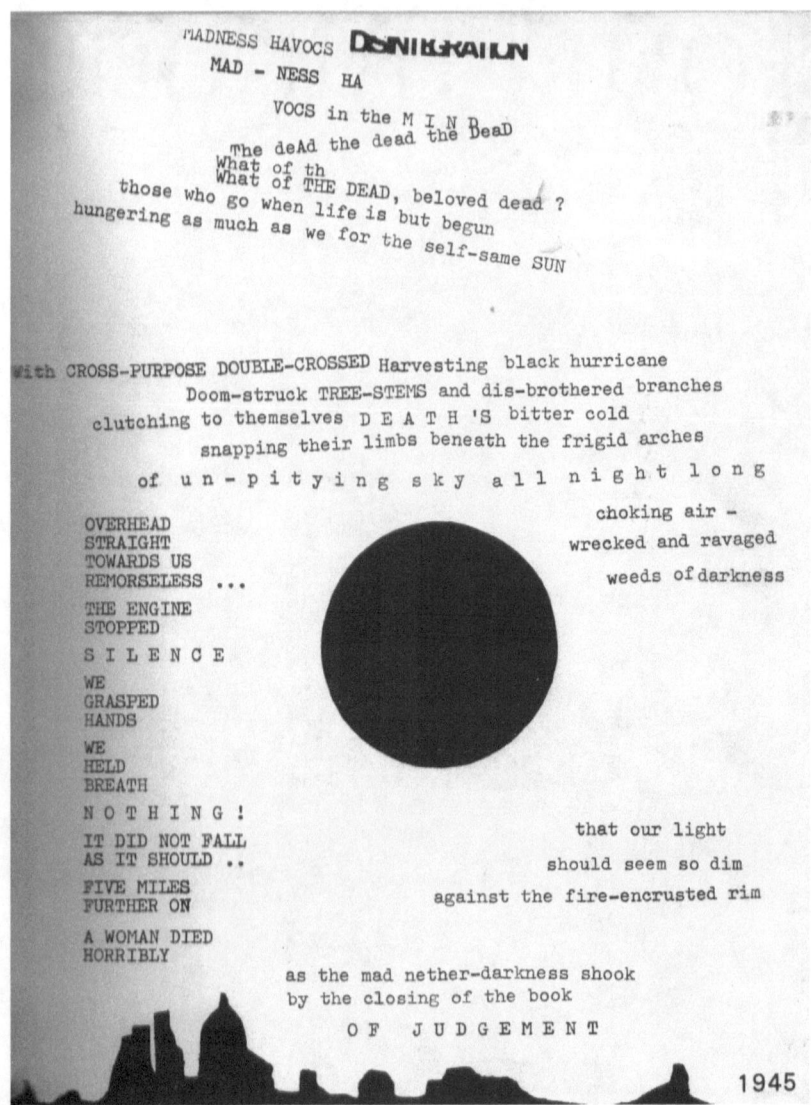

Figures 6.5a and 6.5b Rudolf H. Sauter, "Four Hungers," in *A Soothing Wind*, 16–17. private collection, © Trustees of the Estate of Rudolf H. Sauter.

four main sections: "Time," "In Between," "Lyric Moments," and "Asides and Comments," explaining,

> Unlike what usually happens to me, most of these poems seem to come "out of the blue," so to speak, without conscious connection with

any previous train of thought of immediate stimulus. On one or two occasions I remember waking from a night's sleep with the first few lines upon my lips. What significance, if any, may be attached to this I leave to the reader. The fact remains that this was often only a beginning and days of work may have been required before some of them could be persuaded into their present form. To these have been added a few older poems which seemed to fit into the context of this volume. I hope that you may find something of interest here of what was intended.[48]

All of the 42 poems that followed dated from the 1970s except 2, both dated 1968: a fragment from "The Dream" and "Masks," which Rudolf had brought forward from *The Fifth Hunger*. The prevailing theme of the volume was his sense of his own mortality. He reflected on themes of nature and the divine in order to "speak peace to Mankind, […] to you, my Neighbour and to you who are not even my neighbour," and to ask "What is 'TIME' that lives in us, holds us enthralled or filled with care?—a little twittering of life that passes, who knows where."[49] Equally, and in the spirit and practice of his previous works, Rudolf remained profoundly concerned about the fate of the wider world, including the "Tools" that began to dictate the rhythms of life and the decisions of mankind:

> Of all the tools that man has made
> to lift him from his Primal Day,
> the others slavishly obey
> only the COMPUTER rules.
> Oh save us from this monstrous THING,
> Which, feeding on the Mind of Man
> determining his every plan,
> denies him lift of Heart or Wing.[50]

In concluding the volume, Rudolf hoped for "A Better Day":

> "Hold your horses," as they say,
> this could be a better day—
> Concorde could refuse to fly,
> and fewer planes could pollute the sky,
> Motor cars could cease to smell

---

48. Ibid., "By Way of Introduction," n.p.
49. Ibid., 9–13.
50. Ibid., 37.

and Folk could wish each other well.
Pause and ponder, as you go,
things might be even worse, you know.
So let us think how life could well
be just a little less like Hell,
and how we might grow up and up
by drinking from a "Loving—Cup."[51]

Rudolf's words conveyed in *The Loving Cup* took on even greater meaning when readers learned, under the brief biographical note at the end of the volume, that "on the 12th of June, 1977, before the printing of this book was completed, [he] died at the age of 82 years."[52]

Contemporary Art

As existential themes pervaded Rudolf's multimedia productions and book arts, they also informed his painting in abstract style beginning in the mid-1950s. In the 142nd annual exhibition of the Royal Institute of Painters in Water Colours, held in 1954, he displayed "several strange mystic paintings, which almost defy description," as one critic wrote, with titles such as *The Wind and the Sun* and *Lonely Majesty*.[53] Over the next 15 years he conceived and produced many more abstract works with evocative titles such as *Creational Theme* (Figure 6.6) and *Study in Space*, as well as *Towards the Ultimate, Idea, Leap into Space, Life Unfolding*, and *Life Emergent*, a version of which appeared on the cover of the 1964 pamphlet *Folk Dances of the World*, produced by International Cultural Exchange.[54]

---

51. Ibid., 43.
52. Ibid., 45. According to Rudolf's death certificate, held by Gloucestershire Archives, he died of a heart attack in Stroud General Hospital. His obituaries include "Mr. R. Sauter," *Stroud News and Journal*, June 16, 1977, n.p., "Mr. R.H. Sauter" *Stroud News and Journal*, June 23, 1977, n.p.—the latter of which included details of his funeral service in Stroud's Holy Trinity Church—and Catherine Dupré, "Mr. Rudolf Sauter," *Times* (London, England), June 21, 1977, 16. Following the funeral service, Rudolf's body was cremated at Cheltenham Crematorium.
53. "Midland Exhibits in London Display of Water Colours," *Birmingham Post*, March 20, 1954, 5. Rudolf also exhibited his pastel work "End of the Year" at the Paris Salon. The theme and style of this piece is unknown. "Midland Artists' Work in the Paris Salon," *Birmingham Post & Gazette*, May 31, 1957, 7, https://www.britishnewspaperarchive.co.uk/viewer/bl/0002134/19570531/145/0007.
54. Rudolf H. Sauter, *Towards the Ultimate*, 1964, oil on board, 35 × 46 cm, accessed June 30, 2021, https://redravenarts.com/artists/sauter-rudolf/#jp-carousel-1463; *Idea*, ca. 1964, oil on board, 37 × 55 cm, accessed June 30, 2021,

Figure 6.6 Rudolf H. Sauter, *Creational Theme*, 1967, oil on board, 74.9 × 58.4 cm, private collection, photograph by Stacy Ross, © Trustees of the Estate of Rudolf H. Sauter.

Although Rudolf had displayed some of these works in mainstream galleries, he had largely moved on other venues, as he explained in 1968 to Margaret Turnbull: "I have virtually given up sending to the conventional shows like R.B.A. [Royal Society of British Artists] and R.W.A. [Royal West of England Academy], they no longer have much interest for me."[55] Emblematic of Rudolf moving in this direction was his 1967 "Exhibition of Paintings on

---

https://redravenarts.com/artists/sauter-rudolf/#jp-carousel-1455; *Study in Space*, 1967, oil on board, 40 × 50 cm, accessed June 30, 2021, https://redravenarts.com/artists/sauter-rudolf/#jp-carousel-1461; *Leap into Space*, 1965, oil on board, 50.8 × 53.3 cm, accessed June 30, 2021, https://www.barnebys.com/realized-prices/lot/rudolph-h-sauter-oil-on-board-leap-into-space-1FTo2Tf5Sy; *Life Emergent, ca. 1962, No. 2*, oil on board, 66 × 74.9 cm, accessed June 30, 2021, https://www.barnebys.com/realized-prices/lot/rudolph-h-sauter-oil-on-board-life-emergent-no-NQgzVrIk3X; *Life Unfolding, 1965*, oil on board, 48.2 × 58.4 cm, accessed June 30, 2021, https://www.barnebys.com/realized-prices/lot/rudolph-h-sauter-oil-on-board-life-unfolding-wcGdo5huQD; Life *Emergent No. 3., 1962*, oil on board, 101.6 × 74.9 cm, accessed June 30, 2021, https://www.barnebys.com/realized-prices/lot/rudolph-h-sauter-oil-on-board-life-emergent-no-ivsUhFSm--; *International Cultural Exchange, Folk Dances of the World: Souvenir Programme* (London: International Cultural Exchange, 1964).

55. Rudolf H. Sauter to Margaret Turnbull, October 14, 1968, private collection.

a Cosmic Theme" held in Acacia House of London's Acton Park. It was an elaborate affair, including a reception and a song recital by operatic singer Raimund Herincx accompanied by Howard Greenberg.[56] Curiously, the site was the former home of the film star Sean Connery, which self-proclaimed Universalists Karl Francis and his wife Betty had turned into a spiritualist healing center addressing their interests in "the teachings of mankind and to see that people live right."[57] The publicity leaflet for the program announced Rudolf's "latest paintings, mostly in plastic pigments, reach[ing] towards the Cosmos in an original and distinctive manner unique in contemporary art."[58] Shortly after the opening, the *Gazette and Post* echoed the leaflet as it told readers that Rudolf's work was "a revolutionary idea in visual art." To emphasize the point the paper shared a picture of him, "the man experimenting in plastic pigment painting" actively hanging "some of his own work in preparation for the exhibition."[59]

Galsworthy Reflections

Upon his aunt Ada's death in 1956, Rudolf became the sole trustee of his uncle's literary estate. The responsibility involved many legal "intricacies" that required his attention, but he embraced the trusteeship with as much creativity and curation as had been defining his own artistic interests.[60]

From 1956 to 1962, Rudolf wrote and presented several public lectures about his uncle, at least one of which was broadcast by the BBC.[61] Recordings

---

56. The exhibition was held from 8 October to 16 December. Rudolf H. Sauter to David Carver, September 23, 1967, PEN Archive, 1932–83, 1984.004.71.73, Department of Special Collections and University Archives, University of Tulsa.
57. "Karl Francis: Universalist in Charge," *Gazette and Post* (London, England), September 14, 1967, 6. https://www.britishnewspaperarchive.co.uk/viewer/bl/0002134/19570 531/145/0007. See also on the same page the related article "Healers Open Connery Home: With Veg on the Menu."
58. Rudolf H. Sauter to David Carver, September 23, 1967, PEN Archive, 1932–83, 1984.004.71.69, Department of Special Collections and University Archives, University of Tulsa.
59. "Yoga and Plastic Art Down at the 007 House," *Gazette and Post* (London, England), October 5, 1967, 11, https://www.britishnewspaperarchive.co.uk/viewer/bl/0002 480/19671005/107/0011.
60. Rudolf H. Sauter to David Carver, June 2, 1956, PEN Archive, 1932–83, 1984.004.71.50r, Department of Special Collections and University Archives, University of Tulsa.
61. Of these presentations, the earliest known occurred in late spring 1956, being "a lecture [...] with readings of [Galsworthy's] poems and a foreword by [Viola], followed by a reading of [his] *Salta Pro Noblis* by two local actors and a dramatic version of 'The First and Last' also by local actors." Rudolf H. Sauter to David Carver, June 2,

of these presentations reveal him as a skilled storyteller with a soft, inviting voice, indeed sensitive to describing his uncle's personal and professional character, as well as keenly attentive to delivering well-crafted narratives to captive audiences. Moreover, these spoken-word performances anticipated those which soon would define his contemporary stage production *Four Hungers*. Indeed, they likely influenced how he approached that multimedia project. Equally significant was the fact that during the same year *Four Hungers* premiered at the Cotswold Playhouse, Rudolf chose a performance as a means to preside over the transfer of his uncle's papers to the University of Birmingham.[62] As the *Birmingham Post* reported, Rudolf "conjured up" one of the main characters in Galsworthy's best-selling *Forsyte Saga*, namely Soames Forstye, to be at the "handing-over of the [...] collection and the opening of the [university's] John Galsworthy Room." Dressed as Forsyte, Rudolf introduced himself in the third person and set the stage for the proceedings with a gesture to the Galsworthy papers on display having come from their recent exhibition in the British Museum:

> I make no apology for allowing Mr. Forsyte to gate-crash this distinguished assembly, after all, who should know his creator better than he?

1956, PEN Archive, 1932–83, 1984.004.71.50v, Department of Special Collections and University Archives, University of Tulsa. A subsequent presentation was "Man and Craftsman." BBC Programme Index, "John Galsworthy 1867–1933: Man and Craftsman by Rudolf Sauter," broadcast June 13, 1957, accessed June 30, 2021, https://genome.ch.bbc.co.uk/f97d02faed3f4642b08c0d0e0c799b2e. See also Rudolf H. Sauter, "Portrait of John Galsworthy" (1959) and "An Evening with Galsworthy" (undated), two other contemporary recordings which were likely broadcast on the BBC, JG(II)/11/1, Cadbury Library, University of Birmingham. The former program, produced for the BBC by Richard Keen, was revised and rebroadcast in August 1967 for the Galsworthy Centenary. BBC Programme Index, "John Galsworthy," broadcast August 10, 1967, accessed June 30, 2021, https://genome.ch.bbc.co.uk/44f956d1d d7f474b942d5488ebc49d6a. For a written account of this broadcast, see "Memories of Galsworthy," *Listener* (London, England), August 10, 1967, 166–67. In subsequent years, Sauter also spoke about his uncle in Stroud, Cheltenham and Cirencester and before audiences at Hawkwood International College, Literary Society of Marlborough College and Westonbirt and Malvern Girls Schools. See "John Galsworthy: Script of Talk." Typescript, ca. 1968, JG(II)/11/3, Library, University of Birmingham.

62. "Priceless Gifts to the University to Create a Galsworthy Room," *Birmingham Post*, May 15, 1962, 6. https://www.britishnewspaperarchive.co.uk/viewer/bl/0002134/ 19620515/399/0020. According to the *Times*, Galsworthy had "few connections" to Birmingham. The main reason why Ada chose its university to acquire his collection was because it could "adequately display and provide facilities for scholars in [its] great new library building." "Galsworthy MSS. Handed Over: Loan to Birmingham University," *Times* (London, England), July 27, 1962, 15.

And if they were not always on the best of terms in their youth, they very largely made up their differences in later life. So I thought it only right and proper to ask him to come over from his home in the British Museum to represent all the Characters so beautifully housed in their red Morocco covers in these cases behind me.[63]

Dovetailing with his literary interests of the period, Rudolf drew on his various lectures to write a biography of his uncle, *Galsworthy the Man: An Intimate Portrait*. He published it in 1967, the centenary year of Galsworthy's birth. The early chapters of this book documented aspects of Rudolf's upbringing in Holland Park, revealing as much about him and his parents as they did about the early years of Galsworthy's literary career. Moreover, the fact that Rudolf's biography of Galsworthy and his own *Crie du Coeur*, were published a year apart suggests that he was working on both projects simultaneously, likely reflecting on one as he did the other. As creative projects, therefore, these books complement each other in much the same way as Rudolf's spoken tributes to his uncle, and no less his planning of at least two Galsworthy centenary exhibitions, intersected with his theatrical interests, becoming windows onto Rudolf's own creativity during the later years of his life.[64]

---

63. "Galsworthy's Relatives; Welcome for Soames Forsyte," *Birmingham Post*, July 27, 1962, 7, https://www.britishnewspaperarchive.co.uk/viewer/bl/0002134/19620727/229/0008. For Rudolf's complete speech on the occasion of the opening of the Galsworthy Room, see Rudolf H. Sauter, "'The Other Side of the Coin': John Galsworthy as We Knew Him," typescript, ca. 1967, n.p., appendix I., JG(II)/12/6, Cadbury Library, University of Birmingham.

64. One of these exhibitions took place at the University of Birmingham and another at the Stroud Festival. See Birmingham University, *Catalogue [of the] Galsworthy Centenary Exhibition Held in the Heslop Room, the Main Library, University of Birmingham, May 19th–June 3rd, 1967*, and Leslie Duckworth, "50 Years of Art at Stroud Festival," *Birmingham Post*, October 17, 1967, 12, https://www.britishnewspaperarchive.co.uk/viewer/bl/0002135/19671017/273/0012. See also Rudolf H. Sauter to Marjorie Watts, April 4, 1967, PEN Archive, 1932–83, 1984.004.71.66r-v, Department of Special Collections and University Archives, University of Tulsa. See also British Museum, *John Galsworthy, 1857–1933: An Exhibition to Commemorate the Centenary of His Birth, King's Library, 13 January to 2 April 1967* (London: British Museum, 1967). Rudolf returned to Wingstone as part of the Galsworthy Centenary, speaking there also about his uncle based on his prepared remarks and recently published book. "Author Unveils New Galsworthy Plaque," *Mid-Devon Advertiser* (Newton Abbot, England), August 19, 1967, 9.

Recalling the Great War: 1975

During the mid-1970s, the editors of two war-themed anthologies asked Rudolf if he would contribute to their respective collections. He obliged both editors with detailed personal narratives representing the first time he had written publicly and at length about his experiences of internment, beyond cursory suggestions of it in his poetry collections. He also offered them selections of his wartime art, marking the first time these works would be seen publicly. The public appearance of these narratives late in Rudolf's life suggested how comfortable he had become with recalling openly his life changing experiences of the Great War period.[65]

David Ball published Rudolf's essay "Between Two Worlds" in his 1977 collection *The Experience of Prison: An Anthology of Prose, Drama, Verse and Picture*.[66] Seven of his wartime drawings, all in pen and ink and wash on paper, followed the piece, depicting stark scenes of internment in the Alexandra Palace, including its main hall filled with partitioned spaces for internees and around and through which they hung their clothing, sparse individual spaces with little to no privacy and littered with belongings and infiltrated by leaking water.[67]

Michael Marland and Robin Willcox published Rudolf's essay "Enemy Alien" in their 1980 collection *While They Fought: An Anthology of Prose and Verse Exploring the Lives of Those Who Did Not Fight, but Who Had to Endure the Second World War*. Herein Rudolf's contribution was introduced as "a specially written memoir of the author's experiences in England as a German-born person during the two world wars, followed by the author's own drawings of the camp for aliens."[68] Four of his wartime drawings, all in pen and ink and wash on paper, followed this piece, depicting stark scenes of internment in Frith Hill Camp, Surrey, including the barbed wire fence surrounding the tents of the camp, a seemingly endless row of tents separated by a shallow muddy trench

---

65. Patrick Howell, *Consistently Brilliant on a Breezy Hilltop: A History of the Cotswold Players, the First 100 Years* (United Kingdom: Quicksilver, 2016), 143.
66. Rudolf H. Sauter, "Between Two Worlds," in *The Experience of Prison: An Anthology of Prose, Drama, Verse and Picture*, ed. David Ball (London: Longman, 1977), 128–43.
67. All seven of Rudolf's drawings reproduced after his essay "Between Two Worlds" were uncaptioned. Discernable detail near his signatures on four of these drawings reveal them to be "A Battalion," "B Battalion," "The Clockmaker" and "The Letter Home, A Battalion." One of the three untitled works later illustrated the cover of The Fine Art Society, *Rudolf H. Sauter, 1985–1979 [sic] Internment Drawings—Alexandra Palace 1918–19, 7–25 June 1993* (London: Fine Art Society, 1993).
68. Rudolf H. Sauter, "Enemy Alien," in *While They Fought: An Anthology of Prose and Verse Exploring the Lives of Those Who Did Not Fight, but Who Had to Endure the Second World War*, ed. Michael Marland and Robin Willcox (London: Longman, 1980), 86–94.

and a pair of internees playing chess while another pair stand on the barbed-wire perimeter looking outside the camp.[69]

"Between Two Worlds" and "Enemy Alien" appear in their entirety in the epilogue below to give Rudolf himself the last word in this first book about the arc of his creative life in war and peace. As for his final paintings, they recalled another major event in his life—namely his visit to the Grand Canyon—providing him inspiration to pursue one more exhibition, a meaningful coda to his artistic life.

Recalling the Grand Canyon: 1975–76

Rudolf marked his 80th birthday—in 1975—by taking his first glider flight on the grounds of the Cotswold Gliding Club. The occasion inspired him to "turn over a new leaf," as he explained to Michael and Margaret Harrison, "from revising and re-writing old poems and other material, till the words stuck in my throat." He explained further that

> the big picture of the Canyon which I painted in 1928 happened to be propped up at the foot of my bed. Morning after morning I woke to find it rebuking me, daily more and more, for a too *literal* translation of it and I felt what I must do, was to try, anew to portray that *inner* feeling which has remained with me from the first moment when I stepped out of the train and saw The Canyon shimmering and iridescent through the trees—one of the greatest experiences of my life! So I set about it—and the pictures which has so far "erupted" (one might say) are very different from those painted on the spot, 47 years ago. Though based on them and on photographs, drawings and sketches done at the time, I am now rather short "skeleton-wise," of basic forms of material to go further on this project. I have already completed eleven canvases (new ones) and they are entirely different in outlook from the old ones. You may of course not like the way the Canyon is treated in them, but I am trying to express the *inner* impression, the inner exaltation of that magic place.[70]

---

69. As in the volume edited by Marland and Willcox, all four of Rudolf's drawings reproduced after his essay "Enemy Alien" were uncaptioned. While there is no discernable detail to determine the titles of these works, the final image remains extant and is reproduced above as Figure 2.8.
70. Rudolf H. Sauter to the Harrisons, November 1975, BANC MSS 89/72z, The Bancroft Library, University of California, Berkeley.

In assessing his progress and welcoming informed feedback, Rudolf added that "not many people have seen them so far, but 2 friends who have, in their time, visited the Canyon twice (and have some knowledge of painting) were very impressed." He went on to ask the Harrisons for their help in achieving his new vision of his long-beloved subject that had fundamentally helped him realize his identity as an artist. "I suppose you cannot tell me of any further 'material' I could get," footnoting, "Photos, postcards, anything!" because, he explained,

> The library here doesn't know anything, travel agencies are not very helpful, because of course I can't undertake a journey, which of course would have been what I would like to do. I hasten to say that it is not literal, geological exactitudes that I want, but something to re-juvenate and stimulate my aging memory (photographs or cards).

Rudolf concluded, "do let me have some news of you" and added a poignant fact rooted in his experience of 50 years earlier, that "your little Indian doll mascot still presides over my studio activities."[71] And to convey the profundity of his recent flying experience and how it motivated him to recall the vast space of the site he wished to recall more vividly than he could, Rudolf included two poems with his letter, the first with an etching of a glider circling high above the Grand Canyon:

> To stroke the Sky with thin aspiring Wing
> and, rising on the thermals of the mind
> find all things changed and from this moment New!
> Not grappling with rock as climbers do
> nor wrapped in the wrinkled Canyons of the Wind
> but at the gates of Sunrise moved to Sing
> and, looking down un-tethered to the Earth,
> see all Men "one"—all linked by Human birth ...
> When morning breaks above its rim
>   of gray
> So be my Wish for you—this very day!

The other poem Rudolf included in his letter to the Harrisons was "Three Graces":

> The MOON—and a bright star
> lone, beside,

---

71. Ibid.

and winged clouds all around!
and dark sky
and silent cry
that can find no uttering sound!

A yellow gleam along the hill—
Day not yet begun!
But NO pain
in the gentle rain,
and—afterwards—the SUN!

For Sun-Shine,
and *no* decline
is what I wish for YOU:
a breath of air,
and touch to share!
and loving moments—too!

In thanking Rudolf for his thoughtful holiday greetings, Harrison noted that when he and his wife

> saw what you had done with your greeting, we had a very warm spot in our heart for you and felt very close to you. The Canyon with the sun peeping over the rim brought back very fond memories for me. If only we could turn back the clock to that long ago—almost 50 years—and all be together again.[72]

Moreover, Harrison sent Rudolf "some pictures of the Canyon—mostly winter scenes—that appeared in *Arizona Highways*."[73] Rudolf appreciated these images because he had been "lacking" such "snow aspects" among his own kept photographs. He recalled Harrison saying that the Canyon would appear "quite differently" in the winter and that he would be able to paint the scenery "100% better" than during the summer. "Well that's what I'm trying to do," Rudolf wrote to Harrison:

> Though the time is 50 years and my return only by way of the "mind."
> I just live in it and hardly have time for anything else. Studying my diary

---

72. Michael Harrison to Rudolf H. Sauter, December 19, 1975, BANC MSS 89/72z, The Bancroft Library, University of California, Berkeley.
73. Ibid.

of the time, I notice that hardly a day passes without some reference to "snow," so your photos are most appropriate [...] I feel you may well be shocked at some of the liberties I have been taking. When things are a little more advanced I will certainly take some transparencies and let you have them. But, be prepared for the worst. Perhaps, however, the little mascot—Indian Doll-dancer—which still presides over my studio you gave us when we were out there may preserve me from committing the worst errors of bad taste.[74]

Informed by the winter images Harrison offered and by his own diaries, photographs and memories, Rudolf's creative return to the Grand Canyon manifested itself fully in a series of paintings which he intended to form the basis of a new exhibition which he described in *The Grand Canyon: How These Pictures Came to Be Painted, 1975–76. Journey into Color. Reflections after 80*.[75] Among the works Rudolf likely had planned to include were *The Last Glow* (Figure 6.7), *Snow and Cloud*, *Pearl and Rose*, *Sun's Last Glow* and at least two more, both entitled *The Grand Canyon*.[76]

In the exhibition program, Rudolf explained the origin, meaning and purpose of the project, drawing directly from the thoughts he had recently shared with Michael Harrison in their correspondence. Beginning with the question "Why?" Rudolf began his lengthy answer:

---

74. Rudolf H. Sauter to Michael Harrison, February 17, 1976, BANC MSS 89/72z, The Bancroft Library, University of California, Berkeley.
75. Rudolf H. Sauter, *The Grand Canyon: How These Pictures Came to Be Painted, 1975–76. Journey into Color. Reflections after 80* (Nympsfield, Gloucestershire: Nimsfeilde Press, 1976). It is unclear if Rudolf actually realized this exhibition, or if it was the unrealized project mentioned in his obituary, for which he had been painting, had "planned to hold in the George Room Gallery, Stroud," and which went ahead as "a memorial exhibition for him." See "Mr. R. Sauter," *Stroud News and Journal*, June 16, 1977, n.p.
76. Rudolf H. Sauter, *Snow and Cloud*, non-canvas laid down on board, 40.5 × 50.7 cm, accessed June 30, 2021, https://www.barnebys.hk /%E6%88%90%E4%BA%A4% E5%83%B9/%E6%8B%8D%E5%93%81/rudolf-helmut-sauter-jdb5ZRUWtj; *Pearl and Rose: The Grand Canyon*, accessed June 30, 2021, https://www.barnebys. com/realized-prices/lot/rudolf-sauter-b-1895-7PxxIVQqC; *Suns Last Glow: The Grand Canyon*, oil on board, framed, 29 × 42 cm, accessed June 30, 2021, https:// cuttlestones.co.uk/salecatalogue/ FA090318.htm?s=133&c=303&f=374&display=50; *The Grand Canyon*, 1975, oil on board, 30 × 40, accessed June 30, 2021, https://www.barnebys.com/realized-prices/lot/oil-painting-rudolf-sauter-1975-the-grand-canyon-on-board-5b8saE0Gdp; *The Grand Canyon*, 1976, oil on board, 40.7 × 50.8 cm, accessed June 30, 2021, https://www.barnebys.com/realized-prices/ lot/the-grand-canyon-4Bn9BDak23.

Figure 6.7 Rudolf H. Sauter, *The Last Glow*, 1976, oil on board, 23.4 × 41.9 cm, courtesy of Philip Serrell Auctioneers & Valuers, © Trustees of the Estate of Rudolf H. Sauter.

> As one grows older in years, one finds oneself reflecting with renewed urgency on the past—if only to try and discover how it could contribute to some sort of creative future. Such moments may well provide an edge on which to "stand and stare." They may also provoke the uncomfortable reflection that, if one cannot do still better, what purpose has been served by the Past?[77]

He continued, adding more detail beyond that which he shared privately with Harrison:

> With such reflection in mind I looked with new eyes on the picture which happened by chance to be propped up at the foot of my bed. It was a large Oil-painting of the "Grand Canyon of Arizona," painted at the age of 30 immediately after my return from a visit in 1926. It had been exhibited with some success in London, New York, Cincinnati, Stroud and elsewhere and has remained one of my most treasured possessions ever since, because of its *associations*. But, as morning after morning I woke to find it facing me, I became less and less satisfied with the

---

77. Rudolf H. Sauter, *The Grand Canyon: How These Pictures Came to Be Painted, 1975–76. Journey into Color. Reflections After 80* (Nympsfield, Gloucestershire: Nimsfeilde Press, 1976), 1.

painting itself. Structure and colours were recorded with loving care—the creamy limestones at the top, down the Earth's mile-deep history of successive layers, from the shales and red sandstones to the schists and granites of two thousand million years ago between which the Colorado, the coloured River, still carries the crumbling rock away [...] a fascinating enough study which appeals to the intellect; but I could no longer see it in this way, something was missing.

Where, I asked myself, was the essential *Spirit* of this magic place? I missed the exaltation of fifty years ago when my Wife and I had stepped out the stuffy train in to the clear dawn at 7,000 feet—and first saw the Canyon through the trees, shimmering in early light, undefinable—remote [...] and for a moment I had wondered whether we might not have perished in the train and whether this might not be a pre-view of Heaven itself.

We stood transfixed, in a Silence so intense it seemed as if all sound on Earth had ceased [...] all activity suspended.[78]

Their tour began, Rudolf explained further:

Presided over by Tom the guide, my Wife and I were, I believe, one of the very first parties ever to go down the steep, as-yet-unfinished Yaqui Trail—slithering round the frosty hairpin bends on what we hoped were sure-footed mules...across the newly-built suspension-bridge at the bottom—and back again—in one day. It was certainly a memorable Day. The mules, we were told, are trained to walk within six inches of the edge so as not to brush their riders off against the steep walls of rock on the inside. Beyond—is a thousand foot drop. Sometimes on the bends you feel as if suspended over Space as the mule turns and you look between its ears at—nothingness.[79]

Reflecting on this experience 50 years later, Rudolf wondered about

Memories which may have lain dormant perhaps for many years can become more potent and return with added force when the moment is ripe. Could those three weeks on the edge of the abyss half a Century ago, I wondered, be the stimulus for which I had been subconsciously waiting, the challenge needed to start me off painting again after a long break engrossed in writing?[80]

---

78. Ibid., 1–2.
79. Ibid., 3.
80. Ibid.

Evidently, Rudolf believed this was the case as he explained further that

> the Spirit of a *place* does not lie only in what the eye can see. It is compounded of many things. Its impress is on the body as a *whole*. Each nerve, each sense vibrates in tune, if it is to come alive. Time and circumstance take part [...] and the viewer himself is part of the circumstance—and of the picture he views. Must we so often be governed in our outlook by facts and objects and material values? Why not allow ourselves more often to be taken out of our Selves by something transcendent, by which we can renew our fading perceptions and dwindling energies? Only when the Mind is undistracted by detail does the Spirit reveal itself.[81]

Such was his approach—indeed his state of body, mind and spirit—as he

> began by experimenting in all directions. [...] But what an undertaking! How even begin to express this in terms which might do justice to such a Theme? [...] how to pay tribute to such a tremendous Subject! It was like trying to pack all Heaven into a nutshell. *Each* picture became an exploration. *Each* new aspect required its own technique and refused to be imposed on by preconceived notions. *Each* mark of brush or painting-knife became a new step, an adventure in itself.[82]

Sensitive to his mortality as an artist, Rudolf concluded:

> They say our material bodies are replaced completely every seven years. Perhaps our minds are no more stable. Be that as it may, I could no more have painted these present canvases 'seven generations' ago, than I could now in all conscience paint that picture which continues to provoke me from the foot of my bed. The relationship had changed [...] the *outlook* was quite different. It is with a Landscape—admittedly unscalable by human foot—that we are concerned—a landscape where the Mind and the Sense can wander and renew themselves and where it seems quite natural that Man's imagination should have once been moved to call the summits by such names as "Shiva's Temple," "Osiris' Temple" or "Wotan's Throne," or make his way along the "Bright Angel Trail." It is not the purpose of this Exhibition to merely display a number of unrelated pictures. It is rather—if that is possible—through their combined

---

81. Ibid., 4.
82. Ibid., 5.

presence to share an experience with other people and, as far as lies on one's power, to pay tribute to that supreme quality in Nature, which still seems able at times to lift the heart and mind of Man *above* his material preoccupations.[83]

So, it could be said that it was nature—in the form of the glorious and memorable Grand Canyon—which lifted Rudolf's heart and mind during his final days. This exhibition and all he dedicated to realizing it was a fitting coda to his creative life, indeed to the totality of his experience as a sensitive English artist dedicated to his craft and to the challenges of capturing the human condition.

---

83. Ibid., 6.

Conclusion

LEGACY

During the late 1960s, when Rudolf became a regular visitor to Stroud Typewriting, Rotaprinting and Duplicating Service to begin work on his first artist's book with Patricia Scrivins and her son John, their conversations touched on the fact that Viola had been ill for several years and recently suffered a stroke. Patricia had nursing qualifications and offered to assist Rudolf with caring for Viola. The three formed a close bond. When Viola died, Patricia continued to be a companion to Rudolf, visiting him daily, accompanying him on his travels around Stroud and helping him publish his three volumes of poetry, *Crie du Coeur*, *A Soothing Wind* and *A Loving Cup*. In addition to thanking Patricia by name in all these volumes, Rudolf wrote and dedicated number of poems to her, among them one which conveyed his deep appreciation of their companionship:

> I
> We must have dialogue—
> all the time, my dear,
> let word descend between us
> like a dove—
> no hawks between!
> and may our tongues be lit,
> as now, with love.
>
> But if at times
> the dove is sick
> and ecstasies grow dull.
> caress again with life
> the bird of peace.
> Touch me, my dear,
> and I will understand.
>
> II
> In life together
> There are many things—

strange, unaccustomed things—
a thousand marriages to make
between the various aspects
of our lives.

For you have fifty years
of living in one world,
I more than seventy
in another world—
True marriage of two worlds
is not an easy thing.

But where love is
the subtle current flows
through everything—
as we are linked;

so when the shadowing hawk is dark
between us and the sun

touch me—and I
will try to understand.[1]

The strong relationship between Patricia and Rudolf deserves attention for fundamental reasons: it helped to preserve Rudolf's work after his death and, ultimately, it helped to make this book possible.

Rudolf named Patricia an executor of his will along with Alan Meyer, an attorney with the firm Halsey, Lightly and Hemsley.[2] In this way, Rudolf passed to them equally the copyright in his entire body of work. In turn, and per Rudolf's wishes, they arranged for the preservation of his papers in the University of Birmingham, alongside the papers of his uncle and aunt. The *Birmingham Post* reported this news, closing a final chapter in Rudolf's life and opening a new one for researchers.[3]

---

1. Rudolf H. Sauter, "For Pat with Love," unpublished typescript, August 1969. Oldmeadow Collection.
2. Meyer's firm had handled legal matters for Rudolf and his aunt Ada when they became stewards of Galsworthy's literary estate, including the donation of Galsworthy's papers to the University of Birmingham.
3. "Forsyte Bequest Completes Archive," *Birmingham Post*, September 1, 1977, 2, https://www.britishnewspaperarchive.co.uk/viewer/bl/0002135/19770901/033/0002; Ian Small, "Special Collections Report: The Galsworthy Collection and Its Fate," *English Literature in Transition*, 1880–1920, 27, no. 3 (1984): 236–38.

When Patricia died in 2005, the copyright held by her passed to her children. Their stewardship of this copyright together with Alan Meyer—indeed their collective willingness to grant permission to use Rudolf's work—allowed this book to be written and published, and now the world to begin to appreciate the singular creative life of Rudolf Sauter in war and peace.

EPILOGUE:
IN HIS OWN WORDS

Between Two Worlds*

It was a huge building with a tower at each end, situated high on a hill and dominating the whole of North London. Once an Entertainment Centre and now the home of the B.B.C., *Alexandria Palace* had been converted into a great Prisoner of War Camp to house so-called "Enemy Aliens" married to British wives. It had the advantage that families of those living in London could more readily visit. It was surrounded by extensive grounds which were supposed to be kept in order by the prisoners, presumably against eventual "Peace." I can only speak of this one camp, for, though threatened with removal to the Isle of Man where single men were incarcerated I was never transferred, on compassionate grounds ... .

With the exception of myself and one or two others, perhaps the youngest in the camp, the three thousand or more inmates were married men of all conditions of life: Business men and Labourers, Waiters, Carpenters, Joiners, Watch-repairers, Bakers, Gardeners, Cobblers, Jewellers and we had Chefs from the best Hotels—if there had only been the material to cook. Thanks to the intervention of the Quakers and a committee of well-wishers under Dr Markel, facilities were arranged and materials supplied so that they might carry on trades or hobbies as best they could, working in difficult conditions on their beds. But this kept them going, and those who could do some work were the lucky ones. The changes were that if you took a broken watch to Harrods in those days it would be repaired in the "Palace."

For those who find themselves by circumstances "between two worlds" so to speak, there are always special problems. In my case, it happened that I was born in Germany in 1895 of parents living in England. My father, George Sauter, as a young painter, had emigrated to this country in 1889 where he

---

* This essay by Rudolf H. Sauter appeared posthumously in David Ball, ed., *The Experience of Prison: An Anthology of Prose, Drama, Verse and Picture* (London: Longman, 1977), 128–43.

hoped to find greater freedom than under the academic outlook of this native Munich. Here he married Lilian, elder sister of the author John Galsworthy, the creator of the Forsytes, and became involved in her traditional and near-Forsyte background. He made a career for himself, and our London home was open house for Artists, writers, musicians and men of distinction from all over the world. Here, too, he was able through his influence and connections to promote the interests of British artists at home and abroad. My parents were devoted, and we lived a full, happy and creative life, It was in this atmosphere that I was brought up and educated and which made what occurred later all the more distressing.

When the First Word War descended upon us, things were different. Prejudice was whipped up, our freedom restricted and my truly English mother was subjected to all kinds of ignominy. Even long-standing friends "passed by on the other side." It was at least some compensation to feel that they may have been embarrassed. But we had become Untouchables.

German by birth and with my father's nationality, English by up-bringing and my mother's heritage, to fight on either side against the other would have been for me unendurable torture. Fortunately I was spared this.

There were some who stood by us, of course, but whipped up by Press and propaganda such as was never known in the Second War, anti-German feeling became intense. It was not long before most of the so-called "Enemy Aliens"—even those married to British wives—were interned. My father, in spite of a long petition signed by fellow artists was escorted to Wakefield Camp. Here, though distressed beyond measure, he still managed to retain his sanity by painting, but was never able to reconcile himself to the treatment he had received from his adopted Country. Later he was sent back to Germany, under an arrangement for the exchange of elderly civilians over military age, and never lived in England again. Thus, though contact was always maintained, a family separation began which did not a little to accelerate my mother's early death in 1924.

In spite of my uncle's guarantee of good behaviour, as feeling grew more embittered, I also was arrested and escorted to Alexandra Palace.

I mention these things because similar experiences became for others as well the background of this particular aspect of Prison Life. It was distress of mind rather than body which undermined the spirit, for, unlike the Concentration Camps of the Second War, conditions in the Alexandra Palace were not unduly harsh—*in themselves*. It must be remembered that these "prisoners" were mostly elderly men, who had had voluntarily adopted this country as their home, had lived here many years and had spread their roots into her soil. They were deeply disturbed by the fate of their families, becoming more destitute, surrounded by a barrage of hate, for there was no dole, and many people would not employ the wives of "Huns." There was also the fear of molestation. It was a situation comparable to Nazi hatred of the Jews. Through my mother, who did what she could to help, I learned how desperate the plight could be of the families outside of men I came to know inside. Most of the internees had English-born children, some had had some in the forces. If their sons were killed, this amnesty no longer applied, and they were immediately interned. As a comparative youngster it did me the world of good and enlarged my outlook be concerned in all this, and I soon found myself crying out against the monstrous insanity of such things—and to question what was happening.

Though the Camp was under military control, most of the actual administration devolved on a Committee of the prisoners themselves, for we were not actually dangerous criminals! Prisoners were detailed for work in the extensive grounds and to maintain the tennis courts against better days. On these those who assisted in the administration were permitted to play. Surveillance was not over-strict and games were encouraged, at any rate in later years when I was there. Like every other group of people, forced to live huddled together in idleness and too great proximity for years, we organised sports and classes of anything and everything from Spanish and accountancy to fencing and single-stick. We got up a pantomime for the visiting children at Christmas, we held concerts of popular music, for there were a number of musicians, and we arranged film-shows of the flickering pictures of those days. These activities helped to distract us.

> But it was more than that, it was thought itself that mattered to keep us going ...
> ... little thought—mere atom of the sun
> that breathes in man—whom man has made to run
> and venture all, how bravely you set out! ...
> You little thought, behind our bars remaining,
> dear as freedom ... *You are* Freedom here.

Visits were allowed on certain days—and these were looked forward to as the climax of our lives. Families climbed painfully up, through the guard-house at the bottom, up the steep hill which led to the Palace, and arrived panting. The visits themselves took place in a large space, a small corner of which two other prisoners and myself had been allowed to curtain off and use as a studio. This was shut away from the main part of the building. Only certain innocuous things could be brought in, and all visitors were scrutinized by the military guards. But, of course, smuggling was carried on by all. I remember on one occasion the wife of a friend of mine, burst into our "studio" in a state of great alarm and embarrassment, clutching her bosom! "Eet ees zo hot, the butter eet ees melting. What shall I do? what shall I do? You must 'elp!"

Discovery would have led to reprisals on her husband, perhaps cancellation of the next visit or transfer to the Isle of Man Camp. However we eventually sorted it out, and she returned pacified to the visiting Area. It was easier to solve the "butter" problem than that of the lady whose bottle of red-wine, tied round her waist, became accidentally broken.

My uncle John Galsworthy, disgusted with the whole business, but powerless to do anything about it and anxious to discover personally what conditions were really like, allowed himself to be smuggled through while the guard's attention was being distracted, to make a tour of the whole building—and out again. The sight of that well-known and dignified figure, Creator of Forsytes, disguised as a prisoner and trying to look as inconspicuous as possible, was a sight to be seen to be believed. He was horrified by what he saw, and the experience provoked him to send me copies of his works—"the whole lot," as he put it in the accompanying letter, all personally inscribed, "To relieve the tedium of such surrounding." These books, however, were promptly censored as "Subversive Literature" and impounded, but not destroyed, so that we soon found means to smuggle them through—and they were widely read. This may have been the reason that he knew no protest would have been of any avail, if he had pressed for better conditions in the camp. Perhaps he realized that under the circumstances no better conditions were possible.

The "Big Hall," which alone housed some thousand men, was a dreadful place, in which no one could have either privacy or quiet, especially at night. Designed to accommodate symphony concerts and Handel's Messiah, it was hardly the most suitable place to house the thousand plank beds which jostled one another under the vast roof-space, and round each of which men erected little barriers or grey blanket, to provide some pretense of privacy. Moreover it was very cold and not entirely weather-proof ...

> Drip ... drip!—drip!
> A monster morgue, this,
> Framed in dusk,
> And, ranks on ranks
> Of "living corpses"
> On their planks! ...
>
> Thick, thick with smoke!
> A smudge of light—
> among shadows of thieving
> through the cold—
> a face shows white

Drip … drip!
No sleep!
Rain taps the floor,
the minutes lag,
the shadows toss,
rats creep
and gnaw the woodwork …

Sick … sick! …
a cough … another cough!
With stare like glass
one dream-torn creature
mutters—Light!
The rest is dark.

There were, however, other battalions, smaller halls with fewer men, where conditions were a little better, but not much. We were always hungry, of course and what little meat there was—was inevitably horse. We could write a certain number of letters—official letters—on specially prepared paper, which passed through the censor. But there was no end to the number of notes which could be smuggled out.

On the whole, as far as I remember it was nearly fifty years, the military eye was not *too* strict, and with the Commandant working members at least had reasonably good relations. In fact concessions could sometimes be obtained through those who worked in the office. In some ways we might be termed lucky, in others not—so much depends on the point of view.

In spite of the many personal tragedies, all thought became relative to what was happening elsewhere—the news of the fearful slaughter, which filtered through even into our isolation, though newspapers were not supposed to reach us. These events obsessed us even more because there was so much time to think about them. But our surroundings could not be ignored; and I was encouraged to try and record them in drawings and words—the people about me, whose personal miseries were so heart-rending. I tried to put down in line and word what was going on about me as War Artists in their way were portraying the horrors at the front. In all, I made some fifty drawings on the spot, in this camp and the one to which we were sent after the closure of hostilities, and wrote poems which were afterwards published as "SONGS IN CAPTIVITY" (Heinemann 1922, now out of print) in an attempt to give a picture of this little and perhaps forgotten corner of the major tragedy which was unfolding all round us. For, in the end, is not *Great Tragedy* only really measurable by all the small, personal, calamities of which it is composed?

> ... The letter shivered in his hand—
>   "She's been a good wife, understand ...
>   "and now?"
>   He tore the letter through.
>   "Was this the goal of four whole years"
>   "captivity?"
>   "How gay he'd been
>   "thinking of her!"
>   Now, idiot fears
> like caterpillars crawled (ugh!) green
> about his brain—
>   "Gone? Can't be true'"
> "An' me in 'ere!
>   "With 'khaki', too!"
> "My Missus! ... Christ!"
>   His face grew wan,
> his slow jaw striving to express
> he moved up and down—expressionless.
> Next morning, when the "Roll" was cried,
> they found him—on the wire, outside.

The main fear that obsessed us, as war began to draw to an end, was that we might be deported to Germany, a country from which so many of us had long been severed, and we should then be parted—perhaps forever—from those whom we loved and who might not be able to follow us. Some were sent away, others, like myself were spared. Every day the notice boards were anxiously scanned, to see if our names were on the dreaded list.

The total experience may not have been in any way comparable to that in the concentration camps and extermination centres of later years, but I think no one can have gone through it and failed to come out a somewhat differing being. As I look back in 1975 from the age of 80 years at the young fellow who went through the gate of that prison in 1918, I can only say how grateful I am to have had the experience. If, perhaps, one learned from close contact with others a touch more of compassion, it was not time wasted ... as I wrote in 1919:

> Have you ever seen a horse "dead-beat"
> that won't, because it can't move up the street?
> or even marked the apathy—and cried—
> to see the eyes of old dogs wandering
> along death's shore with feeble shaky feet?

or watched a cat, unwell and pondering
for hours on nothing? Ever noticed, too,
the hungry lounge of creatures in a Zoo
condemned in loneliness to run to seed—
and felt ashamed when they looked over you
at things you couldn't see ... while you, the freed,
went hurrying about—to watch them feed?

That's how they feel, who pass their days "inside."

* * *

Years of Captivity

Gold, that a mill-race
dusted world-over—gone
in the Forever!
where hunger is rich.

Chaff in the market-place
eddied and trampled-on—
days of endeavour
cast into the ditch!

Enemy Alien[*]

I have been asked to record my experience of war in connection with some drawings I made at Frimley POW[1] Camp, ironically enough six months after fighting ceased. But the after-effects of war may be, for some, as devastating as the war itself.

For those who are, so to speak, born between two worlds, there are always special problems. It happened that, by a curious combination of circumstances, I was born in the Bavarian mountains in 1895, of a German father and an English mother. My father, who became an internationally known artist, was engaged on a series of portraits and my mother was taking a cure, in Pfarrer Keeipp's famous Cold-water Establishment at the time. In a few months, when the work was completed, my parents returned to my mother's homeland, where I was brought up and with which I have always identified myself.

---

[*] This essay by Rudolf H. Sauter appeared posthumously in Michael Marland and Robin Willcox, eds. *While They Fought: An Anthology of Prose and Verse Exploring the Lives of Those Who Did Not Fight, but Who Had to Endure the Second World War* (London: Longman, 1980), 86–94.

1. Prisoner of war.

When the 1914 war broke out, I was a young man of nineteen years, who found himself between the jaws of two opposing forces: born in Germany and with my father's nationality and yet English by upbringing and my mother's almost "Forsyte" heritage, for she was a sister of John Galsworthy.[2] In these circumstances I was indeed fortunate in not being called upon to fight for either side against the other, which would have been intolerable. But it was a tremendous shock, and in the despite of youth I voiced my agony:

> My God! How I loved the great sky,
> the big wind running across the stars,
> the light of suns tossed on the sea,
> and stillness, too!
> Then—out of the sky tumbling—raucous Death!
>
> its very vileness stinking on the wind—
> Death in the world, aping the form of man
> who terribly gave birth to this mad child.

and, questioning the whole situation, continued:

> Am I that man? For, that I am a man,
> Oh God!—could I
> have helped to bring about this awful thing?
>
> But, after it, what then? Will there be light again?
> will there be song of birds, and will the sight
> of loveliness return to man again
> after he's felt the savagery of pain?
> Is there forgiveness for this awful dearth
> of love … or do I dream?
>
> Whatever man has done—
> there *must* be beauty, and who says there's none
> has bound his eye and cannot find the knot.
> Forgive me—God!
> I, too, have seen it and perceived it *not*.

In the context of today, with its even more callous disregard for the sanctity of human life, such words seem perhaps rather naïve, but as an expression of emotion at that moment, it may be they were not over-emphatic.

---

2. Author of the series of novels about the Forsyte family, *The Forsyte Saga*.

My parents were both people of great integrity, with international views, artistically, philosophically and spiritually inclined and regarding peace in the world as a prime condition of life. Now restricted to a five-mile radius, shunned by people whom they had been accustomed to regard as friends, under police supervision (not unfriendly, be it said), we had nevertheless become untouchables. We could not separate suffering into national compartments—we mourned for both sides and could share the meaning of the words of Wilfred Owen found after his death at the front among his papers, and so movingly used by Benjamin Britten in his Requiem: "I am the enemy you killed, my friend."

It was not long before my father was interned, though for the time being I was spared, on compassionate grounds, to be near my mother whose health was already a source of anxiety. Immersed in the little oasis of my home, confronted by the threatened eclipse of all that I held most dear, bewildered by the prejudice and aura of hatred with which we were surrounded, and unable to resolve this mystery by participation in any outside activity, I felt that the only way to retain sanity was to occupy this period of idleness with something creative. Encouraged by my parents and one or two remaining friends, I was able to continue painting scenes of the London surrounding me, and to write poems and songs in which to express something of that which was uppermost in the mind, and thereby sublimate to some extent the immediate misery. One of my main relaxations was a visit to the Proms, then in the old Queen's Hall, where thanks to Sir Henry's[3] blunt refusal to be influenced by public opinion, the "Three B's" (Bach, Brahms and Beethoven) had been saved from deportation and were still being played.

Meanwhile, the knowledge of what my father must be going through after all he had done at home and abroad to further the interests of British artists, added to war conditions, further affected my mother's health.

At length, however, as the tide of hatred grew, I too was interned.

I have described in more detail elsewhere (in *The Experience of Prison*, Longman Imprint Books) my experience of Alexandra Palace, the Civilian POW Camp for Enemy Aliens married to British wives, in which I was permitted to stay, though unmarried, on compassionate grounds … the noise, the veritable din, the impossibility of any privacy, the squalor of men who, surrounded by hatred, had lost all pride or sense of being, the misery and degradation of those from whom all hope faded after four years of segregation—all that was appalling for those with whom for a mere 15 months I shared internment. That was one side of war. I was at least able to spend much of my time describing and recording it in drawings. It may not have been one of the most spectacular aspects of war, but it was one which left its mark on those who endured it.

---

3. Sir Henry Wood, founder of the Promenade Concerts in London.

The sketches reproduced here were made at Frimley, an arid, wire-enclosed and tented transit camp, to which we were transferred when the Alexandra Palace was closed down some time after the Armistice.

> This bramble-thicket, sprung up overnight
> on the clean earth, unflowering! In the dusk
> some mad end, loosened, taps upon its pole—
> steel thorns tapping—ghosts of dead delight!
>
> Wire … wire! Barbed wire! Behind this dour
> and monstrous serpent round our lives
> we are like creatures mesmerised—
> It glares at us all day, malignant—sour.
>
> "No-man's-land"—where other creatures creep,
> can love and dance together,
> flowers grow unspoiled and crickets cheep,
> birds sing in silent weather!
>
> Fifteen feet of crouching coils to lock
> men out from heaven's wonder!
> And yet, each evening, grey moths come to mock
> and conjure it asunder!

Here we existed more healthily perhaps, but exposed to the torrid heat and swirling sandstorms of that hottest of summers. Here we looked at through the barbed wire at an uncertain future—whether to be allowed to stay in this country, near those we loved, or be deported to Germany to which they might not be able to follow and which to many of us represented a foreign and possibly hostile country. "To be or not to be"—the uncertainty was the hardship.

When at last I was released from Frimley and allowed to return home it was five years before it was possible to become a "nationalized" British subject. We settled down to life in a sort of limbo. I married Viola who had lived with and looked after my mother during my absence and had shared our troubles. Then, overcome by the protracted separation from my father, her health undermined by war-time conditions and a recent operation, my mother died at the early age of 60.

But now, rejected by both Germany (because I had applied to become British) and England (who would not yet accept me), we were stateless and, with appropriate irony, were obliged to travel abroad on Nansen Passports, issued to those without nationality, which guaranteed us nothing and were scrutinized with suspicion by officials at all frontiers.

I was old enough to have been involved in both world wars, but in neither was I destined to become a combatant. The second war posed quite different problems, for I was now a British subject too old to be called up, but again had occasion to see what misery war can bring. In the first war it had been to families divided by national cleavages, in the second to those separated by war from those on active service. It was my job, as an Army Welfare Officer under South Eastern Command, to visit the personnel of remote ack-ack[4] and searchlight sites clustered round the south coast, and to become involved in their welfare and that of their families. I shared their anxieties as the fleets of German bombers growled overhead on their way to London. I visited the wives and children of those from my area who were sent overseas, and whose concern about them sometimes required compassionate leave. It was my turn now to try and heal the wounds which separation brings. These were men cut off from life—not prisoners—human beings isolated from the experience of life and thrust bewildered into the experience of war.

> As war comes and goes
> blowing our cities out
> like candles guttering
> in the winds of hate—
>
> Down the long world reduced we are
> timed to the worm and the weed,
> for the great gold beak of the "Hate-Bird"
> Still pecks at the worm and the seed.

---

4. Nick-name for anti-aircraft fire.

SELECTED BIBLIOGRAPHY

Archival Sources

Archives of American Art, Smithsonian Institution
    Kraushaar Galleries records, 1885–2006
The Bancroft Library, University of California, Berkeley
    Rudolf H. Sauter correspondence with Michael Harrison and related papers, 1926–1976.
Britten Pears Arts
    Papers of Benjamin Britten
Cadbury Library, University of Birmingham
    Papers of Rudolf H. Sauter, Viola Sauter, Ada Galsworthy, and John Galsworthy
Department of Special Collections, Princeton University Library
    Papers of Harrison S. Morris
Department of Special Collections and University Archives, University of Tulsa
    PEN Archive, 1932–83
Gloucestershire Archives
    Official records pertaining to Rudolf H. Sauter and archive of *Stroud News and Journal*
Harrow School
    Harrow School Archive
Harry Ransom Humanities Research Center, The University of Texas at Austin
    Papers of Robert Haven Schauffler
The Huntington Library, Art Museum, and Botanical Gardens
    Papers of Wilfred Partington
Imperial War Museum, London
    Private papers and artwork of Rudolf H. Sauter
Joyner Library, East Carolina University
    Papers of Inglis Fletcher
National Army Museum
    Artwork of Rudolf H. Sauter
Phillips Exeter Academy Archives and Special Collections
    Papers of John Masefield
Research and Cultural Collections, University of Birmingham
    Artwork of George Sauter and Rudolf H. Sauter
Royal Air Force Museum
    Artwork of Rudolf H. Sauter

Special Collections, University of Glasgow
    Papers of the International Society of Sculptors, Painters and Gravers
Taylor Institution Library, Oxford University
    Letters of Rudolf H. Sauter, Georg Sauter, Lilian Sauter, Valda Sauter, and Friedrich Max Müller
U.K. National Archives
    Home Office (H.O.) 144, Nationality and Naturalization

Published Sources

Allen, Tony. *British Prisoners of War 1914–1918*. York: Holgate, 1999.
Anglo-German Family History Society. *An Insight into Civilian Internment in Britain during World War I from the Diary of Richard Noschke and a Short Essay by Rudolf Rocker*. Maidenhead, Berkshire: Anglo-German Family History Society Publications, 2002.
"The Army Welfare Officer." *Spectator*. December 12, 1941, 14.
Ashplant, T. G., Graham Dawson and Michael Roper, eds. *The Politics of War Memory and Commemoration*. London: Routledge, 2013.
Auslander, Leora, and Tara Zahra, eds. *Objects of War: The Material Culture of Conflict and Displacement*. London: Cornell University Press, 2018.
Baker, Elizabeth. *Printers and Technology. A History of the International Printing Pressmen and Assistants' Union*. New York: Columbia University Press, 1957.
Ball, David, ed. *The Experience of Prison: An Anthology of Prose, Drama, Verse and Picture*. London: Longman, 1977.
Barker, A. J. *Prisoners of War*. New York: Universe Books, 1975.
Barker, Dudley. *The Man of Principle: A Biography of John Galsworthy*. New York: Stein and Day, 1963.
Bellony-Rewald, Alice, and Michael Peppiatt. *Imagination's Chamber: Artists and Their Studios*. London: Gordon Fraser, 1983.
Bird, J. C. *Control of Enemy Alien Civilians in Great Britain, 1914–1918*. New York: Garland, 1986.
Birmingham University Library. *The Galsworthy Papers: Handlist of Papers Deposited in Birmingham University Library by the Bequest of R.H. Sauter, Esq*. Birmingham: Birmingham University Library, 1978.
Boddice, Eric, ed. *Pain and Emotion in Modern History*. New York: Palgrave, 2014.
Boime, Albert. "Georg Sauter and the *Bridal Morning*." *American Art Journal* 2, no. 2 (1970): 72–80.
Brandon, Laura. *Art and War*. London: I.B. Tauris, 2007.
Bryans, Dennis. "The Double Invention of Printing." *Journal of Design History* 13, no. 4 (2000): 287–300.
Buckley, Anne. *German Prisoners of the Great War: Life in a Yorkshire Camp*. Barnsley, South Yorkshire: Pen and Sword Books, 2021.
Buren, Daniel. "The *Function of the Studio*." Translated by Thomas Repensek. *October* 10 (Fall 1979): 51–59.
Burke, Peter. *Eyewitnessing: The Uses of Images as Historical Evidence*. London: Reaktion Books, 2001.
Burton, Stacy. *Travel Narratives and the Ends of Modernity*. Cambridge: Cambridge University Press, 2014.
Bush, Harold K. "Cradling Lives in Our Hands: Towards a Theory of Cultural Biography." *Christianity and Literature* 57, no. 1 (2007): 111–29.

Butt, Maggie. *Ally Pally Prison Camp*. Devon: Oversteps Books, 2011.
C.W. Kraushaar Art Galleries, *Exhibition of Paintings and Lithographs by R.H. Sauter, April 14–30, 1928*. New York: C.W. Kraushaar art Galleries, 1928.
———. *Paintings, Drawings and Etchings by Rudolf H. Sauter, 30 March to 11 April, 1931*. New York: C.W. Kraushaar Art Galleries, 1931.
Cain, Barbara. *Biography and History*. Basingstoke: Macmillan Education, 2010.
Carr, Gillian, and H. C. Mytum. *Cultural Heritage and Prisoners of War: Creativity behind Barbed Wire*. New York: Routledge, 2012.
Cesarani, David, and Tony Kushner. *The Internment of Aliens in Twentieth Century Britain*. London: Routledge, 1993.
Celant, Germano. *Book as Artwork 1960–1972*. Brooklyn: 6 Decades Books, 2010.
Colton, Harold S. *Hopi Kachina Dolls with a Key to their Identification*. Albuquerque: University of New Mexico Press, 1959.
Conn, Peter J. *Pearl S. Buck: A Cultural Biography*. Cambridge University Press, 1998.
Conrad, Joseph. *The Collected Letters of Joseph Conrad*. Cambridge: Cambridge University Press, 1983.
Cooper, Robert M. *The Literary Guide & Companion to Southern England*. Athens, Ohio: Ohio University Press, 1985.
Cope, Bill, and Diana Kalantzis, eds. *Print and Electronic Text Convergence*. Champaign, IL: Common Ground, 2001.
Crang, Jeremy A. *The British Army and the People's War, 1939–1945*. Manchester: Manchester University Press, 2000.
Crawford, Elizabeth. *The Women's Suffrage Movement: A Reference Guide 1866–1928*. London: Routledge, 2001.
Cresswell, Yvonne M., ed. *Living with the Wire: Civilian Internment in the Isle of Man during the Two World Wars*. Douglas, Isle of Man: Manx National Heritage, 1994.
Crawford, Elizabeth. *The Women's Suffrage Movement: A Reference Guide 1866–1928*.
Csikszentmihalyi, Mihaly, and Eugene Halton. *The Meaning of Things: Domestic Symbols and the Self*. Cambridge: Cambridge University Press, 1981.
Culkin, Kate. *Harriet Hosmer: A Cultural Biography*. Amherst: University of Massachusetts Press, 2010.
Dakers, Caroline. *The Holland Park Circle: Artists and Victorian Society*. New Haven, CT: Yale University Press, 1999.
Das, Santanu, ed. *The Cambridge Companion to the Poetry of the First World War*. Cambridge: Cambridge University Press, 2013.
Dearinger, David B. *Paintings and Sculpture in the Collection of the National Academy of Design, 1826–1925*. Manchester, VT: Hudson Hills, 2004.
DiCenzo, M., Leila Ryan and Lucy Delap, eds. *Feminist Media History: Suffrage, Periodicals and the Public Sphere*. London: Palgrave Macmillan, 2010.
Dixon, Joy. *Divine Feminine: Theosophy and Feminism in England*. Baltimore, MD: Johns Hopkins University Press, 2001.
Dominic Winter Auctioneers, *Fine Art & Antiques, 29 June 2016* (catalogue). Cirencester: Dominic Winter Auctioneers, 2016.
Dove, Richard. *"Totally Un-English"?: Britain's Internment of "Enemy Aliens" in Two World Wars*. Amsterdam: Rodopi, 2005.
Drucker, Johanna. *The Century of Artists' Books*. New York: Granary Books, 2004.
Dupré, Catherine. *John Galsworthy: A Biography*. New York: Coward, McCann & Geoghegan, 1976.

Durey, Jill Felicity. "Alien Internment in John Galsworthy's 'The Bright Side' and 'The Dog It Was That Died.'" *Literature & History* 30, no. 1 (May 2021): 45–61. https://doi.org/10.1177/03061973211007349.

Einhaus, Ann-Marie, and Katherine I. Baxter, eds. *Edinburgh Companion to the First World War and the Arts*. Edinburgh: Edinburgh University Press, 2017.

Evans, Martin. *War and Memory in the Twentieth Century*. London: Bloomsbury Academic, 1997.

Fahlman, Betsy. *Kraushaar Galleries: Celebrating 125 Years*. New York: Kraushaar Galleries, 2010.

Feltman, Brian K. *The Stigma of Surrender: German Prisoners, British Captors, and Manhood in the Great War and Beyond*. Chapel Hill: University of North Carolina Press, 2015.

The Fine Art Society. *Rudolf Sauter, 1985–1979 [sic] Internment Drawings—Alexandra Palace 1918–19, 7–25 June 1993*. London: The Fine Art Society, 1993.

Fletcher, Inglis. *The Story of My Life: Pay, Pack and Follow*. New York: Henry Holt, 1959.

Fréchet, Alec. *John Galsworthy: A Reassessment*. Totowa, NJ: Barnes & Noble Books, 1982.

Ford, Ford Madox. *Memories and Impressions*. Harmondsworth: Penguin Books, 1979.

Foss, Brian. *War Paint: Art, War, State and Identity in Britain 1938–1945*. London: Yale University Press, 2007.

Fosse, Marit, and John Fox. *Nansen: Explorer and Humanitarian*. Lanham, MD: Rowman & Littlefield, 2015.

Fussell, Paul. *The Great War and Modern Memory*. Oxford: Oxford University Press, 1975.

———. *Abroad: British Literary Traveling Between the Wars*. Oxford: Oxford University Press, 1980.

Galsworthy, Ada. *Ex Libris: John Galsworthy*. London: William Heinemann, 1933.

———. *The Dear Dogs*. London: William Heinemann, 1935.

———. *Over the Hills and Far Away*. New York: Scribner's Sons, 1938.

Galsworthy, Jocelyn. *White Hats and Cricket Bats: My Painting life*. Shrewsbury, England: Swan Hill Press, 2000.

Galsworthy, John. *Awakening*. New York: Charles Scribner's Sons, 1922

———. *Ex Libris*. London: William Heinemann, 1933.

———. *Memories*. New York: Charles Scribner's Sons, 1918.

———. *The Works of John Galsworthy*. Manaton edition. With plates, including portraits. London: William Heinemann, 1923.

Gardiner, John. *The World of Netlam Bigg: A Centenary Celebration*. Stroud: J. F. Gardiner, 1999.

Gardner, Brian, ed. *Up the Line to Death: The War Poets, 1914–1918*. London: Methuen, 1964.

George Graham and His Creation Paintings: Appreciations and Extracts from His Letters. London: W. P. Griffith and Sons, 1952.

Gianfaldoni, Serena, Georgi Tchernev, Uwe Wollina, Maria Grazia Roccia, Massimo Fioranelli, Roberto Gianfaldoni, and Torello Lotti. "History of the Baths and Thermal Medicine." *Open Access Macedonian Journal of Medical Sciences* 5 no. 4 (2017): 566–68.

Gindin, James. *The English Climate: An Excursion in a Biography of John Galsworthy*. Ann Arbor: University of Michigan Press, 1979.

———. *John Galsworthy's Life and Art: An Alien's Fortress*. Ann Arbor: University of Michigan Press, 1987.

Goodrich, John. "The Private Language of Painting, Revealed in Artists' Images of Their Studios," Hyperallergic, April 13, 2015, https://hyperallergic.com/198769/the-private-language-of-painting-revealed-in-artists-images-of-their-studios/.

Gray, H. Branston. *The Public Schools and the Empire*. London: Williams & Norgate, 1913.

Friends of Stocks Mill. *A Guide to Stocks Mill, Wittersham, Kent*. Wittersham, Kent: Friends of Stocks Mill, 1995.

Gutman, Robert W. *Mozart: A Cultural Biography*. Boston, MA: Houghton Mifflin Harcourt, 1999.
Hammond, Mary, and Shafquat Towheed, eds. *Publishing in the First World War: Essays in Book History*. London: Palgrave Macmillan, 2007.
Hanley, James. *The German Prisoner*. Holstein, Ontario: Exile Editios, 2006.
Harris, Frederick, ed. *Service with Fighting Men: An Account of the Work of the American Young Men's Christian Associations in the World War*. New York: Association Press, 1922.
Harry Moore-Gwyn British Pictures. *Rudolf Sauter: Observations from Nature, Spring 1916*. Exhibtion as part of stand C6, Art Antiques London, June 12–19, 2013. London: Harry Moore-Gwyn British Pictures, 2013.
Harvey, Charles, and John Press, "The Ionides Family and 1 Holland Park." *Journal of the Decorative Arts Society* 18 (1994): 2–14.
Hill, Jeffrey. *Sport, Leisure and Culture in Twentieth-Century Britain*. Houndmills: Palgrave, 2002.
Historic England. "1, Holland Park Avenue." Accessed December 23, 2016. https://historicengland.org.uk/listing/the-list/list-entry/1380239.
Hoare, G. G. "Delius Slept Here?" *Delius Society Journal* 54 (January 1977): 6–7.
Hoffmann, Jens. *The Studio: Documents in Contemporary Art*. London: Whitechapel Gallery and the MIT Press, 2012.
Hoffmann, Jens, and Christina Kennedy, eds. *The Studio*. Dublin: Dublin City Gallery The Hugh Lane, 2007.
Hogg, Jonathan. *British Nuclear Culture: Official and Unofficial Narratives in the Long 20th Century*. London: Bloomsbury, 2016.
Hoppé, E.O. *The Book of the Exhibition of New Camera Work by E.O. Hoppé*. London: Goupil Gallery/Millais House, 1922.
Howell, Patrick. *Consistently Brilliant on a Breezy Hilltop: A History of the Cotswold Players, The First 100 Years*. United Kingdom: Quicksilver, 2016.
Hudson, Edward, ed. *Poetry of the First World War*. London: Wayland, 1989.
"Humphrey Spender." *Independent*. Accessed December 30, 2013. http://www.independent.co.uk/news/obituaries/humphrey-spender-6053.html.
Hunt, Nigel C. *Memory, War and Trauma*. Cambridge: Cambridge University Press, 2010.
Hynes, Samuel. *The Edwardian Turn of Mind*. Princeton, NJ: Princeton University Press, 1968.
Isherwood, Ian. *Remembering the Great War: Writing and Publishing the Experiences of World War I*. London: Bloomsbury, 2017.
"Inside the Artist's Studio." Art History Today. Accessed December 20, 2020. https://artintheblood.typepad.com/art_history_today/2011/05/inside-the-artists-studio.html.
Jackson, Robert. *The Prisoners, 1914–18*. London: Routledge, 1989.
Jones. Edgar, and Simon Wessely. "British Prisoners-of-War: From Resilience to Psychological Vulnerability: Reality or Perception." *Twentieth Century British History* 21, no. 2 (2010): 163–83.
Jones, Heather. *Violence against Prisoners of War in the First World War: Britain, France and Germany, 1914–1920*. Cambridge: Cambridge University Press, 2011.
Karman, James. *The Collected Letters of Robinson Jeffers, with Selected Letters of Una Jeffers: Volume Two, 1931–1939*. Stanford University Press, 2011.
Keenan, James P. *The Art of the Bookplate*. New York: Barnes and Noble Books, 2003.
Kern, Stephen. *The Culture of Love: Victorians to Moderns*. Boston, MA: Harvard University Press, 1998.
Kirkby, Mandy, ed. *Love Letters of the Great War*. London: Macmillan, 2014.

Kirwin, Liza, and Joan Lord, eds. *Artists in Their Studios: Images from the Smithsonian's Archives of American Art*. New York: Collins Design, 2007.

Lago, Don. "Haunted by Time: British Writers Discover the Grand Canyon." *Ol' Pioneer: The Magazine of the Grand Canyon Historical Society* 25, no. 2 (Spring 2014): 6–15.

Lampe, Lilly. "What Goes On in the Artist's Studio." *New Yorker*, April 16, 2015. https://www.newyorker.com/culture/photo-booth/what-goes-on-in-the-artists-studio.

LeBourdais, George Philip. "A Brief History of the Artist's Studio." Accessed December 20, 2020. https://www.artsy.net/article/artsy-editorial-why-do-we-care-about-an-artist-s-studio.

Leeds City Art Gallery, *Catalogue of the Permanent Collection of Paintings and Drawings*. Leeds: City Art Gallery, 1900.

Leonard, Trevor. "'Guilded Squalor': An Evaluation of Francis Bacon's 7 Reece Mews Studio." Irish Georgian Society. https://www.igs.ie/education/list/category/trinity-college-dublin/p6.

Lerner, Paul. *Hysterical Men: War, Psychiatry, and the Politics of Trauma in Germany, 1890-1930*. Ithaca, NY: Cornell University Press, 2003.

Leslie, Henrietta. *Go as You Please: Memories of People and Places*. London: Macdonald, 1946.

———. *More Ha'Pence Than Kicks, Being Some Things Remembered*. London: MacDonald, 1943.

"The Little-Known Passport That Protected 450,000 Refugees." Atlas Obscura. Accessed December 20, 2020. https://www.atlasobscura.com/articles/nansen-passport-refugees.

Local Army Welfare Officer [pseud.]. "Six Years of Army Welfare." *Journal of the Royal United Services Institution* 91, no. 561 (1946): 52–55. http://www.tandfonline.com/doi/abs/10.1080/03071844609433898.

Lochnan, Katharine. *Holman Hunt and the Pre-Raphaelite Vision*. Toronto: Art Gallery of Toronto, 2008.

Llewellyn, Sacha, and Paul Liss, eds. *World War II War Pictures by British Artists*. Published on the occasion of the exhibition at Morley College London. October 28–November 23, 2016. London: Zenith Media, 2016.

Malafronte, Allison. "The History of the Plein Air Movement." *American Artist* (October 2009): 20–24.

Malvern Public Library. *Pictures by C. W. Edwards, R.B.A., R.I. and R.H. Sauter, R.B.A., R.I.*, April 1–22, 1950. Worcestershire: Malvern Public Library, 1950.

Mangan, J. A., ed. *"Benefits Bestowed"?: Education and British Imperialism*. Manchester: Manchester University Press, 1988.

Mark, Graham. *Prisoners of War in British Hands during World War I: A Study of Their History, the Campus and Their Mails*. Exeter: Short Run Press, 2007.

Marland, Michael, and Robin Willcox, *While They Fought: An Anthology of Prose and Verse Exploring the Lives of Those Who Did Not Fight, but Who Had to Endure the Second World War*. London: Longman, 1980.

Marrot, H. V. *The Life and Letters of John Galsworthy*. London: William Heinemann, 1935.

Marshall, Alan. *Changing the Word: The Printing Industry in Transition*. London: Comedia, 1983.

Masefield, John. *The Taking of the Gry*. London: William Heinemann, 1934.

"Memories of Galsworthy." *Listener*. August 10, 1967, 166–67.

Merrill, Linda. *The Peacock Room: A Cultural Biography*. London: Yale University Press, 1998.

Metropolitan Museum of Modern Art. *A Century of Artists Books. 23 October 1994–24 January 1995*. Accessed December 20, 2020. https://www.moma.org/calendar/exhibitions/439.

Micale, Mark S., and Paul Lerner, eds. *Traumatic Pasts: History, Psychiatry and Trauma in the Modern Age, 1870–1930*. Cambridge: Cambridge University Press, 2010.

Minford, John, and Claire Roberts, eds. *China Heritage Quarterly*, special issue on Zhai, the Scholar's Studio, number 13 (March 2008). http://www.chinaheritagequarterly.org/editorial.php?issue=013.

Mottram, Ralph Hale. *For Some We Loved: An Intimate Portrait of Ada and John Galsworthy*. London: Hutchinson, 1956.

Moynihan, Michael. *Black Bread and Barbed Wire: Prisoners in the First World War*. London: Cooper, 1978.

Mytum. Harold, and Gilly Carr, eds. *Prisoners of War: Archaeology, Memory and Heritage of 19th- and 20th-Century Mass Internment*. New York: Springer-Verlag, 2013.

"Nansen Passport." Dead Media Archive. Accessed December 20, 2020. http://culturea ndcommunication.org/deadmedia/index.php/Nansen_Passport.

"Nansen—a Man of Action and Vision." UNHCR. Accessed December 20, 2020. https://www.unhcr.org/en-us/events/nansen/4aae50086/nansen-man-action-vision.html?query=nansen.

Neiswander, Judy. *The Cosmopolitan Interior: Liberalism and the British Home 1870–1914*. New Haven, CT: Yale University Press, 2008.

Nelson, Carolyn C., ed. *Literature of the Women's Suffrage Campaign in England*. Peterborough, Ontario: Broadview Press, 2004.

Noakes, Lucy, and Juliette Pattinson, eds. *British Cultural Memory and the Second World War*. London: A&C Black, 2013.

Orlando Project. "Gladys Henrietta Schütze." Accessed July 17, 2014. http://orlando.cambridge.org/public/svPeople?person_id=schugl.

Owen, Joan M. "John Galsworthy: Radical Edwardian or Proto-Modernist?" PhD diss., Edge Hill University, 2016. https://research.edgehFigureac.uk/en/studentTheses/john-galsworthy-radical-edwardian-or-proto-modernist.

Panayi, Panikos. *Prisoners of Britain: German Civilian and Combatant Internees during the First World War*. Manchester: Manchester University Press, 2012.

Parsons, Ian. *Men Who March Away: Poems of the First World War*. New York: Viking Press, 1965.

Pathé, Anne-Marie, and Fabien Théofilakism. *Wartime Captivity in the Twentieth Century: Archives, Stories, Memories*. New York: Berghahn Books, 2016.

Pennell, E. R., and J. Pennell. *The Whistler Journal*. Philadelphia, PA: J. B. Lippincott, 1921.

Plamper, Jan, and Keith Tribe. *The History of Emotions: An Introduction*. Oxford: Oxford University Press, 2015.

Powell, Anthony. *Under Review: Further Writings on Writers, 1946–1990*. Chicago: University of Chicago Press, 1994.

Pugh, Martin. *Women and the Women's Movement in Britain since 1914*. London: Palgrave,

Rachamimov, Alon. *POWs and the Great War: Captivity on the Eastern Front*. Oxford: Berg, 2002.

Reynolds, Mabel Edith. *Memories of John Galsworthy*. London: Robert Hale, 1936.

Reznick, Jeffrey S. *John Galsworthy and Disabled Soldiers of the Great War: With an Illustrated Selection of His Writings*, Manchester: Manchester University Press, 2009.

Richardson, Phyllis. *The House of Fiction: From Pemberley to Brideshead, Great British Houses in Literature and Life*. London: Random House, 2017.

Robbins, Keith. *Great Britain: Identities, Institutions and the Idea of Britishness*. London: Longman, 1988.

Roper, Michael. *The Secret Battle: Emotional Survival in the Great War*. Manchester: Manchester University Press, 2009.

Rotberg, Robert I., and Theodore K. Rabb. *Art and History: Images and Their Meaning.* Cambridge: Cambridge University Press, 1986.

Roth, Michael S. *Memory, Trauma and History: Essays on Living with the Past.* New York: Columbia University Press, 2012.

Royal Blue Book: Fashionable Directory and Parliamentary Guide. London: Kelly's Directories, 1899.

Ruedy, Ralph H. "Ford Madox Ford and the English Review." Doctoral thesis, Department of English, Duke University, 1976.

Sanderson, I. C. M. *A History of Elstree School and Three Generations of the Sanderson Family.* Privately printed, 1979.

Sauter, Lilian. *Through High Windows.* London: Curtis and Davison, 1911.

Sauter, Rudolf H. *Crie de Coeur.* Stroud: Stroud Typewriting, Rotaprinting and Duplicating Service, 1968.

———. *Erda: Poem for the Earth, The Trial of Man: A Masque for 1972.* Self-published, unknown printer, 1972.

———. *The Fifth Hunger.* Self-published, unknown printer, 1971.

———. *Galsworthy the Man: An Intimate Portrait.* London: Peter Owen, 1967.

———. *The Grand Canyon: How These Pictures Came to Be Painted, 1975–76. Journey Into Color. Reflections After 80.* Nympsfield, Gloucestershire: Nimsfeilde Press, 1976.

———. *The Loving Cup.* Stroud: Stroud Typewriting, Rotaprinting and Duplicating Service, 1977.

———. *Songs in Captivity.* London: William Heinemann, 1922.

———. *The Soothing Wind.* Stroud: Stroud Typewriting, Rotaprinting and Duplicating Service, 1969.

Sauter, Rudolf H., and Viola Sauter, *Book of the Studio.* Bury, Sussex: privately compiled, 1931–32.

Schäfer, Peter. "Georg Sauter und seine Jenaer Professorenporträts." *Das Kulturhistorische Archive von Weimar – Jena* 1/2 (2008): 97–109.

Small, Ian. "Special Collections Report: The Galsworthy Collection and Its Fate." *English Literature in Transition, 1880–1920* 27, no. 3 (1984): 236–38.

Smith, Carrie, and Lisa Stead, eds. *The Boundaries of the Literary Archive: Reclamation and Representation.* London: Routledge, 2013.

Smith, Robert F. W., and Gemma L. Watson, *Writing the Lives of People and Things, AD 500–1700.* London: Taylor and Francis, 2016.

Spiller, G. *The Ethical Movement in Great Britain.* London: Parleigh Press, 1934. http://archive.org/details/ethicalmovementi029667mbp.

Stalla, Bernhard J. *Lebenswege eines Malers und Zeichners: George Sauter.* Brannenburg: Peter Drexler, 2011.

Stein, Jesse A. "Masculinity and Material Culture in Technological Transitions: From Letterpress to Offset Lithography, 1960s–1980s." *Technology and Culture* 57, no. 1 (January 2016):, 24–53.

Stibbe, Matthew. *Civilian Internment during the First World War: A European and Global History, 1914–1920.* London: Palgrave Macmillan, 2019.

Stroud Festival. *Festival Poems.* Stroud, Gloucestershire: Stroud Festival Poetry Committee, 1967.

Stumpf, Rudolf. *Zwischen Deutschland und England: Die Geschichte des Malers Georg Sauter.* Berlin: Deutscher Kunstverlag, 1940.

Tames, Richard. *London: A Cultural History.* Oxford: Oxford University Press, 2006.

Taylor, Alex. *Perils of the Studio: Inside the Artistic Affairs of Bohemian Melbourne*. North Melbourne, Victoria: Australian Scholarly Publishing, 2007.
Tebbutt, Melanie. *Making Youth: A History of Youth in Modern Britain*. London: Palgrave, 2016.
Thompson, Carl. *The Routledge Companion to Travel Writing*. London: Routledge, 2012.
Thompson, Paul. *The Edwardians: The Remaking of British Society*. London: Weidenfeld & Nicolson, 1975.
Twyman, Michael. *The British Library Guide to Printing: History and Techniques*. Toronto: University of Toronto Press, 1998.
Tyerman, Christopher. *A History of Harrow School, 1324–1991*. Oxford: Oxford University Press, 2000.
Tylee, Claire M., ed. *Great War and Women's Consciousness: Images of Militarism and Womanhood*. London: Palgrave, 1990.
United Artists' Exhibition in Aid of the Lord Mayor's Red Cross and St. John Fund and the Artists'General Benevolent Institution. London: Royal Academy of Arts, 1940.
The Second United Artists' Exhibition in Aid of H.R.H. The Duke of Gloucester's Red Cross and St. John Fund and the Artists'General Benevolent Institution. London: Royal Academy of Arts, 1942.
The Third United Artists' Exhibition in Aid of H.R.H. The Duke of Gloucester's Red Cross and St. John Fund [and the Artists'General Benevolent Institution. London: Royal Academy of Arts, 1943.
University of Glasgow. "The Correspondence of James McNeill Whistler." Accessed July 27, 2015. http://www.whistler.arts.gla.ac.uk/correspondence/people/biog/?bid=Saut_G&initial=S.
Vanderpool, Derek, Vivian Wang and Jonathan Fetter-Vorm. *Never Such Innocence: British Images of the First World War*. Published in conjunction with the exhibition held at the Hoover Institution Library and Archives, January 10–March 1, 2008. Menlo Park, CA: American Printing, 2008.
Vischer, A. L. *Barbed Wire Disease: A Psychological Study of the Prisoner of War*. London: John Bales, Sons & Danielson, 1919.
Wallace, Ian. "The Evolution of the Artist's Studio, from Renaissance Bottege to Assembly Line." Artspace, June 14, 2011. https://www.artspace.com/magazine/art_101/art_market/the-evolution-of-the-artists-studio-52374.
Walling, John. *The Internment and Treatment of German Nationals during the First World War*. Great Grimsby: Lincolnshire: Riparian, 2008.
White, Eric Walter. *Silver Jubilee Stroud Festival. 10–24 October 1971*. Stroud: Stroud Festival, 1971.
Wikipedians, "Windmills in Kent. Mainz." Germany: PediaPress, n.d.
Wilkinson, Oliver. *British Prisoners of War in First World War Germany*. Cambridge: Cambridge University Press, 2017.
Wilkinson, Tom. "Typology: Artist Studio," *Architectural Review*, February 17, 2017. https://www.architectural-review.com/essays/typology-artist-studio/10017316.article.
Wohl, Robert. *The Generation of 1914*. Boston, MA: Harvard University Press, 1979.
Yarnall, John. *Barbed Wire Disease: British & German Prisoners of War, 1914–19*. Stroud: History Press, 2011.
Zuelow, Eric G. E. *A History of Modern Tourism*. London: Palgrave, 2016.

INDEX

The Aberdeen Press and Journal 81
After the Raid (ca. 1940) 125–27
Alexandra Palace 44–45, 48–62, 112, 171, 186–87, 193, 194
Aliens Restriction Act 41
"And a lovely smell of whitewash" (1920) 79–80
America, travel to 102–5, 108–11
Annunciation (1940s) 146–47
Argonaut 28
Arrest of Rudolf 43
Art history 6
Artistry (1924–50)
    America, travel to 102–5, 108–11
    Bury House 105–6
    Bury Studio 111–13, 116
    citizenship 101–2, 125
    Coddington 136–39
    enlistment 130
    future and passing of Georg Sauter 100
    Homo Sapiens: MCMXL (1940) 125–28
    Italy, tour of 95–100
    peace, finding 135–39
    responsibility and family roots of Rudolf 113–23
    Stocks Mill, Wittersham 116–17
Art Record 20
"The Aviator" (Lilian Sauter) 27–28
Awakening (Galsworthy) 77–78, 80, 82–83, 85

"B" *Battalion from the Workshops* (1919) 58
Bacchus and Ariadne (Titian) 11
Bailey, R. F. 32
Ball, David 171
Ballin, Ada S. 18
"Barbed Wire" 55–56, 85, 154, 157
"Barbed Wire All Round" 54–55, 85

Barbed Wire Disease: A Psychological Study of the Prisoner of War (Vischer) 45–46, 69–70
Barrie, J. M. 89
Bashford, Robert 146
Bavaria 15
"The Before and After: A Confession" 85–87
Beginnings (1890–1914)
    Bavaria 15
    Elstree 31–32
    Georg and his circle 21–25
    Harrow 32–37
    Holland Park 17, 25–27, 28–30, 40, 77, 78–79, 101, 170
    Holland Park, Sauters in 21
    Lilian and her circle 25–31
    Summertime travel of Rudolf with parents 25
Bell, Miss Evans 18
Belloc, Hilaire 26
Bennett's Welcome (Fletcher) 138–39
Berbank, Albert E. 127–28
"Between Two Worlds" (1977) 171–72, 185–91
"Big Hall" 188–89
Birmingham Post 1, 4–5, 168–69, 182
Bishop, Michael 146
Blundell, Rachel 146, 150
Blunden, Edmund 154
Bookman 82
Book of the Studio (1931–32) 111–13
The Bookseller, Newsdealer and Stationer 80–81
Brace, James 18
Braley, Berton 28
Brandes, Georg 98
The Bridal Morning (Georg Sauter) 23
British Camp, The Bare Figure 137–38
British Camp, The Hot Summer 137–38

British Camp, The Scorched Hill 137–38
British Camp from Evendine 137–38
British Camp in Mist 137–38
Britten, Benjamin 151, 152–54, 158–59
Broad, Valda 100
Broadbent, Maurice 144, 146, 148, 150
Brooke, Rupert 154
The Brooklyn Daily Eagle 109–10
Bryce, Alexander J. C. 127–28
   Bury House 105–6
   Bury Studio 111–13, 116

Campden Hill Square 17
The Canteen, Alexandra Palace (1919) 59
Cantwell, Robert 17
Carnations in a Glass Vase (1926) 105
Carnegie Art Institute 23
Carver, David 159–60
Castle Mattsies 15–16
"The Cause" (Lilian Sauter) 30–31
Change-of-address card (1934) 116–17, 118
Chapman, Arthur 28
Chrysler Building 110
Cincinnati's Closson Galleries 108–9, 112
"The Circle" 157
   Citizenship 101–2, 125
Clark, Leonard 159
Closson Galleries 108–9, 112
Coddington 136–39
Comrades (Georg Sauter) 20–22, 77
Connought Rangers 38–40
Conrad, Joseph 24, 28, 82–83
Contemporary art, 166
Cotswold Gliding Club 172
Cotswold Players 146, 148–49
Covent Garden 100
Creational Theme (1967) 166, 167
Crie du Coeur (1968) 154, 156, 157, 158–59,
   170, 181–82
Cultural biography 4

Daily Colonist 126–28
"Dark Hills, Dusk" 43
"Dawn Over Camp" 85–87
"The Day the World Went
   Backwards" 144
D-Day landings 135
Death of Rudolf 1, 166

De Bosschère, Jean 82–83
Dejeuner sur L'herbe (Édouard Manet) 23
"Despair" 85–87
Dodsworth, June 146
"Doing Time" 53–54, 85–87
Doodlebug Alley—Death on the Way
   (1944) 132–34
Doodlebug Alley—The Crooked Cross
   (1944) 132–34
Downfield Press 162–65
Dundee Evening Telegraph 101–2
Dutton, Thomas 17–18

Education of Rudolf 36–37
   Elstree 31–32
   Harrow 32–40
Edwards, C. W. 137–38
   Elstree 31–32
Empire State Building 110
Enemy alien 1, 2, 3, 8–9, 56–60, 135
"Enemy Alien" (1980) 171–72, 191–95
English Review 25–28
Englishwoman 28, 30–31
   Enlistment 130
Erda (1972) 151
"The Etching Room" (1931–32) 115
Evans, C. S. 89
Evans, John 146, 150
Evening Telegraph 129
Ex Libris: John Galsworthy 113–15
*The Experience of Prison: An Anthology of Prose,
   Drama, Verse and Picture* (Ball) 171, 185

Family tree of Rudolf 12, 115–16
Fiedler, Ethel 84
Fiedler, Hermann 93
The Fifth Hunger (1971) 144, 149, 165
Fletcher, Inglis 138–39
Folk Dances of the World 166
Forbes-Robertson, Norman 116
Ford, Ford Madox 18, 25
"Foreboding" 85–87
Forsyte Saga (Galsworthy) 77–78, 168–69
Four Hungers (1960) 144, 147, 162,
   164, 168–69
Fourth-Sunday At-Homes 20–21
"Fragments of Memory" 85–87
Frances Knight-Bruce 11

INDEX

Francis, Karl 167–68
Francis Drake Hotel 108
Frith Hill Camp 61, 65–68, 70–71, 73, 112, 171–72
Frontispiece (1920) 78
Furst, Herbert 20
Fussell, Paul 154

Galsworthy, Frank 106
Galsworthy, John 1, 67–69, 89, 168, 185–86
Galsworthy, Mabel Edith 11, 13–16, 74
Galsworthy, reflections by Rudolf 168
Galsworthy Senior, John 20–21
Galsworthy the Man: An Intimate Portrait (1967) 170
Gardner, Brian 154
Gazette and Post (1967) 167–68
"Gedanke" (Thought) 43, 85–87
Gibbs, Philip 121–22
Go as You Please: Memories of People and Places (Leslie) 136–37
Grace before Ploughing (Masefield) 92
Graham, George 141
The Grand Canyon 161, 175
Grand Canyon (1975–76) 103–4, 172, 173
Graves, Robert 154
Great War 8–9, 17, 92, 113–15, 135, 136–37
Great War (1964–68) 152
Green Bay Press Gazette 110, 111
Greenberg, Howard 167–68
Guardian 30

Hardy, Thomas 28, 89
Harraden, Beatrice 28–30
Harris, Ruth Green 109
Harrison, Margaret 172
Harrison, Michael 116–17, 120, 172
Harrow 32–40
Harrovian 36–37
"The Harvest" 121–22
Hearn, Peter 144
Hemingway, William McGregor 31–32
Henry, John Sollie 17–18
Herincx, Raimund 167–68
Highgate West Hill, London 135–36
Holiday greeting cards by Rudolf (1932, 1935–36) 114, 119, 123

Holland Park 17, 25–27, 28–30, 40, 77, 78–79, 101, 170
Holland Park, Sauters in 21
  Georg and his circle 21–25
  Lilian and her circle 25–31
The Holland Park Circle 17
Homo Sapiens: MCMXL (1940) 125–28
Hoppé, Emil Otto 105–6
Houseman, Laurence 28–30
Howe, W. T. H. 108–9, 112–13
Hueffer, Ford Madox 25–27
Hullah, Annette 28–30
Hunt, Charles 146
Hunt, Violet 28–30
Hunt, William Holman 18

In Chancery (Galsworthy) 77
International Cultural Exchange 166
International Society of Sculptors, Painters and Gravers 23
Internment (1914–19)
  Alexandra Palace 43–45, 48–62, 112, 171, 186–87, 193, 194
  Arrest of Rudolf 43
  Frith Hill Camp 61, 65–68, 70–71, 73, 112, 171–72
Into Battle: Thunderbolts Supporting a Bomber Sweep at Dawn (1943) 131–32
"The Intruders" 157–58
Isle of Man Camp 187–88
Italy, tour of 95–100

James, Henry 14–15
Jus Suffragii 30–31

Kachina Doll 113, 116–17
Kendall, Guy 27–28
Knee, Ronald 146
Kneipp, Father Sebastian 15–17
Kneipp health resort 15
Kraushaar, John Francis 107–8
Kraushaar Galleries 108–10

Lancet 45
The Last Glow (1976) 176
Lavery, John 100
Lawrence, D. H. 28
Lee, Laurie 144

INDEX

LeFevre Gallery 107
Leighton, Lord Frederic 17
Leslie, Henrietta 136–37
Lewis, Wyndham 28
Lichtenfeld, Joseph 17–18
Lion, Leon 89
Little Towers of Terreno 109
Living Age 27–28
Local Army Welfare Officers 125, 130–31
Lonely Majesty (1950s) 166
"Lost Days" 85–87
The Loving Cup (1977) 162, 172, 181–82
Lowndes, Marie Belloc 28–30
Luker, Jeanette 146

Manaton edition (Galsworthy) 89, 92
The Man of Property (Galsworthy) 77
Map of the Story (1934) 91
Marland, Michael 171–72
Masefield, John 89–92
Maternity (George Sauter) 20–22, 77
McClintock, William K. 38–40
McKinnel, Norman 89
"Meadows with Yellow Flowers" 43
Meynell, Alice 28–30
Militarism 57–60
Milton, Ernest 89
Modern war, history of 8
"Morgengesang" 43
Morris, J. F. 31–32
Moss, John Cottam 32–33
Mott, F. W. 45
Mottram, Ralph Hale 18–20
Music composition by Rudolf 146
Muswell Hill 44, 51

Nansen passport 95
National Gallery 11–12
NEVER MORE…! (a modern Triptych) (1936) 122
New York from South End of Central Park (1931) 110
New York Times 109
"Night in the Big Hall" 54, 85–87
Nottingham Evening Post 94
Not to Be Removed (ca. 1940) 128

"Ode to the Doodle-Bug" 132–34
Old Barns, Chalfont St. Peter (Berbank) 126–28

The Old Town, Menton (Bryce) 126–28
O'Sullivan, Curtis Dion 80, 108
The Ottawa Journal 129
Ottobeuren 153–54
Our Time and Age (ca. 1957) 142–43
Out of the Dawn: Thunderbolt about to Take Off (1944) 131–32

The Pall Mall Gazette 87
Paths in the Moonlight—Bombers Going Out Over the Channel (1944) 131–32, 133
"The Pause" (Lilian Sauter) 28–30, 93, 100–1
Payne, Edward 148–49
Peace, finding 135–39
Pearl and Rose (ca. 1975) 175
Phantom Eye—Phantasy (ca. 1940) 131–32
Phillimore Estate 17
Plan of Aliens Internment Camp, Frith Hill (1919) 67
Plan of Bury Studio (1931–32) 112
Plants Springing from a Barren Landscape (ca. 1947) 137
The Poet, John Masefield (1923) 90
"Poet's Work" (Lilian Sauter) 28–30
Pound, Ezra 28
Prinsep, Valentine 17
Prodigal Son (Britten) 158–59
The Publishers' Circular and Booksellers' Record 87
The Puente Nuevo (untitled) (ca. 1925) 95–96

Reconstructing a creative life
   art history 6
   cultural biography 4
   modern war, history of 8
Recovery (1919–24)
   Awakening (Galsworthy) 77
   domesticity 83, 85
   illustrations for Galsworthy's Manaton edition 89
   Masefield and Sauter 89
   Red Cross 132–34
Reflections (1950–77)
   contemporary art 166
   Galsworthy reflections 168
   Grand Canyon (1975–76) 103–4, 172–73
   Great War (1964–68) 152

Music composition 146
   Stroud Festival 144
   Responsibility and family roots of
      Rudolf 113–23
Requiem (Britten) 154
Return at Dawn: Spitfires on Patrol (1943) 131–32
Ridgeway, Reverend N. V. 32
Robin Hill 78–79
Robins, Elizabeth 28–30
Robins, William Palmer 107
Robinson, Charles Newton 25–27
Robinson, W. Heath 82–83
Royal Academy 11, 126–28, 143–44
Royal Commission on the Manufacture
   of and Trade in Armaments
   Commission 121–22
The Royal Crescent 17
Royal Institute of Painters 17–18
Royal Scottish Academy 146

Sackbut 30–31
Sailboats, drawing of (1913) 27
Salute the Soldier Week campaign 131
Samuel, Herbert 41–42
San Giorgio (1950s) 96–97
Sassoon, Seigfried 113, 154
Sauter, Blanche Lilian (née Galsworthy) 11,
   20–21, 30–31, 73–75
"The Aviator" 27–28
   becoming a parent 15
   "The Cause" 30–31
   christening son of 16–17
   circle in Holland Park 25
   intellectual pursuits of 14–15
   literary and political interests of 14–
      15, 25–31
   marriage to Georg 15
"The Pause" 28–30, 93, 100–101
"The Poet's Work" 28–30
Through High Windows 28–30
Victorian separate spheres and 14
"Women's Highest Please for
   Suffrage" 28–30
"Women's Song of Freedom" 29–30
Sauter, Georg 11–12, 20–21, 23, 60–61,
   99–100
   becoming a parent 15
The Bridal Morning 23
   Comrades 20–22, 77

   christening son of 16–17
   circle in Holland Park 21–25
   future and passing of 100
   marriage to Lilian 15
Maternity 20–22, 77
Sauter, Viola Ada Emily (née Wood) 48–49,
   51–52, 67, 73, 75, 111–12, 137–38,
   142–43, 146, 181–82
   Lilian and 73–75
   Rudolf and 48–52, 61–62, 65, 73–75,
      84, 102–3, 108, 111, 113, 135–38, 144
   William Leendert Bruckman
      and 48, 84
Schauffler, Robert Haven 88
Schreiner, Olive 28
The Scotsman 87
Scott, G. A. 32–33
Scott-James, R. A. 25–27
Scribner's Magazine 80
Scrivens, John 154–55, 181
Scrivens, Patricia 154–55, 181–82
Searchlights along the Thames Estuary
   (1940) 131–32
"The Seekers" 144
Self-portrait of Rudolf (ca. 1920) 75, 76
Sharp, Evelyn 28–30
Sinclair, May 28–30
The Sinister Insect: The Dragon Fly
   (ca. 1940) 131–32
Sketch of a woman (1910) 26
The Skin Game (Galsworthy) 148–49
Sky Battle (1940) 131–32
"Sleepless" 52–53, 85–87
Snow and Cloud (ca. 1975) 175
Songs in Captivity (1922) 85–88
A Soothing Wind (1969) 160, 162, 181–82
The Spectator 87
Spiritual Militancy League 30
St. John Prisoner of War Fund 132–34
Stallworthy, Jon 154
Stephen More 89
Stephens, James 26
"Stepping-Stones" 158
   Stocks Mill, Wittersham 116–17
"Storm over a Tor" 43
Stroud Festival 144
Stroud News and Journal 146–48
Studies of Contrails (1940) 131–32
Study in Space (1967) 166

Suburban Back Gardens in Snow (ca. 1920) 75–76
Sullivan, J. F. 82–83
"Sun through a Thin Mist" 43
Sun's Last Glow (ca. 1975) 175
Swan, John Macallan 24

The Taking of the Gry (Masefield) 90–91
"The Three Trees" 153
Through High Windows (Lilian Sauter) 28–30
"Time" 52, 85–87
Toulson, Shirley 144
Turnbull, Margaret 159, 167–68

"Under Canvas—On the Eve of Peace" 85–87

Villa Rubein (Galsworthy) 14–15
Vineyard 28
Vischer, Adolf 45–46, 69–70

Wakefield Camp 186
Walpole, Hugh 26
War Artists 125, 189–90
War Requiem (Britten) 152–53
Wartime law, rule of 41–42
"Waste" 85–87
The Watchmaker, Alexandra Palace (1919) 59
Watson, William 27–28
Watts, George Fredric 17
Wells, H. G. 26
Western Mail 136–37

While They Fought: An Anthology of Prose and Verse Exploring the Lives of Those Who Did Not Fight, but Who Had to Endure the Second World War (Marland and Willcox) 171–72, 191
Whistler, James McNeill 23
"Why?" 70–71, 85–87
Wightman, Richard 28
Willcox, Robin 171–72
The Wind and the Sun (1950s) 166
Windmill (ca. 1940) 121
"Windswept Clouds" 43
Woman Suffrage 30
"Woman's Song of Freedom" (Lilian Sauter) 29–30
Women Writers' Suffrage League (WWSL) 28–30
Women's Charter of Rights and Liberties 30
"Women's Highest Plea for Suffrage" (Lilian Sauter) 28–30
Woods, Margaret 28
Wörishofen 15–16
World Refugee Year (1959–60) 146

"Years of Captivity" 85–87
Yorkshire Post and Leeds Intelligencer 128–29
Young Men's Christian Association (YMCA) 45

Zangwill, Edith Ayrton 28–30

www.ingramcontent.com/pod-product-compliance
Lightning Source LLC
Chambersburg PA
CBHW021141230426
43667CB00005B/205